The Invention of Palestinian Citizenship, 1918–1947

The Invention of Palestinian Citizenship, 1918–1947

Lauren Banko

EDINBURGH
University Press

Edinburgh University Press is one of the leading university presses in the UK. We publish academic books and journals in our selected subject areas across the humanities and social sciences, combining cutting-edge scholarship with high editorial and production values to produce academic works of lasting importance. For more information visit our website: edinburghuniversitypress.com

Edinburgh University Press Ltd
The Tun – Holyrood Road
12 (2f) Jackson's Entry
Edinburgh EH8 8PJ
www.euppublishing.com

Typeset in 11/13 Adobe Sabon by
IDSUK (DataConnection) Ltd

A CIP record for this book is available from the British Library

ISBN 978 1 4744 1550 7 (hardback)
ISBN 978 1 4744 1551 4 (webready PDF)
ISBN 978 1 4744 1552 1 (epub)

Contents

Acknowledgements

This book is the product of not only my own research and writing, but it comes out of the encouragement and support throughout several years from supervisors, colleagues, friends and family members. My long-standing interest and research in the history of the Middle East has always been supported despite the fact that it has surely seemed strange to a number of family members and friends. An ample number of individuals and institutions have acted as guides along the way. This monograph came out of a PhD thesis, submitted to the History Department at the School of Oriental and African Studies (SOAS), University of London. The focus on citizenship and nationality came somewhat indirectly out of an academic and personal interest in the history of Palestine during the Mandate and the ideologies, political, social and civic forces that shaped this history. However, this focus is not entirely history – its implications loom large today in the nature of citizenship and nationality granted to, revoked from and manipulated by a number of actors in Israel, the Palestinian territories including East Jerusalem and European and American governments. In addition, the narrative of Palestinian Arab émigrés in the decades before 1948 has been crucial to the civic identity of Palestinian refugees post-1948. While I have attempted to shine light on these Ottoman and interwar Palestinian emigrants and their citizenship status, this remains a field for further historical and political enquiry.

Throughout the process of the PhD research, and the research and writing of the manuscript, my former colleagues at SOAS have provided an overwhelming amount of encouragement. I owe a big debt of gratitude to my doctoral supervisor, Nelida Fuccaro, whose ever-patient and critical advice, suggestions and corrections always left me feeling energised and inspired about the initial project and then the manscript. Thanks are also owed to Benjamin Fortna, Konrad Hirschler, Laleh Khalili, Michael Talbot, Fabian Stremmel,

David Beamish, Jacques Rouyer Guillet, David Lunn, Aparajita Mukhopadhyay, Jared McDonald, Katie Natanel, Philipp Wirtz, Arash Sedighi, Jake Norris, Nadim Bawalsa, Engin Isin, Ilan Pappe, Mutaz Qafisheh, Justin McCarthy, Julie Peteet and William Clarence Smith.

A number of individuals, archives and institutions in Great Britain, Palestine, Israel, and Beirut, Lebanon have graciously donated their time, archival materials and funds throughout the research and writing process. Although I will inadvertently leave some people out, thanks go to Penny Mitchell and Hadeel Qazzaz at the Palestinian American Research Centre (PARC), Salim Tamari and the Institute for Palestine Studies (IPS) (Ramallah), the Institute for Palestine Studies Library in Beirut, the Ibrahim Abu-Lughod Institute of International Studies, Roger Heacock, Assem Khalil, Musa Budeiri, Adnan Musallam, Butrus and Naila Abu-Manneh, Khader Salameh, Mudar Kassi, Haifa Khalidi, the lovely individuals of the Friday Shat-ha group and many others.

The archivists at the National Archives in Kew, the British Library, the Churchill Archives Centre at Churchill College, Cambridge, and the Kenyon Institute (KI) in Jerusalem were always helpful, as was Debbie Usher at the Middle East Centre Archive in St Anthony's, Oxford. Despite the language barrier, I received a great deal of help from the archivists at the Israel State Archives and the Hebrew University Library. The funding from PARC, the Council for British Research in the Levant (CBRL), the Palestine Exploration Fund (PEF) and SOAS during 2011 and 2012 made the bulk of the research that forms the manuscript possible. The Arabic and Middle Eastern Studies Department of the University of Manchester and Moshe Behar have been accommodating, providing me with a base and a position from which I was able to finish the manuscript.

The manuscript has benefited from the discussions, questions and engagement with its major and minor themes at a number of conferences and workshops, including those held by the Moise A. Khayrallah Center for Lebanese Diaspora Studies and Akram Khater, Institut français du Proche-Orient (IFPO) and Claire Beaugrand, the Institute for Palestine Studies (Ramallah), Experts and Expertise in the League of Nations conference (Paris, Institut National des Lanques et Cultures Orientales (INALCO)) and the Institute of Historical Research (IHR) (London). The editorial staff at Edinburgh University Press (EUP), including Nicola Ramsey and Ellie Bush, have been patient and accommodating. I must also sincerely thank the two anonymous readers, whose critical, engaging and well-informed comments have shaped this manuscript.

A huge expression of thanks goes to Nathan who read partial and full drafts of the chapters and whose non-specialist comments have been ever-helpful. Finally, my parents, Blaise and Dana Banko, receive the greatest amount of thanks for their love and encouragement despite their often raised eyebrows at my excursions and research. None of this would be possible without them. Any omissions or mistakes are my own.

For my mother, Dana Banko (1948–2015), who very much wanted to see this book, and for my father, Blaise Banko, who will see it published.

I

Introduction

In August of 1929, shortly after the end of the outbreak of violence that had flared up over access to the Wailing Wall (or Western Wall) in Jerusalem, one Arabic press editorial concluded that the riots stemmed from the Palestine Citizenship Order-in-Council issued four years prior, in 1925. That citizenship order-in-council, the author of the editorial wrote, supported not only Jewish immigration in large numbers into the territory but it did not foster any sense of loyalty between newly created Jewish Palestinian citizens and the Palestine Mandate Government. He described many of the Jewish immigrants to Palestine as English, Italian or French and argued that they remained English, Italian or French after their arrival. Not only did they fail to truly integrate into local society, they did not immediately naturalise as Palestinian citizens. This, the writer claimed, was contrary to the post-war principle of nationality. Within Palestine, the journalist added, their lack of naturalisation created an impossible situation wherein Jewish residents would not be solely loyal to the Government of Palestine; rather, they were loyal to what the government termed their 'country of origin' despite habitual residence within the territory of the mandate. In the journalist's opinion, the problem with this was that such Jews who did not take Palestinian citizenship could individually and collectively influence the governments and other residents of their home countries with respect to policy towards Palestine.[1] In the wake of the 1929 riots such an accusitive type of news editorial was not unusual: in the previous three years, a generous amount of page-space in the Arabic press had been given over to opinion pieces, editorials and letters related to the 1925 Palestine Citizenship Order-in-Council and what most of their authors felt to be its detrimental effects upon the Arab emigrant population. The order itself, according to press reports, served only the Jewish immigrants since it offered European Jews almost unfettered access to naturalisation and citizenship while at the same time it denied ipso facto citizenship to Palestinian Arabs who happened to reside, even temporarily, outside of the borders of the mandate.

In studies of Palestine under the mandate the term 'citizenship' has been used as if it was an accepted and uncontested reality for the population of Palestine from the earliest years of the British Administration. Indeed it was not; rather, the provisions, status and terminology of citizenship continued to be contested and reshaped through the 1940s and until the creation of Israel in 1948. Such assumptions of the term's ubiquity are misleading and do not consider the historical processes through which Palestinian nationality and citizenship came into existence in a particular colonial, interwar context. The 1925 Palestine Citizenship Order-in-Council and its amendments spurred a wide-reaching debate over what constituted Palestinian nationality and citizenship and, importantly, the origins and definitions of Palestinian civic and political identity during the years of the mandate. This debate took place within Arab society and in political circles as well as at the highest levels of the Palestine Administration in Jerusalem and the British Government in London.

National identity at the close of the First World War had been pinned down by a generation of post-Second World War scholars in absolutes, influenced by sources penned within a certain nationalist discursive field. More recently, postcolonial and so-called 'new imperial' historians have framed national identity in light of its ambiguities and focused on those aspects of identity, particularly colonial identity, for which the public opinion and popular discussions found within primary sources neglect to overtly demonstrate. Yet, the rhetorical language of the League of Nations and the post-war imperial powers supported the former type of linear nationalist history during the first half of the twentieth century. These imperial powers themselves, and a generation of scholars who emerged from within their academies by mid-century, justified British and French assumption of sovereignty in the Arab Levant with the argument that protectorates, mandates and trusteeships would bring the region's inhabitants closer to a higher political and social standard necessary for self-determination. The impact of such arrangements of territorial control and the system of quasi-colonial trusteeship over indigenous inhabitants upon processes of legal and civic identity formulation by these inhabitants has not been the traditional focus of 'nationalist' scholarship.

More recently, historians have posited identity as a category of analysis, used to break down and understand the impact of the multiple classifications into which colonial or imperial powers placed individuals. In particular, categories of subjecthood manipulated by colonial officials from the late eighteenth century onwards used the headings of nation, race, ethnicity and a so-called civilisational or developmental level, among others. With few exceptions, the Arab Levant has been largely absent from historical studies on how certain European powers classified and managed subject populations at the turn of the twentieth century and during the years between the two world wars.[2] Indeed by the twentieth century, the inhabitants of the former provinces of the Ottoman Empire were rarely classified by Europeans as 'natives' or 'uncivilised' souls in need of development assistance in order to bring them politically, morally, culturally and economically into the age of modernity. The founding covenant of the League of Nations, approved in 1919, noted that Greater Syria (*Bilād al-Sham*) and Mesopotamia needed some form of trusteeship in order to foster self-governing institutions before the League could grant complete sovereignty to the inhabitants of these territories to run their own political and national affairs. However, the victorious Allied Powers and the United States recognised what the French delegation to the twenty-fourth session of the League of Nations Council referred to in 1923 as the 'differences between the natives' state of civilization' when they compared West and East Africa, or even Algeria, with Syria, Lebanon, Iraq or Palestine.[3] These differences of civilisation had a clear bearing on the methods used by the League and the Allied powers to create new categories for 'citizens' and 'nationals' of post-war entities.

During the course of the nineteenth century the principle of nationality, which Rogers Brubaker defines as the concept of states *as* and *for* certain nations, became the major factor in the organisation and imagination of territorial space as political space.[4] Essentially, this concept translated into the nation-state, the political entity that embodied the 'nation' and whose institutions privileged the centralisation of administrative power in the hands of the majority ethnic or otherwise historically dominant group in a particular territory. The League propagated the same concept, and its Permanent Mandates Committee visualised the Arab mandates as states-to-be for certain 'nations'. The Allies divided these territories detached from the defeated Ottoman Empire with the promise to hand them over as sovereign states-in-the-making to the nationality that formed the majority of the population resident within each. Yet the actual meaning of 'nationality' did not remain a static concept linked to ideas of race and ethnicity, and its definition in the nineteenth century did not transfer over to the twentieth. In fact, nationality and sovereignty complicated the implementation of the entire mandates system from its inauguration to its end. The practical application of this principle of nationality in the Levant has yet to be fully explored by historians of the Middle East or historians of imperial citizenship. This book attempts to begin that exploration for the case of Mandate Palestine.

The mandate is fascinating as both a period of time and an institutional structure. It represents a transition on a number of levels in the Arab Levant: on the one hand, that between Ottoman modernist and reformist changes in political, social and civic realms and, on the other, the spread of indirect colonial rule marked by the contradictory policies of self-determination and 'ethnic unmixing' in anticipation of the nation-state becoming the primary, internationally accepted political organisation. After the end of the First World War the entirely new mandate category, a territory held in trust, did not theoretically allow for imperial powers to make claims of outright sovereignty. Rather, the ideas behind the style of indirect rule popularised by Frederick Lugard in West Africa influenced the structures of administration and control by France and Great Britain over their mandates in the Arab Levant. For the study at hand what is important to stress is that without British or French nationality, mandated citizens (indirectly ruled) could not claim to be subjects of the Crown in the case of Great Britain nor nationals of France. Even so, as historian Rieko Karatani has shown, the interwar period marked the beginning of the development of nation-state citizenship in Great Britain, in contrast to imperial subjecthood.[5]

In the former Ottoman Arab provinces, the political and civic identities of the region's inhabitants underwent gradual – although at times more drastic – changes directly related to the demise of the Ottoman Empire and the Arabs' subsequent integration into the British and French imperial systems. As part of these transitions, pre-war reforms and notions of legal and political modernity informed the growing arguments by the region's inhabitants that the imperial, mandate powers surely had to grant what sociologists and political theorists now refer to as the 'bundle of rights' associated with membership in a nation-state polity. Within French and British colonial territories from the Caribbean to India the rise of nationalism, pan-Islamism, pan-Africanism and pan-Arabism among subject populations are represented by the multi-faceted demands of individuals and groups to a legally recognised and rights-bearing status – that of the citizen – vis-à-vis the state.

Marking Nationals, Making Citizens

After 1918 to the mid-1940s, both nationality and citizenship became less like abstract political concepts as mandatory officials, the British government and the Arab population negotiated, manipulated, shaped and integrated them into political, social and civil life as markers of civic, national and international identity in a changing society. The ultimate aim of the chapters in this book is to trace the historical process of, in the words of Engin Isin, 'making citizens'. Such a process involves more than paper decrees that determine a legal status as issued from the imperial centre; instead, making citizens involves practices that are social, political, cultural and symbolic. Isin's work, which influences this project, interrogates and probes at the conditions under which subjects act as citizens and thus transform into citizens, as well as how they make claims to rights, benefits and responsibilities.[6] The making of the Palestinian citizen entailed not only an ideological process through which notions of citizenship and the rights associated with that citizenship were crafted by the British administration and redefined by the Palestinian Arabs, but it also involved changes to the political language and the vocabulary of identity and belonging as well as engagement with certain types of behaviours. By the end of the First World War, citizenship began to take on a rather different meaning, apart from European and Ottoman understandings of nationality. The citizen came to be defined as much by political and civil rights and activities as by his or her historical membership in, and engagement with, a particular broader community.[7]

The mandatory powers in the Levant, under the auspices of the League of Nations, represented a different institutional form of authority markedly separate from older methods of colonial government and territorial control. This authority was manifested in a number of ways, one being in the relationship between the mandate as a state-in-the-making with the population of the territory under mandatory control. The following chapters trace this manifestation in Palestine under mandate administration through the creation of the categories of legal citizenship and internationally recognised nationality. The institutionalisation of citizenship as a legal status of identity conferred by the government stirred tensions in Palestine among those Arabs who professed social, civic, cultural and, ultimately, communitarian understandings of nationality as an identity granted by birth or descent in the Arab world. These intellectuals and leaders perceived nationality as a status imbued with certain inherent rights that gave nationals alone the ownership of the territorially defined nation-state and its government. In Palestine in the first two decades under the mandate, this understanding of nationality and citizenship as linked to primordial national identity and exclusive political rights based on membership in a particular historic community resulted in discourses, vocabularies and behaviours that underscored and emphasised multi-faceted acts of resistance on the part of Arab nationalist and populist leaders as well as émigrés outside of the territory against Great Britain's legislative constructions of the national and the citizen. In particular, Palestine's educated Arab nationalist leadership both in Palestine and in the diaspora were well-versed in the meaning of citizenship and the rights associated with it in the Western European context, as well as in the meaning of and the rights associated with a particular Arab-Ottoman nationality. The mandates system not only dismantled most Ottoman imperial institutions, but it also caused a progressive rupture of the Arabs' understandings of Ottoman subjecthood and national belonging. The institutions introduced by the British colonial officials in Palestine challenged traditional and Ottoman reform-era understandings of identity and cultural belonging in the Levant. Significantly, the style of government by Great Britain challenged the Palestinian Arabs' own, often wildly optimistic, understandings of British democracy, liberal citizenship and governmental duties towards citizens.

The book presents a new understanding of the Arabs' reactions to colonialism and Jewish immigration into Palestine by framing resistance to mandate policies and the early stages of the development of the political project of Palestinian nationalism through the articulated appeals, discussions, ideologies and demands for a *political*, as opposed to simply legal, identity. Political citizenship came to be linked to Arab nationality and an understanding of the inherent nature of political, social and civil rights and duties for the Arabic-speaking or otherwise formerly Ottoman population. These interpretations existed by the nineteenth century in Ottoman Syria but the advent of the mandate and new political languages in the post-war era reformulated them. Contrary to European or North American understandings of contemporary citizenship, Palestine's Arab leaders framed demands for a communitarian style of citizenship whereby birth or descent in a particular national community granted that community the ownership over its territorially bound political entity and its resources. Anti-mandate sentiment and resistance developed in tandem with the Arabs' agitation for rights *to* the state, particularly as the Palestinian Arabs began to frame the mandate as the tool by which Great Britain allowed a foreign, non-Arab group to take control over and have the rights *to* Palestine. Neither citizenship nor nationality, according to these demands, could be imposed upon natives by a foreign power, and neither rights nor duties could be granted by governmental, or colonial, authorities. Instead, national identity and the accompanying rights and duties existed as natural elements of membership within a nation.

To focus purely on the political demands and conditions for citizenship and nationality in Palestine would neglect the varied understandings and meanings of both statuses for the British, the Arabs both in Palestine and in the diaspora and the Jewish immigrants. Citizenship, as understood by natives of Palestine, did not immediately become political – citizenship in 1920 evolved in meaning and practice and it had a different set of accompanying vocabulary by 1937, for instance. The book aims to trace how, and to what extent, citizenship became politically linked to nationality and civic identity as a reaction to the legal parameters of the British-created citizenship status in the post-1918 period. Similarly, the civic component of citizenship did not appear immediately or fully formed in the Palestinian Arabs' reactions against the policies and laws of the mandate government from 1920 onwards. The so-called 'bundle of rights' that went along with citizens' membership in the state – civil, social and political – was understood in various localised ways by the Palestinian Arabs. However, only once 'citizenship' became tied to political projects of belonging as well as to an understanding of ownership over the nation did particular written and ideological discourses, responsibilities and behaviours become associated with the concept of 'the Palestinian citizen'. It is useful to cite William Hanley's argument in favour of historians who offer a more nuanced understanding of the multiple layers of citizenship in the Middle East in the early twentieth century. He stresses that, for the case of Egypt, any study of citizenship that focuses solely on political agency or that is purely through the lens of political citizenship 'impoverishes analysis of Middle Eastern citizenship'. To do so would be to give the conventional, European definition of citizenship as the prescription to political, colonial and post-colonial ills. This sets historians of the Middle East who 'seek to restore honor to the region's past' on an 'impossible quest for something like indigenous citizenship' that had inherent political elements before its supposed destruction by outsider, colonial forces.[8] My intent here is to steer away from falling into the trap of framing the history of the Palestinian Arabs' understandings and notions of citizenship and nationality as dictated by and based primarily upon political – and more contemporary European – meanings of citizenship.

After 1918, the understanding by Palestinian Arabs of subject-hood, nationality and citizenship experienced a significant shift. Under the institutions of the Ottoman Empire, Arabs constituted Ottoman citizens in a legal sense, but as subjects of the sultan they could expect protection from the state in return for loyalty. Changes underway in Europe and in a number of colonial posses-sions even before the outbreak of war conceptualised subjecthood as based on allegiance (by the collectivity of subjects) to a state or ruler with populations and territories coming under the sovereign control of that state or ruler. The British in Palestine emphasised a type of individual allegiance to their own authority but in the eyes of many Palestinian Arab politicians and nationalists, the British offered few of the expected protections in return. Similar to what Hanley describes as part of the Egyptian nationality laws created under the British Government in Egypt, the eventual passage of the citizenship order-in-council in Palestine did not delineate rights but rather jurisdiction. It focused on who was a Palestinian citizen, and how one could became a citizen through naturalisation.[9] The key problem for the Palestinian Arabs was what they continually stressed to be the lack of British protection of their 'majority' rights in Palestine. Unrestricted (European) Jewish immigration and settlement and the laissez-faire attitude of the British in Palestine towards this angered the Arabs more than the colonial nature of the mandate itself: its policies signified a lack of British protection for Palestine's Arab citizens. Citizenship was a recognised legal status but it offered none of the rights for the Arab population that would have enabled the latter to mount a challenge to the perceived lack of protection by the local administration.

An ongoing point of conflict between the colonial administration of Palestine and the Palestinian Arab leaders was the lack of rep-resentative institutions. As Benjamin Thomas White has shown for Syria during the interwar period, alongside representation, institu-tions such as citizenship are necessary in order to facilitate a sense of commonality upon which a public sphere develops.[10] Citizenship is thus a key part of the formation of civil society and the institu-tions through which inhabitants of a territory and the state negotiate rights and duties. The discussions articulated within civil society and political institutions linked empire and the place of the Palestinian Arabs within a larger imperial system to colonialism, the Palestine Administration and the definitions of citizenship and nationality.

Although Arab populist and nationalist leaders might not have initially demanded a modern, rights-bearing notion of citizenship, they emphasised the aspect of protection of the 'native' community of Palestine and saw themselves as akin to British subjects with some sort of legal standing.[11] These leaders assumed that due to the raison d'être of the mandates system, this legal standing would soon translate into political standing within a nation-state controlled by, and for, the majority Arab citizens.

Not surprisingly for colonial powers, the Palestine Administration and the British Government failed to take into full account the Palestinian Arabs' own discourses of nationality. As a result, the figures of the national and the citizen have been in conflict with each other not only during the mandate but also since the creation of the state of Israel through to today. The book uses the term 'discourse' often, and refers largely to political and ideological discourses. The ideologies, notions, discussions, interactions, and debates over the primordial nature of nationality, race, citizenship and belonging, and rights combined to create the discourses under study here. The British administration had its own set of discourses on the meanings and applications of citizenship, nationality and rights, framed by understandings of Britain's role in Palestine, the mandate's position within a larger imperial system and a number of values and categorisations of race and identity. The Palestinian Arabs, too, had their own discourses on citizenship and nationality based on historical experiences and traditional understandings of identity; similarly Zionist and non-Zionist Jewish immigrants were informed by a number of discourses on these two terms, although these themes are outside the scope of the book. We cannot overlook the fact that colonial, or mandated, subject-citizens did not act as passive receptors of imperial policies. Whether in decisions to assimilate or in the realm of self-definition, the Palestinian Arabs and their notions of identity fit within wider trans-imperial networks that contributed to multiple definitions of 'the citizen' and that shaped multiple civic identities.

And yet Palestine has been left out of British 'imperial' history studies, even though we can categorise the mandate administration and its institutions as serving what John Darwin terms a 'bridgehead' between the imperial centre and the colonial sphere. As the entire book shows, the institutions of the mandate – the different bridgeheads – were certainly not oriented towards compatible imperial aims, a not uncommon phenomenon in British imperial history as Alan Lester notes. The incompatible nature of these institutions, including those directed by Foreign Office and Colonial Office advisers, further stimulated what postcolonial historians such as Ann Laura Stoler and Frederick Cooper refer to as 'the tensions of empire' among the colonialists themselves.[12]

It is useful here to turn to an analysis on the British precedents for categorising subject populations. In the eighteenth century, for British and French colonialists, race in the context of imperial nationality and citizenship is best analysed in reference to culture and lineage. Racialised notions as applied to colonial subjects allowed Great Britain to define the grounds of inclusion or exclusion with cultural characteristics such as language, descent and religion as the primary factors by which to judge the prospects for assimilation into the realm of 'Britishness' or 'whiteness'. Kathleen Wilson has shown that such racialised notions developed in the eighteenth century during a period of accelerated British imperial expansion and were channelled through the discourses, cultural understandings and practices that accompanied that expansion.[13] As Stoler has shown in reference to one of the principle architects of colonial law in the Indies, by the nineteenth century colonialism made obsolete *jus sanguinis* (by descent) and *jus soli* (by domicile) as the sole determinants of nationality. In the late nineteenth century, colonial officials felt that these two qualifications no longer determined whether an individual shared qualities of his fellow nationals: a common culture, history, language and morals.[14] Indeed, shared qualities became the all-important factor in imperial decisions as to which individuals or groups acquired a certain nationality. In British colonies, as in Dutch and French colonial possessions, new criteria to mark citizens and nationals included middle-class values and morals as well as privileged 'white' backgrounds.[15]

By the nineteenth century, nationality came to be conceived of as related to legal status. At home and abroad, subjects of Great Britain were subjects of the monarch rather than to a state. Until 1870, British subjects did not commonly lose their nationality even if they settled in a foreign country. Imperial experts constructed British nationality regulations after that date to keep pace with international norms and increased emigration (and, importantly, economic emigration) of subjects from British possessions. Only in 1907 did a new law standardise nationality for all British subjects in the empire including in the Dominions. In 1914, the British Nationality and Status of Aliens Act assumed that all British subjects were bound together through allegiance to the Crown. Birth or naturalisation of an individual (male) in British territory conferred British nationality, and these nationals were recognised as such internationally. Ethnicity or 'race' had far less to do with this status, but rather nationality came through the shared allegiance and loyalty to Great Britain – assumed to be a given for individuals born or naturalised in imperial territory.[16]

As early as the late eighteenth century, a range of groups in British and French territories used their sense of a protégé-type nationality to make claims to citizenship *as* political subjects.[17] In influential and illuminating studies, Stoler and Cooper have both shown how colonialism, colonial subjecthood and imperial citizenship reflected and even extended racial hierarchies and hierarchies of the 'protégé'. This type of citizenship was also highly stratified despite the supposedly equal grant of it through domicile in imperial possessions.[18] Indeed, British colonial citizens in one territory (for example, India), were treated by imperial officials according to racial hierarchies once those citizens entered other British colonies or possessions (such as South Africa or Egypt). The hybrid subject-citizen, which existed in British India, as an analytical category of colonial identity represents a clear anomaly if approached from the vantage point of the post-imperial age. Citizenship, particularly the liberal citizenship of the late nineteenth and early twentieth century in the metropole, assumed that individuals held certain rights and performed certain duties as free men. The colonial citizen, by contrast, only exercised rights and duties vis-à-vis his or her colonial or settler administration.

By the early twentieth century, even as empire began to slowly lose some of its grandeur and meaning, empire *as a practice* provided a particular arena that allowed for discussions, notions, rhetoric, and examples of behaviour to circulate between metropoles, colonies and diasporic sites within which colonial officials made their home and exercised political sovereignty. This circulation influenced the British and French perceptions of the League of Nations mandates as quasi-colonial trusteeships. Indeed, colonial subjecthood, protection and citizenship came to be redefined through the first decade of the twentieth century. In particular, as both France and Great Britain established protectorates from the latter half of the nineteenth century, their role in the assumption of control over affairs translated into the provision of protection. The categories of imperial protection transitioned alongside international norms of diplomacy. In the cases of Morocco and Egypt, French and British protectorates respectively, inhabitants held a different juridical status than did subjects in outright colonies such as Algeria or India. Protectorates had their own nationality separate from the nationality of the power that administered their affairs. However, as Stoler notes, imperial powers had more of a stake in ensuring that subjects become integrated into the social, cultural, moral and political life of the metropole before true assimilation into the national status of that particular sovereign. Cooper argues this as well, noting that, for French Algeria, individual colonial subjects could only become citizens of the wider French Empire if they reached a certain degree of evolution.[19]

In his work on colonial citizenship in French West Africa, Cooper notes that just as citizenship defines inclusion and exclusion in communities it also melds a person's rights to that person's state.[20] The British concept of citizenship is not one that necessarily came with certain citizenship rights and duties. Of course, Great Britain has never had a basic law or bill of rights that listed rights and duties of its subject-nationals.[21] It is no surprise, then, that in Palestine under the British-administered mandate, colonial officials and Cabinet members promoted an apolitical citizenship. As Ilana Feldman explains, this citizenship transcended nationality as it offered rights in a social and perhaps diplomatic, rather than political, sense.[22]

Contextualising the 'Mandated National'

In studies on the ideological development of the nation, scholars such as Jurgen Habermas have posited two types of nationhood whose roots lie in the eighteenth and nineteenth centuries. The French notion has been discussed above as a nation of citizens whose identities do not come from common ethnic, cultural or linguistic properties but instead from the practice of citizens exercising their civil rights as participants in the state. Political unity as related to the territorial and institutional structure of the French state has been the deciding factor of inclusive belonging to the nation as citizens (*demos*).[23] Therefore, citizenship was a right through the provision of *jus soli*. The German notion of the nation differs from the French notion in that national identity developed before the nation-state in the territory that became modern Germany. Citizenship and nationality were much more exclusive than in France: the community formed the nation through its shared culture, language and ethnicity (*ethnos*). The right to citizenship came from the provision of *jus sanguinis*.[24] To put this into perspective for the Levant, the Ottoman Empire recognised both *jus soli* and *jus sanguinis*.

Nationality as defined by Brubaker as *jus sanguinis* ethno-cultural membership in a nation developed out of the concept that the ethno-cultural nation came to define the political identity of its citizens.[25] Once the nation-state comes into existence with sovereign borders and democratic political and legal structures, it becomes responsible for deciding the terms of citizenship as a legal and recognised status and then granting rights associated with it. National identity, as opposed to nationality and citizenship, is a more abstract collective consciousness and a nation can exist without being sovereign. A sovereign entity, however, is essential to regulate citizenship and provide the proper identification to its citizens.[26] By the nineteenth century, people slowly became dependent on the state that they lived under to legislate their identity in terms of borders. As John Torpey notes, nationality is implemented through a state's bureaucratic measures (such as the passport) to control movement and borders.[27] Citizenship, then, refers to the legal relationship between an individual and the state, and the individual's full membership in a community with civil, political and social rights and responsibilities. T. H. Marshall, the notable scholar on citizenship, stresses that the rights of citizenship must be shared equally by all citizens in a given community.[28] Importantly, citizenship status determines access of an individual to the resources of the state and is used as a way to distribute power. Bryan Turner defined citizenship as a set of social practices of rights and obligations that define the nature of social membership of a community.[29]

The importance of nineteenth-century Ottoman history for understanding the post-1918 evolution of claims to nationality and citizenship in Palestine cannot be understated. Ottoman nationality can be placed into the broader history of citizenship in the nineteenth century.[30] Nineteenth-century Ottoman law classified inhabitants as nationals in a territorial, rather than ethno-cultural, sense. Central to its Tanzimat reforms, the Ottoman Government actively promoted a new national ideology termed Osmanlilik (Ottomanism) in order to reinforce an Empire-wide concept of equality of subjects.[31] Prior to the law, the population's relationship to the state was mediated through their *millet*, or religious community. By the turn to the twentieth century and after the 1908 Young Turk takeover of the Ottoman government, the notion of Turkish nationality as separate from Arab nationality became incorporated into citizenship legislation, and citizenship became more akin to nationality in the imperial codifications of identity.[32] In sharp contrast with this, by the turn of the century Great Britain could no longer adhere solely to grants of nationality by birth *and* by descent within amendments to Empire-wide legislation. Upon later assumption of the Palestine Mandate, in part to maintain their position as the ultimate sovereign, Great Britian refrained from grants of explicit liberal citizenship rights such as to representation in a legislative council or proportional voting rights. These types of proposed democratic measures, while implemented partially by the Ottoman government in the Arab provinces before 1914, severely challenged the foundation of British policy in Palestine – the facilitation of a Jewish national home. Palestinian citizenship had to be created in order to legally – and diplomatically – classify the inhabitants of the mandate, and to regulate who could acquire such a status.

For officials who served in the government of Palestine, the construction of legal and internationally accepted identity was a complicated process. In the early years of the civil administration, the colonial administrators' notions of nationality were influenced by their empire's own citizenship legislation and history of colonialism in the 'Orient' (including India and Egypt), the perception of Palestine as divided into Muslim, Christian and Jewish religious communities and the Jewish national home policy that the mandate encompassed.[33] The entire process of inventing citizenship in the crucial early 1920s resulted in unanswered questions that pertained to the changing statuses, sovereignty and political and civil rights of Palestinian Arabs and Jews. The process also formally separated Arab from Jewish Palestinian citizenships as both communities received, lost and used their citizenship in different ways. Aside from the separation of Arab and Jewish citizenship acquisition and loss, officials in London and Palestine did not consistently use the terminology of nationality and citizenship in the same ways. The empire's bureaucrats – in this case, colonial and mandate officials – had their own clear understandings of nationality and citizenship in the context of British policy in the metropole and in colonies and protectorates but this understanding was situated at a unique juncture in the history of empire.[34] The tutelage system of the mandates in the Levant called into question traditional, colonial practices of delineating identity.

The National and the Citizen in Vocabulary and Behaviour

The current study focuses on two broad groups: the native, largely Arabic-speaking population of Palestine, and the largely English imperial and local officials and administrators who essentially formulated and applied British policy in Palestine. In order to better define 'discourse' as throughout the chapters, a brief note of vocabulary is necessary. The terms of reference used by the two groups to describe political and civic identity rarely coincided in terms of their meanings and definitions. In fact, Palestinian Arab leadership did not use consistent terminology in reference to nationality and citizenship during the interwar period, and so it is often hard to pin down the best Arabic-to-English translations of the terminology used in documentary sources without a good deal of context. Consequently, any attempt to pin one specific meaning or set of values and practices to the Arabic and Ottoman terms such as 'nationality', 'citizenship' and 'rights', is to step onto subjective grounds and indeed making such an argument is not the purpose of the study.[35] Arab nationalist and more populist leaders seemed to have picked and chosen the words that they used and the concepts they attached to them in order to suit certain circumstances, slogans, audiences or locales. By the early 1920s if not before, the terms for 'nationality' ('*jinsiyya*'), citizenship ('*muwātana*') and civil rights ('*huquq midaniyya*') took precedence in written discussions of identity and political membership in the nation. Their meanings in the context of the Palestine Mandate became familiar to a larger segment of Palestinian society as the readership of newspapers grew throughout the first decade of British rule. Most commonly, writers and politicians used 'citizenship' and 'nationality' interchangeably and incorporated other meanings for citizenship such as '*midaniyya*', which denoted a greater sense of *urban* civic identity. The terms that accompanied this discourse such as '*qawmiyya*' (in reference to pan-Arab nationalism) emphasised the synthesis of Palestinian nationality with a pan-Arab national identity. As Helen Haste has shown, in the construction of the citizen the historian must take into account the ways in which individuals negotiate rhetoric, meaning and definitions of citizenship and particularly the narrative that explains and justifies the citizen and the nation.[36] In the case of Palestine during the era of British mandatory rule, the representation and the understanding of the citizen was directly linked to Ottoman-era social categories of (Arab) nationhood, community (southern Syria) and a sense of an Arab ethnic identity.

The year 1918 did not represent a clear break in the history of Palestine's Arab population, nor did it represent a break or transformation for the wider region. As the book demonstrates, self-identification by the Arab population of Greater Syria in particular, including those Arabic-speaking peoples who migrated away from these provinces, remained in line with late-Ottoman era identification. The end of the Ottoman Empire did not signal a singularly new conception of political selfhood or even nationhood by the Palestinian Arabs; rather, they continued to stress their legal and ideological identifications as that of

Arab, yet former Ottoman, nationals.[37] This is in line with the argument of Awad Halabi who maintains that the Palestinian population nurtured strong links with their Ottoman identity into the 1920s and during the Turkish War of Independence.[38] Although the year 1918 marks the start of British administration in Palestine, it cannot be characterised as the year of any abrupt change in political or ideological identification from that of Ottoman citizens to strictly Palestinian nationals. Indeed, the two were not mutually exclusive in the early years of the mandate.

The place of Mandate Palestine, as well as the other Arab mandates, in the global context of the emergence of nation-states and international and diplomatic norms is understudied. The book attempts to shed light on a small corner of this dimension in the history of the Levant and its diasporic and migratory population and their *practice* of citizenship. The nationalism of the twentieth century shaped laws on nationality and immigration and the authorities in states determined which individuals or ethnic groups belonged to which nation-state as its nationals.[39] Hanley has written that just before the First World War identity documents were 'portable signs of sovereignty' that defined 'the human boundaries' of the state.[40] Residence documents, or nationality documents as they came to be known, conferred an obligation of consular and diplomatic protection to their holder by the state or colonial power that granted them. Pre-First World War citizenship was a local status and largely irrelevant in international contexts. Imperial systems incorporated bureaucratic measures to differentiate between categories of human beings and to classify peoples according to their subject status, race, religion, and, until the end of the war, their nationality.

It is in this context that the issue of Palestinian Arab emigration from Ottoman Greater Syria and Mandate Palestine becomes significant. Arab emigrants, while the subject of newer studies in recent years, have been almost entirely left out of the historical discourse of national politics in the Levant. The political agency of the Palestinian Arab emigrants (*muhājarīn*) is significant in its connection with the process of 'making citizens' during the mandate period, particularly through links of civic associations. The Palestinian Arab diaspora (*mahjar*), especially the emigrants in Latin America, played a major role in crafting a counter-definition of Palestinian citizenship intimately linked with that of Arab nationality. Until quite recently, historians of Palestine have long neglected the role played by Ottoman emigrants from southern Syria in ideological and political movements against the mandate government and its policy of support for the establishment of a Jewish national home.[41] The emigrants' discourses on the questions of identity and belonging – shaped within the varied discursive fields of the diaspora – demonstrate that their 'outside-in', ethnically segregated existence in the Americas allowed for these diasporic Arabs to make clear the realities of the British administration to their families, to the national movement and to socio-political organisations in the homeland. Sections of the book approach citizenship from the standpoint of the Palestinian Arab diaspora in order to offer a more nuanced understanding of multiple meanings of citizenship, Arab nationality and civic and political identities that at times converged with or diverged from the development of these same meanings and movements within the mandate's territory. The diaspora also offers a third community through which the historian can understand the impact of British policies in Palestine, especially in light of changing imperial policy. The history of the *mahjar* is also crucial to contemporary understandings of Palestinian statelessness and refugee status.

In order to trace the legislative development of Palestinian nationality and citizenship, historians must rely on records of the Colonial, Foreign, Home, Dominions, and India Offices, as well as records from Parliamentary debates, Trade and Treasury Offices, the Crown Agents and the Law Officers. The opinions of British (and French) officials in Egypt and elsewhere in the Middle East, India and Africa influenced the drafts of the nationality order, and so too did the Zionist Organisation. Mandate legislation, the Arabic press and documents of nationalist and local societies and leaders are all crucial sources to trace the construction and evolution of the post-war national and citizen. The Arabic sources for the topic of citizenship in the diaspora (such as letters, files of civic associations and newspapers printed in places such as the Americas, the Caribbean and the Philippines) are numerous and widespread particularly since citizenship and nationality became important issues for Palestinian Arabs and Jews who lived across the globe. Unfortunately, a number of these sources outside of the Levant and Great Britain have not been consulted due to the focus of this project as well as a number of uncertainties over their locations – however, sources from the Syrian and Lebanese Arab diaspora from the interwar period have only recently been uncovered by other historians. This book has used documentary sources located in personal archives, libraries, and state archives in the United Kingdom, Israel, the West Bank and Beirut.

A certain amount of the historiography on Mandate Palestine has emphasised Britain's creation of dual structures of administration and society.[42] Chapter 2 delves deeper into this, to investigate whether the structures put in place by Great Britain for the acquisition of Palestinian citizenship favoured Jewish immigrants in any way, and the chapter demonstrates how and why Great Britain felt the dual administration structure necessary to preserve its own sovereignty from 1918 through 1925. In terms of legislation and administration, the mandate officials took cues and direction on policy from London, and Great Britain acted as a colonial power in Palestine in its legislation and administration. Perhaps most significantly for the early years of the Palestine Administration, Foreign and Colonial Office permanent members were guided by their mission to ensure that legislation in the mandate territory was in line with post-war norms and that it did nothing to prejudice the establishment of the Jewish national homeland. The main focus here is on the history of British legislation in Palestine and the main actors – and tensions between these actors and their departments – involved in making that legislation, including the mandate's first attorney-general, Norman Bentwich. The aim of British legislation, however, was to simply create a legal citizenship for the mandate's inhabitants, and to provide the means by which this citizenship could be acquired.

The third chapter is somewhat in debt to the theoretical work on democracy, civil society, belonging and communitarian citizenship formulations by Raymond Rocco. The chapter shifts focus from the British aspect of nationality and citizenship legislation to the Arab inhabitants of Palestine, in order to analyse the development of the civic and political community during the early years of the mandate administration. The new types of spaces and institutions introduced by the new administration in Palestine challenged traditional, Ottoman-style ways of understanding identity, community and nationality. The challenges and disruptions wrought by the incorporation of Palestine into a new imperial system reconfigured social relations and communal and national boundaries. These disruptions strengthened the Arabs' sense of communitarian belonging to Palestine, allowed for the formation of new civic and political associations and laid the foundation for engagement of Arab society with particular notions, ideologies and claims frequently discussed in a plethora of press articles. These would later constitute a series of demands and appeals for citizenship rights. At its core, the chapter traces how citizenship and nationality took on a specifically political and rights-based understanding of Arab civic belonging in Palestine.

Chapter 4 contextualises the discourses, influences, notions and political transformations that informed the Palestinian Arabs' understanding of nationality and citizenship in the diaspora (particularly in Latin America) and at home in the years leading up to and just after the 1925 Citizenship Order-in-Council. Importantly, it focuses on the impacts of these understandings in Palestinian society and as part of Arab relations with Great Britain as the mandatory power. Just as significantly, the Arab nationalists and local, civil society leaders began to change their perceptions of the identity of Jewish immigrants, largely informed by the situation of the Arab emigrants outside of Palestine. It offers an entirely new history of the emigrants and their reactions to, and counter-definitions of, the type of legal and apolitical nationality and citizenship that Palestine Mandate and colonial officials attempted to craft during the same time period. With reference to work by Engin Isin, the chapter analyses how citizens were 'made' in the diaspora and the roles played by civil society organisations to link Palestinian natives abroad with their homeland as mandate institutions and Jewish immigration became ever more an entrenched part of life for the Arab population of Palestine. The impact of citizenship legislation on the diaspora frames the introduction of debates, discussions and slogans within Palestine, such as the demand for the 'right to return' and letters of protest to the British and international community that underscored the grievances of the emigrants who lacked citizenship. The emigrants, for their part, historically represent both civic and political belonging in the entity that Arab nationalists increasingly stressed their right of ownership to – the Palestinian nation-state.

British rule in Palestine, as elsewhere in the overseas Empire, was reinforced through laws, regulations and orders-in-council. The power and rule of Great Britain, as Chapter 5 demonstrates, was sovereign – British officials often neglected or selectively applied the League of Nations, international treaties and international and regional norms. However, other layers of history can be added to British rule in Palestine in the decade after 1925: tensions between London and Jerusalem and between individual officials hindered attempts by local administrators to implement regulations and policies that would ease the increased ill-feelings and discord between the Arab and Jewish communities. Certainly, this was the case with citizenship legislation, although the Arab leadership attributed British reluctance to turn the citizens' legal status into a political one to British favouritism for the Zionist movement and Jewish immigrants. The reality was far more complicated, not only due to internal tensions between officials but also because of insistence by members of the Cabinet and various corners of Whitehall to promote imperial standards with respect to any policies or regulations on Palestinian citizenship and nationality. The chapter demonstrates how Palestinian citizenship was offered and revoked in different ways for Arabs as opposed to Jews, and that the differences between administrators specifically with respect to policy towards Jewish immigrants had an effect on changes to citizenship legislation. Although the distinctions created by legislation were very much a part of the wider colonial project and the changing fortunes of the British Empire, the chapter also emphasises that the unique nature of the mandate and its national home policy meant that administrations had to account for a certain internationalisation of Palestinian citizenship.

By the latter half of the 1920s and the early 1930s, British and Arab misunderstandings of each other's intentions with respect to identity and citizenship status encouraged even stronger claims by the Arabs to the bundle of rights that they felt entitled to in accordance with their own particular understandings of nationality and citizenship. Different socio-economic Arab groups in Palestine used a number of ways to express their wishes, demands and comprehension of rights *to* the state, rather than the civil and religious rights they were offered within the state. The sixth chapter ties the discussions of citizenship that circulated in the territory from 1918 through the mid-1930s to the projects of belonging that the nationalists, populists and the Arabic press attended to and actively worked towards. The active engagement of the press and social groups in political actions with the aim of changing mandate institutions fostered a new vocabulary of rights, political and civic identity and citizenship belonging in the years just before the start of the Palestine Revolt in 1936. The chapter frames certain discourses on citizenship and national identity as more dominant and others as more subaltern during the latter half of the 1920s and 1930s. The key case study within this chapter is that of the Palestinian Arab Istiqlal (Independence) Party, whose policies aimed to redefine citizenship and access to rights under the mandate.

Chapter 7 chronicles the changes to the various meanings of citizenship and civic identity during the three years of the Palestinian Arab Revolt. Effectively, citizenship claims became rather 'stalled' in Palestine upon the outbreak of the nationwide revolt against the British. Rural rebels and revolt commanders co-opted certain claims, which in turn influenced newer meanings of patriotic loyalty and practices of citizenship. In particular, the Peel Commission report, which offered recommendations on policy in Palestine following the initial disturbances, is described in terms of its impact on citizenship in order to offer a historical explanation of the continuities and changes of both the British and the Arabs' perceptions of nationality, citizenship and rights by 1937. The concluding chapter, Chapter 8, offers further insight on citizenship in Palestine after 1939 and until the end of the mandate in 1948 and the changing levels of the Arabs' political subjectivity. The differences between the multiple doctrines, vocabularies, expressions and concepts of citizenship during the first two decades of the mandate administration are reflected in the legislation on citizenship passed by the British administration and in the reactions by the Arab citizens to that legislation. It explores the immediate reactions of Great Britain and the Palestine administration to the increased Jewish immigration to the territory and the changes made to the mandate's citizenship legislation in the wake of the Peel Commission's recommendations. The conclusion demonstrates that on the eve of the Second World War, citizenship claims, particularly that of the right to administer Palestine, continued to be a central and defining issue for Arab residents and emigrants as the two groups increasingly feared the impact of the increased Jewish immigration and the demographic and political changes to the citizenry.

After Great Britain rescinded control over the mandate and when the state of Israel came into being in 1948, it remained a fact that the territory's native Arab population had been constituted as political subjects as well as legal citizens for more than two decades: they did not simply exist in nationalist imaginings but were defined legally in regulations as a demographic entitled to passports, identity documents, measures of civil, political and social rights and international recognition. Palestinian Arab emigrants, especially those in the Americas, also saw themselves as Palestinian nationals entitled to Palestinian citizenship, whether they chose to return to reside in that territory or not. The unavoidable displacement of these native Palestinians due to the 1925 Citizenship Order-in-Council is an unspoken yet crucial element of the Palestinian Arab diaspora today as well as during the interwar years. On the surface, the contemporary political implications of Palestinian citizenship may be few and far between for policy-makers in Palestine and Israel. However, this not-too-distant historical existence of – and the Arabs' own engagement with – notions and understandings of a rights-based Palestinian citizenship cannot be separated from the development of the twentieth and twenty-first centuries of the political, social and civic identity of the Palestinian Arab population both at home, in the occupied territories and Israel, and in the wider diaspora. Palestinian nationalism did not appear in 1918 as a movement whose adherents had a clear political identity; rather, citizenship and nationality were forged through reinterpretations of traditional and cultural notions of civic identity, rights and protections of the imperial subjects vis-à-vis the state and Ottoman precedents, alongside acts of political participation, political behaviour and civic engagement.

2

Inventing the National and the Citizen in Palestine: Great Britain, Sovereignty and the Legislative Context, 1918–1925

In October 1922, just two years after the establishment of the mandates system by the League of Nations, the Arab members of the Palestine Mandate's administrative advisory committee met High Commissioner Herbert Samuel in Jerusalem to read through the draft of a law to regulate Palestinian nationality. Nationality did not yet exist as a legal status within the territory ceded to Great Britain's administrative control as a mandate, nor as an internationally recognised identity. By that point Palestine's first attorney-general, an Englishman named Norman Bentwich, wrote a large portion of the draft legislation and submitted drafts to the Colonial Office for approval. Prior to the First World War, Bentwich served as a barrister in England but he had no specialisations in nationality law. None of the officials in the Palestine Administration, whom historian Michael Cohen once classified as either ill-trained or not at all trained for their positions, had such a specialisation.[1] Those seven Arabs who attended the meeting with Samuel and looked over Bentwich's proposal on Palestinian nationality belonged to prominent Palestinian families. Most of these men received a Western-style education, had some knowledge of Ottoman-era law and they all professed sympathies with the anti-Zionist Palestinian Arab nationalist movement. As the men – certainly not specialists in English law – studied the draft, they were struck by Bentwich's plan to give Jewish immigrants 'provisional nationality' while the Arab population in Palestine remained 'former Ottoman subjects' categorised as 'ex-enemy aliens' by Great Britain. One member of the committee, Abdul Khader al-Muzaffer, bewildered as to why the mandate's Arab-majority population was not given the same status as the new immigrants nor even that of officially recognised nationals, proclaimed ironically that 'Palestine is a land of marvels and this new regulation [for provisional nationality] is one of them'.[2]

The so-called provisional status held by the Jewish immigrants reinforced the identity of the Arabs as akin to 'natives' in colonial terminology. By 1922, as the mandatory in Palestine, Great Britain undeniably acted more as an imperial power than as a trustee and the colonial nature of its rule is evidenced by the ways in which the civil administration created and implemented nationality and citizenship as well as other pieces of legislation in cooperation with the British Colonial, Foreign, Home, and Dominions Offices, the Crown and the Zionist Organisation. Until 1938, the Colonial Office's permanent members jointly devised policy for Palestine in cooperation with each high commissioner, and ultimate approval for policy came from the Cabinet and government in London.[3] The members of the short-lived High Commissioner's Advisory Council disbanded soon after the meeting, owing to these Arab members' dissatisfaction with the limitations of their solely advisory role.

When the final draft of the order-in-council to institute Palestinian citizenship came into effect in 1925, its regulations offered more favourable means for the acquisition of citizenship to Jewish immigrants than to Arabs from the former provinces of the Ottoman Empire, Egypt and North Africa. Even Palestinian Arab students or merchants who had temporarily relocated outside of Palestine were disadvantaged by the provisions of the order-in-council. The nationality-turned-citizenship order bolstered the cornerstone of mandate policy: the facilitation of a Jewish national homeland as embodied in the mandate charter. Despite misgivings by certain members of the Colonial Office and the Palestine Administration, this policy influenced most pieces of legislation proposed for Palestine from 1918 to 1925. The intricacies of Palestinian nationality and citizenship legislation reflected the obligation of Great Britain to adhere to the mandate's policy to support the establishment of a Jewish national home. In order to ensure the successful establishment of that national home, which the government professed to be its moral duty, Cabinet ministers in London favoured arrangements that allowed Jewish immigrants to acquire easily Palestinian citizenship upon their arrival to the territory. At the same time, Great Britain worked – albeit with varying degrees of success – to ensure that the legislation in each of their mandates remained in line with new, post-war international regulations. Alongside consideration of the country's obligations to the Zionist Organisation, broader debates on nationality, citizenship and colonialism by Great Britain and, to some extent, other mandate and colonial administrations, framed the specific creation of nationality and citizenship in the quasi-colonial Palestine Mandate.

Discussions and disagreements among colonial officials, inhabitants and immigrants over sovereignty in Palestine and in the mandates system, as well as over the meaning of post-war identity prior to the 1922 ratification of the mandate, influenced the shape of nationality legislation for the territory from 1922 through 1925. These same discussions did not take place only for the case of Palestine, but were replicated in the wider British Empire and throughout the post-Ottoman Levant. In particular, direct colonialism had given way to indirect colonial rule in many parts of the Empire. A number of colonial administrators expounded upon the benefits of indirect rule from the turn of the century, and the trusteeship system proposed for the mandated territories was not construed as outright colonialism. These discussions, ideas, practices and identities developed trans-imperially as officials of empire (and others in non-official capacities) moved between imperial sites. However, as 'new' imperial historians David Lambert and Alan Lester argue, ideas about race, national identity, governance, civilisation and, in our case, citizenship, were not simply imported from the imperial centre or from the periphery, but developed across multiple spaces. Even within the same region, not all imperial ideas, practices and ideologies travelled well from place to place.[4] At the same time, external discussions of the nature of empire impacted these ideas and practices even while they were in transit.

The new language of internationalism and self-determination in a number of locales meant that traditional notions of subjecthood lost their former meanings in the metropole as well as in colonies, protectorates and the Dominions. These changes are reflected in the muddled nature of belonging in Palestine as envisioned by mandate and colonial authorities and policy-makers, as well as those precedents that they turned to for guidance. As demonstrated in what follows, the disagreements over sovereignty and the growing uncertainty by colonial officials over the post-war imperial world-view led to the separate codification of Jewish-Palestinian nationality from Arab-Palestinian nationality as first mentioned in the mandate's 1922 basic law. Through the early 1920s as the British codified nationality provisions, Arab natives were treated differently from Jewish 'provisional' citizens in the practical matters of travel, passports, diplomatic protection and the regulation of the franchise. The latter represent some of the immediate impacts upon Palestine's Jewish immigrants and native Arab inhabitants of the Treaty of Lausanne and the subsequent Palestine Citizenship Order-in-Council as a citizenship order signed by the King of England rather than a nationality law passed by the local administration. The debates over the creation of Palestinian citizenship were not confined to Whitehall and the Palestine Administration, but were framed more broadly by ambiguity and various definitions of nationality and citizenship based upon Britain's experience with imperial subjecthood, national status and imperial consular protection.

Immediately after the end of the First World War and by the time of the Paris Peace Conference in 1919, British officials and the military administration in Palestine grappled with the contradiction between fulfilling both the trusteeship obligations of the proposed mandate and the obligations of the Balfour Declaration that required sovereignty and direct administration of the territory. Although officials found points of comparison with colonial administrations elsewhere in the Middle East and India, the post-war rhetoric of national self-determination and the strength of nationalist movements that inspired the idea of trusteeship over certain groups of people ran sharply against imperial practice. Although, as enshrined in the declaration, the mandate could not prejudice the civil and religious rights of the Arab majority, Great Britain could not offer Jews and Arabs an equal, rights-based citizenship or even equal representative institutions for self-government. Administrators feared that giving political rights to the Arabs to vote or sanction the enactment of legislation would pose a threat to their obligations towards the Zionist movement. Therefore, citizenship had to be framed as a legal, apolitical status with minimal accompanying civil rights, and the ultimate power to give or take away citizenship status rested with the British high commissioners in Palestine overseen by London.

The British in Palestine institutionalised a dual administrative structure that offered Arab and Jewish individuals separate and unequal civil, economic, social and political positions. A number of historians, including Bernard Wasserstein and Zachary Lockman, have debated the limits of classifying the mandate's administration in such a way, but for the creation of legal nationality two different classifications existed for the territory's inhabitants.[5] In light of British practice before and after 1922, the bewilderment expressed by Abdul Khader al-Muzaffer and his colleagues was not misplaced. The foundations of this structure can be traced back to the years immediately after 1918 when the British, in their capacity of military administrators in Palestine, made every attempt to exclude the demands of the Arab leadership on matters of political rights from the commentary on nationality and citizenship. In response to the unwillingness of High Commissioner Samuel to consider certain measures of self-government and to repeal the Balfour Declaration's inclusion in mandate policy, his Arab advisors expressed their disagreement with the nationality law draft in 1922, and not only terminated their service on the advisory committee but also supported a popular boycott of elections to a proposed legislative council that same year. First, however, it is to the parameters of state succession after 1918, and the notions and debates within the League of Nations and by Great Britain on sovereignty in the mandate system, that the chapter now turns.

Great Britain, Palestine and the League of Nations: Sovereignty, Nationality and State Succession, 1919–1922

The end of the First World War did not immediately change the status quo of legislation on the ground in the Ottoman Empire's Arab provinces; in fact, no internationally recognised bureaucratic measures existed to allow for any changes. The practice of sovereign rule by Great Britain, whose soldiers entered southern Syria and Jerusalem at the end of 1917, was ushered into a new era in which direct colonialism of conquered lands could no longer be considered legitimate in the eyes of the newly created international community of nations.[6] Still, despite Woodrow Wilson's declaration of support in early 1918 with groups resisting imperialism, the British Government initially had space in which to claim measures of sovereign control over the Arab-majority provinces that became the mandates of Palestine, Syria, Transjordan and Iraq.

The first order of business for the British occupation forces was to install a temporary administration in southern Syria, which lasted from December 1917 to mid-1920 and became known as Occupied Enemy Territory Administration (OETA) South. The military officials in this area, unofficially referred to as Palestine, decided in 1918 to keep the status quo of Ottoman laws until bureaucratic measures could be undertaken by a civilian administration. The arrival of the first High Commissioner Herbert Samuel in July 1920 marked the start of civil rule. During these two years of military government, and for quite some time after, the most pressing issue was that of sovereignty in the territory that was to become the Palestine Mandate. The basic structures of the League of Nations were not yet fully formed when the Paris Peace Conference of 1919 decided the future status of the Ottoman Empire's Arab provinces of Syria and Mesopotamia (Iraq). The political uncertainty of the early post-war years in the Levant affected the status of the inhabitants of Palestine – one of the most pressing issues linked to sovereignty proved to be the dissolution of Ottoman nationality.

The concept of sovereignty was not clear-cut for any of the parties involved in the creation of the mandate system or even in the creation of the League of Nations. The British, for their part, faced a number of basic questions on the sovereignty of Palestine as related to nationality prior to the ratification of the Palestine Mandate in 1922. Susan Pedersen has argued that the League of Nations mandate system served as a discursive arena – of debate, discussion and ideology – rather than one of practical political action. Here, Britain and France interacted in certain rhetorical ways in order to establish or defend political claims to territory.[7] This left the question of sovereignty over the Arab territories up for debate but delegates to League bodies undertook little concrete action to define the appropriate exercise of power in the cases of trusteeship. Britain, France, and League officials saw themselves as the only legitimate discussants on the issue and British officials held a particularly high view of Great Britain as a leader in the Allies' decision-making. Through the nineteenth century, the British envisioned sovereignty and particular policies of rule to make their empire 'home', familiar and a space that legislation and regulations from the metropole could pass into smoothly.[8] British delegates to the League were reluctant to consider any loss of control over their territories to an international body.

The League of Nations sidelined opinions from nationalist movements and political representatives of the former Ottoman territories, whose ideas of sovereignty over those territories varied greatly from that held by the Allied Powers. A historical analysis of sovereignty, particularly over nationality legislation, can help to answer the question of whether the concept itself mattered to the League and to Great Britain in the early years of the Palestine Mandate. Colonial officials, including the architects of indirect rule, did not have a clear definition of the concept by 1919. The League sought to create and define a new type of sovereignty through the mandates-as-trusteeships concept. Nationality regulations, first in the 1920 Treaty of Sèvres and then in the 1923 Treaty of Lausanne, were one medium through which the international body attempted to define sovereignty.

This early uncertainty over authority in Palestine played a role in the conceptualisation of the nationality of its inhabitants. Initially, the

colonial experts in Britain and in Geneva who supervised the establishment of the mandates did not place much emphasis on the necessity to formulate new provisions to clarify sovereignty and nationality
in each mandate. During 1919 and 1920 officials concerned themselves more with the international validation of Great Britain's
claim to become the mandatory power in Palestine.[9] Locally, from
the beginning of the military administration in Palestine, the British
Colonial Office and the Foreign Office diverged on policy and only
reluctantly worked together. Historian Aaron Klieman, for example,
argues that the two departments had fundamental differences of ori-
entation and priority for Palestine that emerged out of the post-war
tensions over their shared responsibilities for British interests in the
Arab world. With the beginning of the civil administration the Colonial Office and its new Middle East Department (established in 1921)
assumed responsibility and control over the policy and the administration of the Palestine Mandate, but by that point tensions became
apparent locally in Palestine. Meanwhile, the Foreign Office assumed
responsibility for the conduct of relations between the mandates and
independent states.[10] Yet Colonial and Foreign Office power were not
absolute: the India Office, Air Ministry, Home Office, Dominions
Office and other departments also claimed measures of responsibility
for Palestine or its foreign relations.

After the appointment of Samuel in 1920, the Colonial Office
and the Cabinet in London guided the activities of Palestine's civil
administration through the newly established High Commissioner's
Office once the latter passed 'on-the-ground' information to policy-
makers in the British capital. The government formed directives
and issued decrees that it sent to Jerusalem for implementation.
Throughout this process, divergences in opinions became clear:
in 1921, Winston Churchill noted that 90 per cent of the British
officials in Palestine, at that time closely aligned with the Foreign
Office, opposed the Zionist policy of the local British administration headed by Samuel.[11] Although the Colonial Office was concerned with Arab public opinion specifically to maintain political
stability and public security, by contrast the Foreign Office was
aware of Palestine's importance for the wider Arab and Muslim
world and felt more sympathetic toward the general Arab opposition to Zionist policy.[12] In later years the Zionist Organisation
came to view the Colonial Office as especially against its cause.
Tensions went deeper, however: Cabinet Ministers disagreed consistently on policy for Palestine and the Cabinet often disagreed
with the local administration in Jerusalem and the ways in which

the high commissioners could 'set' policy. For its part, the Colonial Office in the 1920s and 1930s suffered from frequent changes to its secretary and under-secretary.[13] Officially, the high commissioners were meant to be unbiased towards either the Arab or Jewish residents of Palestine but in the metropole the situation differed. The Zionist Organisation and its head, Chaim Weizmann, had a great deal of influence in the British Parliament. Unofficially, memoirs by members of the local administration report upon assumed and real biases of various officials and the tensions that these caused in Jerusalem during the early years of the mandate.[14]

The relationship between Great Britain and the League of Nations reflected another dimension of uncertainty over the type of power that the former held in Palestine. As the process of drafting the mandate charters began in 1919, Great Britain recognised that it needed to work with the League of Nations to administer its Arab territories, although the former continued to claim, as it had since 1918, to be the sovereign power in Palestine. In 1919, Lord Robert Cecil, head of the British delegation to the League and president of the League of Nations Union (LNU), stated his opposition to any League interference with future administrative decisions made by mandate governments. Other British statesmen had prominent roles, writing the proposals for the three classes into which mandates came to be divided. Disputes with the other Allied Powers in 1920 over who would take the Arab mandates postponed the actual implementation of the mandate system.[15] From 1919 to 1922, although colonial officials delegated power to other members of the Permanent Mandates Commission (PMC), a largely advisory body, to help formulate the framework of each future British-administered mandate Great Britain greatly influenced the ultimate acceptance or refusal of mandate charters. In the case of Palestine, differences of opinion over these specific preparations for its future independence surfaced between colonial officials in London, members of the civil administration and Zionist Organisation leaders. To varying degrees, the differences of opinion impacted the work of the director of the League's Mandate Section, Switzerland's William Rappard, who supervised the day-to-day running of the PMC and collected data on the proposed mandates. His colleague Sir Frederick Lugard served as Britain's first representative on the commission, despite his lack of diplomatic and political experience.[16]

By the end of January 1920, the British delegation to the League had a general understanding of the structure of the mandates but no consensus existed as to how they would work in practice, especially as to provisions of nationality and the actual status of the inhabitants of the territory.[17] Internally, in the battle between the Colonial and Foreign Offices over the supervision of the mandates, Lugard argued that each fell within the realm of colonial rather than foreign policy. In order to pre-empt further disagreement, control of the civil administration of Palestine was transferred in 1921 to the Colonial Office.[18] The mandatories were officially nominated at the San Remo conference in April of 1920 but the situation in Anatolia and the refusal of the Turkish nationalists to endorse a peace treaty further complicated the practical implementation of the Arab mandates and dissuaded any change in the national status of their inhabitants. British Prime Minister Lloyd George and French Prime Minister Georges Clemenceau decided to grant the Palestine Mandate to Great Britain despite strong Arab nationalist objections, from within the Levant and from the diaspora, as clearly evident from the conclusions of the King–Crane Commission Report.[19]

It must be stressed that the territories of the former Ottoman Empire remained nominally part of that empire until the conclusion of a peace treaty with the forces of Mustafa Kemal and the new Republic of Turkey in 1923. The Turkish nationalists did not accept the 1920 Treaty of Sèvres and therefore Mustafa Kemal remained symbolically at war *as the Ottoman Empire* with the Allied Powers. The Treaty of Sèvres' importance to the current discussion can be related to its provisions for the enforcement of nationality in Palestine and in all of the Ottoman Empire's former territories. The treaty sanctioned the League's consensus on state succession: Ottoman nationality would effectively cease to exist and the new administrations that took the place of the empire would be responsible for the creation and regulation of nationality. However, without Turkey's approval of the treaty, the inhabitants of the mandated territories remained *Ottoman* nationals. They included not only Arabs but also ethnic Kurds, Turkomen, Circassians, Armenians and Eastern European Jewish immigrants.

As the Allied Powers considered questions of nationality in the international, post-war context, the British placed the population of Palestine into categories and accorded different treatment to them. Beginning in 1918 and until the ratification of the Treaty of Lausanne in 1923, the civil administration dealt with two different 'nationality' groups: the native inhabitants, Arab or otherwise, who had all been Ottoman subjects, and the immigrant Jews who arrived after 1914. The method of categorisation was not without imperial reasoning. During the later decades of Ottoman rule, immigrant Jews from Europe who resided in the empire came under the protection of European consuls. In contrast, Jews who came from the other Arab lands, including North Africa, usually took Ottoman nationality.[20] Some groups of Jews from the empire, Egypt or North Africa (such as merchant Baghdadi Jews) acquired British-protected status in the nineteenth and twentieth centuries.[21] The new immigrants, however, did not generally take Ottoman nationality and they did not remain under European protection after the outbreak of hostilities in 1914. When the British officials arrived, one of their priorities towards this group was to define it in provisional national terms.

Prior to 1923, the Euro-centric Zionist Organisation led by Chaim Weizmann (a close friend of Secretary of State for the Colonies at the time, Winston Churchill) lent a great amount of influence in offering commentary and advice, in accordance with Article 4 of the Mandate whose provisions gave the organisation the advisory role on Palestine policy, into the initially nebulous discussions of nationality that affected the Jewish inhabitants of Palestine, the separation of 'national' groups in the territory and the framework of the mandate. Indeed, the mandate charter allowed only for the Zionist Organisation, rather than the Arab leadership, to offer assistance and advice to the British administration. Due to the Balfour Declaration's obligations and the increased Jewish immigration after the war, the British confronted the unique question of how to create a legal and political framework of nationality and citizenship to satisfy the conditions in Palestine. The advice offered by the colonial experts, Cabinet members and the Zionist Organisation shaped both the mandate charter and nationality legislation. After he viewed the earliest draft of the mandate charter in 1919, Weizmann proposed to Britain's Secretary of State for the Colonies that Palestine's inhabitants must have full freedom of religion as part of the 'civil rights' of citizenship. His proposal did not explicitly define 'civil rights' or citizenship. Weizmann's close friend Baron Rothschild added his own commentary to the proposal. He suggested that Jews should receive preferential treatment with a separate citizenship in order to satisfy the Zionist leaders of British sincerity for the national home policy. Rothschild elaborated further by suggesting that the Jews of Palestine should also be given the status of full British subjects. The British noted the potential difficulties of such a measure: Arab demands for the same status as British subjects and widespread opposition to the Palestine Mandate, a mass emigration from Palestine of Jews who had full British protection and the impossibility of maintaining a suitable administration with such a provision.[22] Surely, the British also must have worried about the sincerity of the loyalty to the Crown that such subjects presumably would never cultivate.

While British officials and the League worked on drafts of the mandate, it became clear that departments within the government needed clarification as to the application of Palestinian nationality since colonial precedents could not be used in their entirety. The discussions framed Article 7 of the mandate: the article required the enactment of a nationality law specifically for Jewish immigrants. Colonial legislators, guided by imperial and diplomatic concerns, focused their attention on the means through which they could provide these immigrants with a new national status. Initially, the drafts stated that immigrants who took up residence in Palestine within two years of the ratification of the mandate would lose their existing nationality and automatically become Palestinian citizens.[23] The concept behind the proposal of automatic loss of one nationality and automatic substitution with another did not fit harmoniously with the aim of the Zionist movement: namely, the desire for a self-governing Jewish national homeland was at odds with the forced imposition of the nationality of a non-Jewish, British-administered territory. Until the ratification of the mandates, however, Zionist leaders such as Weizmann requested that the Foreign Office offer consular protection to Palestine's Jewish immigrant population. This request framed Article 12 of the mandate charter, which entitled all citizens to British protection when abroad.[24]

The debates and discussions highlighted above – whether between British administrators in the Colonial and Foreign Offices, officials in London and Jerusalem or members of the Zionist Organisation – informed the practical application of the mandate charter from 1919 to its ratification in 1922. This practical application took into account the visualisation by the local government of two separate national communities resident in Palestine. The international context is no less important to this visualisation. The abrogation of the Treaty of Sèvres by Mustafa Kemal forced the administration to recognise Jewish immigrants as provisional nationals but reinforced the status of the majority Arab natives as former Ottoman subjects who were accorded different treatment. The Palestine Mandate charter stated in Article 7 that the mandatory was to enact a law for the *acquisition* of Palestinian nationality by Jewish immigrants but crucially did not define nationality or citizenship and it made no mention of the Arab population. Arguments over whether Great Britain as a sovereign power separate from the Palestine Administration could offer consular protection to residents further complicated matters. Members of the administration repeatedly failed to come to a unified opinion on the international status of the Palestinian population.

Neither the League nor the Mandate charter stated if authority in Palestine came from the League, the Cabinet, Parliament, the king himself, or an international treaty. The League did not make clear the procedures through which the British could administer the mandated territories, which meant that from 1920 to 1923 the civil administration headed by High Commissioner Samuel hesitated to pass legislation. The charter itself was not a constitution or basic law for the territory. The question of sovereignty remained largely unsolved through Samuel's term of office although the British flew the Union Jack in their mandated territories with the belief – alongside the practical impression that the symbol of the flag gave – that the Crown, rather than the League, was the sovereign.[25] Ultimately, these and other variables forced administrators to delay the completion of a nationality law to regulate citizenship.

Norman Bentwich and the Meanings of Nationality, Citizenship and the Imperial Protégé

In 1939, fifteen years after the implementation of the Treaty of Lausanne, the English mastermind of Mandate Palestine's Citizenship Order-in-Council explained his reasoning as to the differences between nationality and citizenship in an article written for an international law journal. Norman Bentwich maintained that the terminology in the Palestine Citizenship Order-in-Council of 1925 emphasised citizenship, as opposed to nationality, in order to divert from the 'Oriental' definition of the latter. In Oriental countries, he wrote, citizenship marked the allegiance to a state whereas nationality was a matter of race and religion. Both Arabs and Jews were equally Palestinian citizens, stated Bentwich, but throughout his decade-long tenure in Palestine, both groups claimed to have separate Arab or Jewish nationality.[26] In order to avoid instances of friction between an emotive, sentimental status and attachment such as that of national identity with a British-imposed legal and apolitical citizenship, Bentwich intended for the order-in-council to foster a civic (but not political) identity that members of both 'national' categories in Palestine would assume in equal measure.

Discussions on the legal, political and civic meanings of citizenship and nationality in the British and French empires in the late nineteenth century and early twentieth became increasingly common within various indigenous national movements and the members of their diasporas who agitated for measures of self-rule. Before the outbreak of war, citizenship as a specific status began to matter in the context of demands for greater political representation. Indian nationalist leaders, for example, began to make this demand to Great Britain in the years just prior to the war. Several Indian nationalists went as far as to ask for an equality of rights for all British subjects.[27] In French Algeria, Muslims were considered French nationals and subjects but not French citizens and thus they did not have rights of representation in the metropole. In French protectorates, inhabitants came under the protection of France in the decades prior to 1914 with a separate juridical status from that of the native inhabitants of French colonies. After the end of the war, the French continued to insist that any grant of French citizenship to their colonial subjects would jeopardise the subjects' indigenous cultures. The First World War itself, as Frederick Cooper explains, resulted in an even greater number of statuses and classifications of territories and of individuals, a phenomenon that increased the possibility of shifts between these multiple statuses.[28] In large part, these statuses did not reflect the demands for autonomy put forth by burgeoning national movements in colonial and formerly colonial territories. The intricacies of creating legal and documentary identity statuses in the entirely new polity of the Palestine Mandate were magnified once British officials took into account imperial and nation-state meanings of citizenship, international law norms, the opinion of the leadership in the Zionist Organisation and the challenges to imperial subjecthood.

Herbert Samuel, his advisors in the Palestine Administration and Colonial and Foreign Office experts in London spent a great deal of time and paperwork in their attempts to come to an agreement on the categorisation of the status of the native, largely Arabic-speaking (including Ottoman Jews) population. In particular, and largely due to implications at local and regional levels, officials disagreed on whether to treat these inhabitants as British-protected persons, Ottoman subjects, foreigners or as members of an altogether new legal category. As was the nature of the empire by the early interwar period, the officials who served in London and those who had experience in the overseas empire each had their own understandings of nationality, citizenship and subjecthood in the context of British imperial policy. These understandings were situated at a unique juncture in the history of empire, and thus were subject to change in accordance with transformed imperial and international realities.

During the war, both the British and French created two entirely new national statuses for Ottoman Jews who resided in each metropole or imperial possession in order to offer a separate categorisation for those not considered 'enemy aliens'. France categorised thousands of Ottoman Jews in its metropole and colonies as 'of Jewish nationality from the Levant'. The status reflected a fictional category specifically for Ottoman Jews who had been French protégés under the Ottoman capitulations. What the French attempted to do, explains Sarah Abrevaya Stein, was to fit legal imperial categories of personhood into new categories to correspond with the nation-state.[29] Great Britain responded in a similar fashion to the presence of Ottoman 'Turks' in its empire during the war. Aviva Ben-Ur describes the British imitation of French practice: Whitehall invented the category of the 'Ottoman (Spanish) Jew'. These Ottoman Jews had also been protégés of the empire under the capitulations and their new categorisation in 1914 exempted them from deportation or detention as enemies of the Allied Powers. Ottoman Spanish Jews (who did not all claim to be from the Iberian Peninsula) could also naturalise as British subjects.[30]

Ottoman Jews and other Ottoman nationals in the Allied-controlled territories in the Middle East who were not immediately recognised as protégés came under general classification as 'enemy aliens'. Prior to the Treaty of Lausanne's ratification, this classification of the region's inhabitants as 'enemy aliens' complicated diplomatic and consular matters. One of the first practical concerns faced by the Palestine Administration after the demise of the Ottoman Empire in 1918 was the cancellation of protection and capitulations granted by the British Government to some of the empire's Jewish and Christian residents and the effect that this had on the Jews in Palestine. As a result, the Foreign Office failed to come to an agreement with the Colonial and Home Offices as to whether all Ottomans came under British protection or if Great Britain could instead grant Jewish immigrants the status of imperial subjects.[31] As part of these transformations within and outside of the British Empire, officials wondered how other states would treat residents of an international mandate when they left its territory and tried to enter a sovereign state or colony. Practical problems arose when Jewish immigrants and Arabs wished to travel outside of Palestine, whether to places as close as Egypt or as far as Brazil or Chile. While the mandatory powers provided consular protection to inhabitants of B and C mandates, the administration of the A mandates (like Palestine), *not* the home government of the mandatory power, was obliged to offer such protection. The dis-agreements over how Great Britain could regulate protection for Palestine's inhabitants – whom were then neither British subjects nor Palestinian citizens – meant that both Arabs and Jewish immigrants had an ambiguous international and national status. The task of defining the new legal status of Palestinian citizenship, as well as offering advice on other matters of nationality, fell to one man: Norman Bentwich.

In crafting legislation, Bentwich worked closely with Samuel and both men outwardly professed support for the facilitation of a Jewish national home. Shortly after his appointment as Palestine's attorney-general, Bentwich expressed hope that the majority of foreigners in Palestine – the non-Ottoman Jewish immigrants – could automatically receive Palestinian citizenship. Incoming Jewish arrivals received different diplomatic and legal treatment dependent on their country of origin. The administration offered a certificate for the immigrants to claim provisional Palestinian nationality until the time that an official nationality could be created. When the new arrivals made applications for these certificates some lost the nationality of their birth country in accordance with the nationality regulations of that country, while others kept their original nationality even as they acquired provisional Palestinian nationality. It must be kept in mind that these certificates had little international standing but rather conveyed British imperial protection to their holders.

The Foreign Office helped Bentwich to arrange for consular facilities to be offered to provisional nationals as part of the office's overall management of the international relations of the Palestine administration. Bentwich and the Foreign Office legal advisor H. W. Malkin felt it important that Jews who settled in Palestine became full citizens with the right to take part in political and other activities. To ensure this, he advised Bentwich during the early days of the draft nationality legislation process that it would be undesirable to allow foreign Jews who resided in Palestine to be entitled to the protection of their own country. At the time, Malkin doubted that most immigrants would take the necessary steps to naturalise in order to lose their original nationality. He suggested that Palestinian citizenship be automatically given to them – in other words, imposed – and warned that if this was not to be the case Britain 'shall have the spectacle of the Jewish National Home containing quantities of Jews who are not citizens'.[32]

The work of Bentwich had to be done with the standards of imperial policy as the guiding factor. Bentwich worked with the Foreign

Office to draft model regulations for dual nationality, the revocation of nationality, and naturalisation. These regulations needed to conform to British standards and especially to the 1914 British Nationality and Status of Aliens Act and the 1919 Aliens Restriction (Amendment) Act. These acts legally defined British nationality in order to unify the empire. In addition, they stipulated a five-year residency requirement before foreigners could naturalise as British subjects.[33] Meanwhile, the immigrants' entrances to Palestine were coordinated with the Zionist Organisation. A third 'party' was also involved in the process: Bentwich turned to the Treaty of Sèvres as a guide to ensure the compatibility of the Palestinian nationality law with international regulations. However, the latter regulations could not be implemented until the Turkish nationalist forces signed the treaty. Thus, the Arab inhabitants of the former Ottoman Empire remained Ottoman nationals while Bentwich worked on the law.

British consular confusion over how to treat Palestinian Arab residents of neighbouring Egypt in the early 1920s is illustrated in the following example taken from Foreign Office correspondence. The Foreign Office classified Palestinian Arabs and Palestinian Jews who resided in Egypt separately based on their 'race' and 'culture'. British Foreign Secretary Curzon, a man with an extensive background in colonial administration, presented his concerns to High Commissioner Samuel as they related to consular protections and capitulatory privileges for these Palestinians in Egypt and in other British protectorates. In Samuel's opinion, the Palestinian Arabs lost the protection of the Ottoman Empire and therefore in their travels abroad Great Britain assumed the responsibility to provide consular services.[34] He also assumed that the Palestinians could benefit from capitulatory privileges while in another territory under British administration. The frame of reference for Samuel and Curzon was the former system of capitulations between Great Britain and certain nationals of the Ottoman Empire and Egypt: British-protected persons and British subjects were offered favourable diplomatic treatment. In 1920, Curzon asked Samuel for advice on whether to continue to treat certain individuals from Palestine as Ottoman nationals or as British-protected persons in Egypt.[35] In the opinion of the Foreign Office, if the Palestinian Arabs received British protection and privileges such as trial at the Mixed Courts, at the very least this would affirm their international status as British-protected persons without a separate Palestinian nationality. At most, this treatment would indicate that the Palestinians were akin to British colonial subjects not only in Egypt but elsewhere.

The correspondence further reveals the telling attitude of Curzon who argued that the British in Egypt should attempt to grant privileges only to select Palestinian individuals.[36] These 'select individuals' specifically referred to the 'better-educated' Palestinian Arabs and Jews in Egypt. In a letter to Samuel, Curzon stated that the Egyptian administration assumed the Muslim Levantine Arabs to be 'on a lower plane of civilisation than the average Egyptian'.[37] Indeed, the existence of the mandate system justified such an opinion on Levantine Arabs since the structures of the mandates were meant to provide them with further measures of assistance before the populations could manage independence. Curzon's opinion was also backed up with the reality that only educated Jews and a select few Arab Christians qualified for special treatment such as trial in British courts outside of Palestine. Their international statuses, then, mirrored that of subjects under imperial protection in the years before the citizenship order.

The debates over consular protection diverged into related issues including new questions that referred to passports and visas for Arab and Jewish residents of Palestine. Before the implementation of the mandate, travellers used Ottoman passports.[38] After the end of the war, British consulates treated Palestinians in a number of often arbitrary ways: alternately as 'former alien enemies', foreigners or protected persons. As noted above, the British and French treatment of Ottoman Jews during the war underscored the post-war classification of Arabs as former Ottomans and Jewish immigrants as provisional Palestinian nationals. In one particular instance in 1920, immigration officials in Jerusalem treated a Palestinian holding a British passport and an Ottoman passport as a 'former alien enemy'.[39] Because Ottoman passports became invalid after 1918, British consular officials were unable to endorse them for travel to and from Palestine. Neither the Foreign Office nor the Palestine Administration appealed to the League for advice but instead, in contravention of the future mandate charter, the Foreign Office in 1920 advised consular officers not to recognise any claims to British protection by Arabs who lived abroad. In practice, however, the Foreign Office provided emergency certificates for Arabs and Jews that entitled them to receive one-way Palestinian visas or *laissez-passer* in order to travel.

As part of the development of separate 'national statuses', in August 1920 the Foreign Office published the details of the two categories devised for the Arab and Jewish population of Palestine. The first category included those people born in Palestine who possessed Ottoman nationality but whom were not habitual residents.

Ottoman nationals (by birth or descent) who lived abroad but wanted Palestinian nationality could either obtain their nationality by exhibiting their Ottoman passport or other identity documents as proof of paternal descent from an Ottoman subject.[40] The second category featured non-Ottoman residents who wished to adopt Palestinian nationality, and this group consisted mainly of Jewish immigrants. The Zionist Organisation issued certificates to Jews who intended to go to Palestine in order for the mandate administration's immigration officials to grant them a *laissez-passer*.[41] To receive a *laissez-passer*, individuals in both categories needed to reassure the authorities that they would opt for Palestinian nationality as soon as a law passed to that effect and conditional on their permanent residence in the territory. The measure also ensured that travelers did not use their status as provisional Palestinian nationals only to obtain British consular protection.

At this point, the Foreign Office and Bentwich expressed the same belief that Palestinian natives, whether Arab or Jewish, could not have changed their allegiance as Ottoman nationals prior to the ratification of a peace treaty with the empire.[42] Natives did not immediately fall into either of the two classifications listed by the Foreign Office, as the majority remained habitually resident in Palestine. Their Ottoman identities placed them in a sort of diplomatic limbo. By the time of the 1923 formal assumption of the Palestine Mandate by Great Britain, a nationality law had not been promulgated and the concerns of the Foreign and Colonial Offices, Bentwich and Samuel regarding the national status of the Arabs remained unresolved.

The Draft 'Nationality' Order: Definitions, Concepts, and the Status of Palestine, 1922–1924

Although the status of the native and immigrant residents of Palestine did not drastically change before 1924, the administrative status of the territory itself did. Historians have described the system of laws and regulations put into place by the British administration in terms of their impact on land, tax policies, the courts and the economy of the mandate.[43] It was vital that the officials who wrote these laws, including the 1922 constitution (or organic law), the 1922 electoral order and the nationality law drafts, ensured that their articles and provisions did not run counter to any of the obligations to the Arab or Jewish inhabitants. For instance, legislation (at least on paper) could not contradict the trusteeship status of the mandate: laws and directives could not work to re-classify Palestine into a Crown colony or protectorate nor could they impose provisions of British subject status upon inhabitants. According to the mandate system, laws of each mandate had to ensure the well-being and development of the inhabitants.[44]

Nationality and citizenship, and the rights associated with both were connected with the enactment of an organic law and the establishment of a partially elected legislative council. As early as 1921, High Commissioner Samuel expressed hope for the rapid formation of a legislative council and the enactment of a constitution. The administration in Palestine and the government in London debated the framework and function of such a council but decided that an electoral law could not be passed before the ratification of the mandate by the League. However, the administration felt it necessary to issue an order-in-council to regulate Palestinian nationality in order to compile electoral registers. The administration depended on such registers in order to classify inhabitants as citizens entitled to vote, but it first faced the task of defining the parameters of nationality. The British Government outlined three options: the first was to pass a nationality order-in-council; the second was to issue an electoral order-in-council so that an elected legislative council could discuss a nationality law and constitution; and the third was to pass a temporary nationality order-in-council before an elected assembly could work to finalise provisions to regulate nationality. High Commissioner Samuel favoured the first option as he had promised early municipal elections to the Arab leadership.[45] The mandatory government did not opt for any of the three options before the League approved the Mandate for Palestine on 24 June 1922 but instead completed orders-in-council for a constitution and legislative council. Consultation with the League or the Arab leadership over the specifics of the legislation was unnecessary as the mandate charter gave the mandatory full power of legislation and administration.

Following the ratification of the mandate in July 1922, His Majesty's Government approved the Palestine Order-in-Council as an organic law. Enacted on 10 August 1922, it outlined the functions of the Palestine Government and provided for the composition of the legislative council of appointed British officials and elected representatives from each religious community. The text of the 1922 Order-in-Council defined a foreigner as any national or subject of Europe, America or Japan, whereas natives from a British mandated territory or any area under direct British rule, Ottoman subjects or any person who lost his Ottoman subject status were not officially considered foreigners in Palestine (in practice, former Ottoman sub-jects were considered foreigners). Crucially, the order defined the Palestinian citizen for the purpose of enfranchising inhabitants for the legislative council. Citizens included 'Turkish subjects' (mean-ing Ottoman) habitually resident in Palestine, and all other inhabit-ants who did not possess 'Turkish nationality' but were habitually resident in Palestine (referring to Jewish immigrants) provided they applied for provisional citizenship within two months.[46] Jewish immigrants did not need to renounce their birth nationality to be enfranchised since the 1922 Legislative Election Order-in-Council, passed in conjunction with the organic law, did not actually con-fer any nationality.[47] The electoral order-in-council provided Jewish immigrants with provisional nationality while the conditions in the Ottoman Nationality Law of 1869 remained in place as the basis for the provisional nationality of the Arabs. The subsequent citizenship law reproduced this 1922 codification of two distinct categories of 'the national'.

The order-in-council stipulated that the right to vote, the first polit-ical right linked with nationality, would be on the basis of communal identity – an important concept to British rule in Palestine. The pro-posed elected legislative body limited the power of Arab representa-tives to pass laws because the nominated British and Jewish members would outnumber them and the high commissioner (with two votes) could veto or change any legislation.[48] Furthermore, the use of com-munal and religious divisions as the basis of the new voting system did not reflect the realities that secular Ottoman nationality had cre-ated on the ground in the Arab provinces since the mid-nineteenth century. In general, the mandate administration believed that the status of Palestine's inhabitants came from their belonging to a reli-gious – *not* a national – community.[49] Some officials, such as Edward Keith-Roach, suggested that proportional representation was a bet-ter option. Other officials deemed his suggestion too complicated and argued that the Arabs lacked knowledge of self-government due to high illiteracy rates.[50] Instead, the order-in-council implemented a system of secondary electors in electoral colleges and in each district community leaders determined the number of secondary voters for the legislative council's elections. These voters formed electoral col-leges divided by religion and a fixed number of 'provisional' citizens could stand for election from each religious community. The first legislative council elections were held that same year but due to the Arabs' boycott of them, the creation of a legislative council failed. The institutional separation between Arabs and Jews based on their communal identities remained important in the minds of British officials. The British did not devise this separation on their own: the treaties of Sèvres and of Lausanne institutionalised racial separation in the post-war Levant.

Both peace treaties stipulated that nationality orders needed to be passed in each mandate within twelve months from the date of endorsement by Turkey.[51] In Palestine, Attorney-General Bentwich constantly updated the draft of a nationality law in order to adapt it to the conditions stipulated by the peace treaty. In 1920, Bentwich initially modelled the nationality draft on a number of interesting international provisions regarding Palestine in the Treaty of Sèvres. Article 129 of the treaty directly benefited the Zionist ambitions in Palestine. The article allowed for the ipso facto acquisition of Palestinian nationality for all non-Ottoman Jewish residents of Palestine who had resided in that territory for two years on the date of the treaty ratification. This automatic acquisition of nationality meant that Jewish residents could keep their birth nationality. Bentwich argued in 1920 that although political difficulties would arise in Palestine if the article remained in the treaty or if it was used in the nationality law, it could not be eliminated. He was well aware that not all Jews resident in Palestine would want to automatically receive Palestinian nationality. He predicted protests by Jews against the article and suggested an amendment for the Lausanne Treaty that allowed the non-Ottoman Jews of Palestine the option to receive citizenship and renounce their former nationality.[52] The Zionist Organisation seconded this proposed amendment and the Treaty of Lausanne did indeed exclude the text of Sèvres' Article 129.

Some Zionist leaders disagreed with Bentwich's amendment on the grounds that Jewish residents would be forced to give up their birth nationality upon receipt of Palestinian nationality. Both the Joint Foreign Committee of the Jewish Board of Deputies, headed by the British statesman Lucien Wolf, and the Anglo-Jewish Association termed their disagreement 'a very grave objection'.[53] The Colonial Office took up this objection and suggested that Jewish immigrants could also declare their desire not to become citizens and that the mandate administration could authorise them to remain in Palestine. This suggestion allowed for British and American Jews who may wish to stay in Palestine and help establish the national home to keep their own nationality.[54] The Foreign Office agreed and even suggested that non-habitually resident Jews who wished to help build the national home should have the option to acquire Palestinian citizenship 'to take their full part in [the Jewish national home's] political life instead of remaining foreigners'. British and Zionist leaders came to a consensus with Bentwich that Palestinian citizenship should not be enforced on Jews either resident or non-resident but should be made an option just as people resident in other territories detached from Turkey opted for their new nationalities in accordance with international regulations.[55]

Article 125 of the Sèvres Treaty particularly affected Palestine. The article stated that only those individuals who belonged to racial minorities in their new post-war states could opt for the nationality of other territories composed of the racial majority they desired to join. In his position as colonial secretary, Winston Churchill advocated that Palestine be included as one of the territories listed as compliant with this article. The inclusion of Palestine among such territories exclusively benefited the Jewish national home plan: it meant that Arabs of Syria or Iraq could *not* opt for Palestinian nationality since they belonged to the racial majority in their own country. Although Arabs in places like Armenia could opt for Palestinian nationality, the British administrators felt that this would be unlikely and 'would not probably make a serious difference to the balance of the population [in Palestine]'.[56] Since Jews in Arab lands were not considered 'racially' Jewish but rather 'Arab', they could not opt for Palestinian nationality. The lack of options for Jews in Arab lands to become Palestinian citizens is understandable: the Zionist Organisation in the 1920s simply did not consider or reach out to these Jewish groups as part of their aims and agenda, and vice versa. The British, for their part, likely had little knowledge or understanding of Arabised-Jews, and did not give them consideration.[57]

In light of disagreements by Zionist leaders and pro-Zionist British statesmen with certain articles in the Sèvres Treaty, Bentwich attempted to shape Palestine's nationality regulations in order to accommodate for the Jewish national home policy and its increased support from within the Cabinet and Parliament. The Palestine Administration realised that it was not possible to exempt any 'special class' of *European* Jews from the nationality provisions of the peace treaty as applied to the mandate territory. However, Bentwich could insert articles into the nationality law to give the mandate government options for discretion in how it regulated the nationality of Jewish immigrants – as long as the articles did not contravene the treaty.[58] The Home Office initially suggested what would become the most important of these nationality provisions, that *jus sanguinis* (right to nationality by blood) should be limited so that nationality did not pass indefinitely through native-born Palestinian fathers to future generations resident outside of Palestine. Contrary to the Sèvres Treaty, the Home Office recommended that citizenship should pass only to the first generation born outside of Palestine.[59] Officials felt that this limitation should be made clear in the legislation but Bentwich ultimately chose not to mention it explicitly in the final draft of the citizenship law despite its inclusion in that law.[60]

Colonial officials and Bentwich never quite resolved the issue of terminology in the early draft nationality ordinance. The early drafts adopted the terms 'Palestinian subject' and 'Palestinian nationality' to indicate the international status of Palestinians under the mandate. The Sèvres (and Lausanne) Treaty used 'citizen' with the same assumed international dimension. In a memo to the Foreign Office in February 1921, High Commissioner Samuel argued that 'nationality' was the better term to use since it indicated belonging to a nation-state. His opinion ran counter to that of Bentwich. On the other hand, the Foreign Office noted that the phrase 'Palestinian citizen' should be used and argued that the term 'citizen' was used to denote a national of a state whose constitution was not monarchial.[61] 'Subject' seemed unfitting for the Palestinians because it incorrectly indicated that the inhabitants were subjects of the British Crown.

In London, the Foreign and Colonial Offices disagreed on other important practicalities in the law and their disagreements lengthened the process of drafting nationality legislation. One important disagreement concerned the link between habitual residence in Palestine and eligibility for nationality. Here again, the obligation that the institutions of the mandate not prejudice support for the Jewish national home influenced naturalisation and residency arrangements. For his part, Bentwich advocated a short residency period for Jewish immigrants who wished to naturalise, as compared with immigrants to other British-administered territories. By providing for the two-year residency provision Home Secretary Edward Shortt wrote to Bentwich that such 'very special provision' would modify Great Britain's ordinary requirements of residence (five years) for the purpose of naturalisation.[62] However, administration members remained somewhat unsure of setting a precedent different to the standards followed elsewhere in the empire. In their communication with Bentwich, Zionist leaders stressed that all Jews resident in Palestine could become 'Palestinian subjects' but crucially asked that the nationality law allow Jews usually resident in other countries the right to hold dual nationality. Somewhat paradoxically the organisation declared that they would oppose the latter proposal if it meant that Arabs would also be entitled the right to dual nationality.[63] Owing to their influence, the final legislation met the demands of the Zionist leaders such as Chaim Weizmann: immigrants had to surrender documentary papers and passports upon naturalisation but they were not required to actually renounce any other nationality.

On the other hand, the Foreign Office adamantly opposed granting nationality to native Palestinian Arab emigrants who lived even temporarily abroad if any chance existed that applicants would use their status to claim British protection. The office had maintained this position since the first years of the civil administration.[64] In the final months of 1922 in the midst of the above-mentioned debates, the Palestine Administration and His Majesty's Government (HMG) began to receive petitions from Palestinian Arabs stranded in Latin America, Haiti and Cuba. British consuls had not received definite instructions on Palestinian nationality or the dissolution of Ottoman nationality and the qualifications for grants of *laissez-passers* and provisional certificates of nationality were not uniformly recognised by consular representatives. In these early years of the 1920s, consuls sometimes refused to issue passports or visas to Palestinian Arabs (many of whom claimed Ottoman nationality) wishing to return to Palestine or to travel on business, due to either misinformation or a lack of information on how to treat natives of the mandates. These travellers were often forced to remain in one country for extended periods although a number applied to French consuls in bids to obtain Syrian passports or visas to enter Mandate Syria.[65]

Throughout 1923, officials were keenly aware of the debates among delegates to the League over the national status of inhabitants of mandated territories. Members of the PMC grappled with the complex and undefined concept of mandate nationality and the Allied Powers' perceptions of citizenship. For example, one British delegate insisted that a mandate power could *not* grant a status other than its own national status to inhabitants. In other words, the delegate claimed that Britain did not have the power to create a new nationality.[66] Other delegates agreed, noting that 'native inhabitants should not be led to think they were not under the protection of the Mandatory Power'. This posed the danger that 'natives, or those who incited them' would be more difficult to control if they thought their nationality was separate from the nationality of the mandatory.[67] These same themes were mentioned in the debates that took place within the British Government with respect to Palestine prior to the signing of the 1923 Lausanne Treaty. The Foreign Office wrote to the Home Office that Palestine did 'not bear the slightest resemblances to an independent state' and its citizens had no such status as belonging to one. Foreign Office leaders declared that Palestinian inhabitants had a local national status in Palestine but, internationally, they were British-protected persons.[68] The Home Office, responsible for naturalisation, agreed and stated that Palestinian nationality was a 'creation' that gave Palestine a definite status while it remained a state under external British protection.[69]

In a general sense, the debates as well as the uncertainties over the status of Palestine and its place in the wider empire clearly influenced future legislation, including the nationality law. Most notably, if Palestine were a protected state (let alone a foreign country), the king had no jurisdiction over it, yet the king had already ratified the 1922 Palestine Order-in-Council. Even Bentwich, the most senior legal scholar in Palestine, was confused as to the nature of British power in Palestine.[70] In late 1923, the Colonial Office argued that the phrase 'the Government of Palestine' was not just a title but rather 'the instrument by which HMG is exercising his authority under the Mandate' even if Palestine did not fall into any existing Dominion, Protectorate or British-protected state category. In that case, nationality legislation, like the orders-in-council, could be drafted by various departments and by the Palestine Administration, but it could only be ratified by order of the king. By early 1924, the Colonial Office and law officers concluded that the population was under a type of unique British protection.[71] Despite the opinion of departments in Great Britain, the League of Nations did not consider Palestine to be a protectorate of Great Britain.[72]

The Treaty of Lausanne and the Implementation of Citizenship Legislation, 1923–1925

The international recognition of Palestinian nationality (alongside Turkish, Syrian, Lebanese, Iraqi, Egyptian and other nationalities) came as a result of the application of the Treaty of Lausanne between Turkey and the Allied Powers in September 1924 (a year after it had been signed in July 1923). Its regulations for state succession forced the Palestine Administration and the British Government to rush the completion of the Palestine nationality law in order to regulate the relationship between the population and the mandatory power. A little more than nine months prior, in December 1923 High Commissioner Samuel recommended that the Palestine Administration adopt into law the framework for conferring nationality stipulated in the 1922 Legislative Election Order that, it must be remembered, codified separate provisions for the acquisition of nationality. Samuel had postponed municipal elections until the adoption of these provisions in a nationality law so the 'right of voting' could be exercised by all inhabitants with the 'definite and incontestable right to Palestinian citizenship'.[73] In the interim before the completion of the nationality law, members of the Foreign Office argued against the terms of provisional nationality listed in the Legislative Election Order-in-Council. They stated that a class of 'undesirable people' such as communists, prostitutes and fugitives could remain in Palestine as habitual residents who received provisional nationality through the order. These individuals would then acquire citizenship without a waiting period once the proper legislation was ratified.[74] The short residency requirement for citizenship primarily only impacted Jewish immigrants and the requirement itself led to intense debates that further delayed the final draft of the law.[75]

Not all officials agreed with the stance on two-year residency and many certainly were sympathetic towards the number of complaints by the Palestinian Arabs over the liberal immigration regulations for immigrants. One of the chief administrators in Jerusalem, Edward Keith-Roach, opined that the two years' residency requirement for naturalisation would be abused by Jewish immigrants who wanted British protection and not Palestinian nationality. He gave examples of residency requirements in Great Britain and its Dominions, the United States, Switzerland, Belgium, France and Italy that all required at least five years. He maintained that the Jews in Palestine, with their two-year residency qualification, would have been greatly advantaged, and pointed out the Arabs would give a 'tremendous howl' that a Jewish individual from Europe could become a citizen of Palestine in two years.[76] Zionist leaders had accused the local administration of favouritism towards the Arabs, and the Arabs had accused the administration and British Government of favouritism for the Zionist movement; however, the sense one gets from the correspondence of administrators on the ground in Palestine with Whitehall is of attempts from Jerusalem and London to placate both groups in order to ensure political and social stability.[77] Officials in London and the Foreign Office saw naturalisation and nationality in its legal and diplomatic rather than political dimensions. They acted with imperial concerns but also in accordance with changing international norms on nationality and documentary identity. As for nationality and citizenship, little concern for either pro-Zionist or pro-Arab biases or political ramifications is evident in the correspondence from London.

In 1923 the most immediate repercussion in Palestine of the publication of the Treaty of Lausanne was that the Arab inhabitants
would, upon implementation, no longer be treated as former Ottoman
subjects. Still, the treaty presented a new concept: it required native
inhabitants to be *resident* in Palestine on the date that it came into
force and to possess proof of their Ottoman nationality in order to
become subject as citizens to the laws and regulations of the Palestine
administration.[78] Residence in the territory at the specific date that the
treaty went into effect trumped *jus sanguinis* and *jus soli* provisions for
nationality. Previously, descent from an Ottoman national (the *jus sanguinis* route) and birth in Ottoman territory (the *jus soli* route) granted
nationality. However, nationality in the early 1920s was complex and
on a global scale, in evolution and not yet standardised. The situation
was made more complex—particularly for the former Ottoman territories and also in a global scope – by the fact that an ever-increasing
number of individuals had the means and the reasons to emigrate and
settle far from the territory of their birth. Although traditionally in the
Ottoman Empire national status passed through patrilineal descent
without official restrictions upon how many generations could claim
Ottoman nationality, the post-1900 migrations made such claims to
nationality more complex because generations of individuals were
born abroad. Birth in a territory, on the other hand, was far easier to
track and to accord nationality based upon. In part for that reason,
in the early 1920s international lawyers professed preference for the
jus soli acquisition of nationality.[79] From the perspective of the British
Foreign and Home Offices as well as the United States immigration
authorities any allowance for nationality to pass by descent through
more than one generation, rather than for descendants of immigrants
to receive nationality by birth in a particular territory, began to be seen
as potentially suspect and posed the threat that it could create disloyal
elements of the population.

In light of the complications that surrounded nationality in terms
of diplomatic and security concerns, the Treaty of Lausanne and the
British locally in Palestine disregarded the *jus sanguinis* component
of Ottoman nationality. Former Ottoman nationals who lived abroad
upon the date of the treaty ratification in July 1924 were obliged
to first declare their willingness to become nationals of their new
post-Ottoman states within two years and then to return to those
states to reside. By 1924, the circulated draft of the Palestine nationality law nearly conformed to these specific regulations posited by
Lausanne. It stipulated that native-born Arabs who resided abroad

on the date of the enactment of the *law* (not the treaty) had to return to Palestine in order to be considered permanent residents able to opt for citizenship.[80] By the end of 1924, the Colonial Office noted that because of the Jewish policy in Palestine and expected numbers of migrants (termed 'a set of unparalleled circumstances in the history of the world') the draft order required further administrative tweaks. These were completed one year after the implementation of the Lausanne Treaty.

After five years, during which Arabs and Jews in Palestine held ambiguous statuses of varying degree, HMG approved the Palestine Citizenship Order-in-Council and its provisions officially came into force on 1 August 1925. This was the only citizenship order that the British Government enacted in any of its mandate territories. In Iraq and Transjordan, the mandate power placed local Arab authorities in charge of nationality legislation. In Britain's African mandates, inhabitants remained British-protected persons.[81] Article 1 of the order, which mirrored Article 30 of the Lausanne Treaty, declared all 'Turkish subjects' habitually resident in Palestine on 1 August 1924 (the date that Lausanne came into force) to become automatically Palestinian citizens on 1 August 1925. Turkish subjects referred to all Ottoman nationals as defined by the Ottoman Nationality Law of 1869. This article did not account for individuals who had been given provisional nationality under the 1922 Legislative Election Order, most of whom were Jewish immigrants. It also did not take into consideration Ottoman subjects who lived abroad on 1 August 1924 – the number unlikely to have been even considered at that point by Bentwich or anyone else in the administration or the Foreign Office. In total, the number of Ottoman nationals resident in Palestine on the date of the order who became Palestinian citizens was nearly 730,000.[82] A subsequent article addressed the immigrants as the non-Ottoman residents who received provisional Palestinian nationality through the 1922 electoral order and automatically became Palestinian citizens under the 1925 Order-in-Council regulations.

The order did address natives of Palestine who lived abroad. According to Article 2, individuals who were more than eighteen years of age born in Palestine and with Ottoman nationality who had habitual residence abroad on 1 August 1925 could opt for citizenship 'subject to the consent of the Government of Palestine' in accordance with the regulation that they have been in Palestine for six months prior to opting and on the condition that they had not acquired a foreign nationality. This option had to be done within two years from the date of the order, by 31 July 1927.[83] Despite British attempts to keep its citizenship order in line with Lausanne, the discussions within the departments in London and Palestine led to the codification of different terminologies. These differences impacted former Ottoman nationals who lived abroad and considered themselves to be natives of Palestine. Effectively, the difference in wording of Article 2 of the citizenship order from its sister Article 34 in the treaty denied citizenship to those individuals, for the reasons noted above on the post-war complexities of regulating nationality by descent. Article 34 of Lausanne used the phrase 'native of' to reference former Ottomans whereas the order-in-council used 'born in Palestine' in reference to the same individuals. The latter phrase was used due to the recommendation from the Home Office that nationality by birth not be passed on indefinitely for former Ottoman subjects residing outside of Palestine.[84] This change meant certain descendants of Ottomans born in the territory that became Palestine were not to be ipso facto recognised as citizens. It also meant that the order did not conform with prior policy that gave *laissez-passers* to children born abroad to Palestinian parents. It contradicted standards based on Lausanne, British nationality law, the 1869 Ottoman law and also the nationality laws of the French mandates, all of which supported the acquisition of *jus sanguinis* nationality.[85]

The non-Ottoman applicants, mainly Jewish immigrants, who wished to be naturalised or had received provisional certificates of nationality dated prior to October 1922 were required to have been resident in Palestine since that date. They were obliged to surrender any passport or *laissez-passer* on receipt of citizenship documentation. It must be remembered that the surrender of a passport was a different process from the renunciation of birth-nationality. The order required that applicants for naturalisation give a formal declaration that they would permanently reside in Palestine, take an oath of allegiance to the government and show proof of an ability to converse in English, Arabic or Hebrew. Naturalised citizens received a certificate of citizenship that entitled them to (unlisted) political rights and privileges and subjected them to the obligations, duties and liabilities of a Palestinian citizen.[86]

Initially, the citizenship order had arguably positive implications for Jewish immigrants already resident in Palestine (who did not need to surrender passports and received citizenship automatically); while for new arrivals, naturalisation procedures were relatively straightforward. Many of the Arabs who emigrated from Palestine prior to 1918 or even before 1925 found themselves in a difficult position if they wished to be citizens of Palestine due to the two-year time period granted to them in the Treaty of Lausanne to return. That difficulty became magnified by the actions of High Commissioner Samuel who exercised sole power to amend the order: he did so drastically before he left office. In November 1925, Samuel pushed forward the date for option of nationality for these non-habitual residents. Rather than give these individuals two years to choose Palestinian citizenship beginning 1 August 1925, the two-year timeframe for option was put into effect retroactively, from 6 August 1924 – the date that the Treaty of Lausanne came into force. Samuel made the change to bring the order completely in line with the same timeframe given in the Treaty of Lausanne's Article 34.[87] Unintentionally, the change affected Arabs, Jews and any other former Ottoman native of Palestine; however, Arab Christians and Muslims composed the majority of the estimated 20,000 to 25,000 Palestinian-born individuals who lived abroad by 1925. These natives, which included students and merchants who resided outside of Palestine in August 1924, had less than one year to opt for citizenship.

Without any ipso facto nationality, Palestinians resident abroad on 1 August 1924 lost Ottoman nationality with the Treaty of Lausanne and were unaccounted for once the Citizenship Order-in-Council came into effect in August 1925. The order's provisions barred these individuals from citizenship unless they returned to Palestine by 1 August 1926. Emigrants usually needed a valid provisional certificate of nationality or other proof to show that their father was an Ottoman subject, not only to opt for citizenship but to travel. Without this documentation, these individuals often could not travel to Palestine to comply with the six-month residency period before opting for citizenship. In places such as Latin America, Cuba and Haiti, Palestinian émigrés were hit particularly hard. They encountered difficulties to even receive a travel visa to Palestine to visit family. Moreover, the order-in-council was not published broadly *outside* Palestine until at least November 1925.[88] In mid-1923, the Foreign Office reported that in the region south of Peru alone, up to 600 Palestinians held a *laissez-passer* issued by Great Britain that identified them as Ottoman nationals.[89]

To return to the use of terminology, Bentwich and other colonial officials decided only in May 1925 to change the title of the nationality legislation from the Palestine Nationality Law to the Palestine Citizenship Order-in-Council. One month before the order's ratification, the term 'nationality' was crossed out and replaced with 'citizenship' throughout the text.[90] After the ratification of the Treaty of Lausanne, the provisions of nationality were first applied to Palestine, but citizenship remained a term and status in need of legal, diplomatic and political clarification. This again demonstrates the messy definitions of both terms proposed within Great Britain during the 1920s and as applied in indirectly ruled colonies, the Dominions and the non-Arab mandates. With the rise of the nationalism posing a threat to British colonial rule overseas (as well as closer to home, in Ireland) and also creating debate in the League of Nations over self-government in various locales, policies and regulations linked citizenship and nationality to create a status that marked belonging in what would become the political formation of the nation-state.[91]

Conclusion

The 1925 Citizenship Order-in-Council, once in effect, offered a local citizenship independent of British nationality for Palestinians under the administration. When outside of Palestine, the mandate's provisions placed these citizens (but not necessarily natives) in the position of British-protected persons. In an odd twist, they were recognised as citizens of the Palestine Mandate but in the absence of mandatory consulates, these inhabitants came under the same type of protection as did British colonial subjects. Citizenship in this sense was not equal to full nationality as far as international law was concerned since Palestinians became British-protected persons when outside of the mandated territory.[92] The post-war situation was unique in that the Treaty of Lausanne created new principles of nationality that related to state succession in the Ottoman lands. It also attempted to define sovereignty in these territories through internationally established nationality provisions. For the inhabitants of Palestine, the application of the latter principles turned nationals of territories detached from Turkey into nationals of the state to which the territory was transferred – an entirely new international regulation.

Even so, the 1925 Citizenship Order-in-Council did not grant Palestinian citizens the rights they agitated for *as citizens*. The following chapter offers a further analysis of how the Arabs saw themselves in relation to the British Empire and the local administration in Palestine, and how Western European concepts of the rights-bearing citizen, alongside the post-war idealism of self-determination of small nations, influenced these agitations. From the early days of the mandate administration, Arab leaders appealed to the British for control over their own government, rights to their borders, educational affairs, public works, election laws, taxation and tithe rates, and trade laws but Great Britain never intended to grant *political* citizenship.[93] To return to Bentwich's differentiation between citizenship and nationality, the order in Palestine created and regulated a unique type of legal, and internationally accepted, nationality but it did so more for matters of administration and obligation as the mandate charter required – Palestine was certainly not a recognised nation-state. The Permanent Mandates Commission viewed the order more idealistically when it reported in October 1925 that political agitation had diminished in Palestine and that the enactment of the Palestine Citizenship Order-in-Council 'should do much to strengthen a sense of Palestinian nationality' between the Arabs and the Jews who lived there.[94] With the exception of Bentwich's recollection fifteen years after its approval, the British officials who advised on the order-in-council never considered or intended that the legislation would work to bring the two groups together – and it certainly did not. As will be shown, the Palestine Arab Executive leadership disagreed with the citizenship legislation on the basis that through these measures the government continued to neglect what it felt to be the 'natural' civil and political rights of the Arab population. What the order did show was that in contrast to the ways in which citizenship legislation came about in the other Arab mandates through the approval of indigenous legislative bodies, in Palestine the ultimate power to decide on the legal status of the Palestinians was claimed by the British Government and the local administration and with influences from the leadership of the Zionist Organisation.

3

The Notion of 'Rights' and the Practices of Nationality and Citizenship from the Palestinian Arab Perspective, 1918–1925

In early 1925 Lord Arthur Balfour, the former British Foreign Secretary and author of the 1917 Balfour Declaration, visited Palestine for the first time. For the occasion of Balfour's visit, the Palestinian Arab leadership of the Arab Executive Committee (al-lajna al-tanafīdhiyya al-ʿarabiyya) declared a general strike throughout Palestine and emphasised optimistically that the strike would 'instill this patriotism to the youngest of our Palestinian Arab citizens'.[1] The Arabic press ran several features on the visit. Referring to Balfour's planned visit to Tel Aviv the editor of *Sawt al-Shaʿb*, a local Bethlehem politician named ʿIsa Bandak, addressed the nationality of the Jewish immigrants who settled in colonies such as Tel Aviv. He questioned whether they had 'true' Palestinian nationality – as he conceptualised other former Ottoman citizens who were members of the specific Arabic-speaking Ottoman community to have – or if their nationality was simply 'on paper' as granted by the British.[2] Bandak's editorial raises an obvious point: he saw the immigrants as having little more than a British-imposed status that did not require the active exercise of civic loyalty to Palestine as a political entity. Yet even in the late nineteenth century Ottoman world, nationality was not truly the political or legal status that it became in the early to middle decades of the twentieth century. By the interwar period, it took on civic, cultural and political meanings complete with a new (Arabic) vocabulary of reference.

Politicians and nationalists like Bandak helped to develop the political and civic community in Palestine, and by extension advocated particular civic practices that became the source of the Arabs' political identity in the early years of the Mandate Government.

Their understandings of nationality, civic identity and citizenship are analysed in two ways here: the first, in light of the transition of Palestine's population into citizens within a new British imperial context and the accompanying expectations and idealistic visions that the Arabs imagined such imperial membership to convey. These understandings and discussions are also evaluated using the framework of the emergence of new types of spaces and institutions in Palestine, especially that of the mandate as an institution and the growth of civil society. These new spaces and institutions, both legal and civic, challenged traditional ways of understanding identity and community, which had previously been Ottoman in nature. Such a challenge, argues citizenship theorist Raymond Rocco, disrupts long-established political and civic boundaries of identity and transforms notions of identity and membership in the nation-state.[3] Influenced in parts by Rocco's work on communitarian citizenship formulations, the following analysis demonstrates the ways in which the Palestinian Arab national movement developed and publicised notions of nationality and citizenship in the period of transition from 1918 through to 1925, and focuses on the symbols and slogans used to represent the new civic identity and formulations of civic and political belonging for the Arab population of Palestine.

This development of a particular political community by the Arab leadership sharply contrasted with the apolitical citizenship developed by British colonial and mandate officials. These officials did not recognise or grant the rights associated with membership in the metropole of a modern nation-state, and mandate legislation disassociated the concept of Arab nationality (*jinsiyya*) from Palestinian citizenship (*muwātana*) – certainly to be expected due to the nature of colonialism. As described previously, the British administration established different qualifications for Palestinian nationality and citizenship between Jewish immigrants and Palestinian Arab natives. The statuses' ethno-religious determinant reflected the imperial duty of support for Jewish immigration and a Jewish national home in Palestine. In the immediate aftermath of the war Arab leaders and a number of politically aware middle-class intellectuals hoped to gain autonomy and unity with Syria as they increasingly feared future Zionist plans for Jewish immigration and land settlement throughout all of Palestine. To a large extent, the furor over the threat of British and Zionist colonialism and the preparations of the Allies to assume administrative control of the Levant fostered a greater awareness by Arab leaders and the middle-class of their own membership in a post-Ottoman Arab political community that was specifically Palestinian. Still, the educated middle-class, aware of the genesis of civil and political rights in France and Great Britain, tended to assume that the British would offer equal political rights to all inhabitants of Palestine in light of pledges made by American President Woodrow Wilson for self-government and because this class repeatedly argued that the Arabs were more modern than typical colonial subjects.[4]

From this early stage, some educated leaders who identified ideologically as pan-Arab or Palestinian nationalists articulated the clear contradiction between liberal citizenship as legislated in the context of a democracy, and colonial citizenship enforced in Britain's overseas possessions.[5] It is necessary to differentiate between the traditional, notable (*'ayan*) leadership and the middle-class populist (*sha'bī*) leadership. The latter group supported unity with Syria in the early years of the British Administration and emerged as an important political actor by the late 1920s. These populists used civic associations, various symbols, slogans and arguments to represent their ideas of civic identity. It must be remembered that both the traditional and the more populist, younger leaderships came from the same elite socio-economic group in Palestine. Their discourses on the appropriate action to achieve self-government were what characterised the differences in the political vision for Palestine: the younger group generally (but not exclusively) used a more grassroots or populist discourse that advocated action.

In order to position the Arabs' notions of nationality and citizenship, the historical narrative of the two terms must begin earlier than the mandate, in the Ottoman era. Each concept emerged within the political framework of the late nineteenth century. Both the ideology and implementation of provisions of nationality during that period are connected to broader processes of political and social change, most notably the evolution of new power relationships and a fledgling civil society in Greater Syria. By 1920, the Arab leadership in Palestine strongly identified with what Raymond Rocco defines as a communitarian formulation of citizenship, although the influence of liberal and republican citizenship conceptions was clearly expressed in these leaders' words and actions vis-à-vis the local administration in Jerusalem and the imperial government in London. Importantly, as early as 1920 Arabs' discussions of nationality emphasised the idea that by virtue of membership in a primordial, Arab community, Palestine's Arab inhabitants had rights to the state as its sovereigns. Ultimately, this chapter introduces a new historicisation of Mandate Palestine, demonstrating how citizenship and nationality were forged and shaped through acts, understandings and notions of political participation, political behaviour and civic engagement. It is necessary to stress that although these actions, notions and behaviours did not always constitute citizenship claims as understood today, they fostered the conditions under which such claims emerged after the mid-1920s.[6]

Nationalism is an ideology and a movement that cannot be entirely ignored here, both for historiographical purposes and because of the actual influence that the idea of nationalism had in the face of British colonialism and sovereignty over Palestine after 1918. The ideology of Arab nationalism propagated by leading intellectuals in Greater Syria in the second half of the nineteenth century appeared alongside the new Ottoman provisions of nationality. By the end of the First World War, Arab nationalism provided the ideological framework for the articulation of the political aim of national membership in a future nation-state. The ideology influenced the ways in which rights were advocated for by nationalists with a heavy emphasis on the notion of 'primordial' Arab nationality and long-standing membership in the Ottoman political community. When the Allies proposed the imposition of the Palestine Mandate, a strong, largely secular and pan-Arab populist movement developed counter-discussions and actions from those politics of the more traditional leadership based in Jerusalem. A middle-class stratum of writers, educators, lawyers, civil servants and students assumed leadership of this subaltern movement in Palestine. The terms 'populism' and 'populist politics' are used to underscore a specific understanding as to how nationalist groups and individuals mobilised under the banner of 'the nation' or 'the people' to express their opposition to what they saw as the enemy, the mandate administration. They viewed the Zionist movement as the lesser problem and one that would be solved with the abrogation of the mandate. As a final note, while part of the new middle-class, the Palestinian Arab populist groups rarely endorsed the pro-British agenda of men such as Mufti of Palestine Mohammad Hajj Amin al-Husayni, members of the Jerusalem-based political factions of Husayni and Nashashibi family or the members of the Supreme Muslim Council.[7] It must be stressed that a particular civic and political identity emerged from outside the realm of the traditional, factional nationalist politics.

Ottoman Precedents: Imperial Citizenship and Arab Nationality

Histories on the development of the modern nation-state in the Arab world often posit the Tanzimat reforms introduced by the Ottoman Empire in the 1830s as the trigger for the ideological formation of a range of national and civic identities. A more complete history of the modernising reforms in the empire's provinces has been explained in numerous sources.[8] The 1839 Noble Edict of the Rose Chamber, issued by Sultan Abdulmecid, is generally noted as the start of the reform period; as a first step, the edict stated the equality of all imperial subjects. The more specific Ottoman Citizenship Law issued in 1869 codified a definition of Ottoman imperial citizenship (*tabiiyet-i Osmaniye kanunnamesi*) without reference to religion. Article 7 of the law stated that all subjects were to be Ottomans without religious distinction, and that this nationality could be gained (*jus soli* and *jus sanguinis*) or lost according to conditions in the law.[9] As Karen Kern notes, this was a shift from subjecthood to citizenship and, at the same time, a unifying measure to cultivate the loyalty of all Ottomans to the state.[10] According to Kemal Karpat, the wording of the law attempted 'to reconcile the Ottoman concept of nationality stemming from the *millet* [religious community] experience with the European idea of citizenship' by its creation of a direct relationship between the individual and the state.[11] In practical terms, the law simply concerned the means towards the acquisition of Ottoman nationality.

However, a rather different approach to what the 1869 law did and meant is perhaps more illuminating for the later study of communitarian citizenship ideology in Palestine after 1918. Clearly, the political and civic dimensions of nationality and citizenship did not appear because of the Tanzimat law, although Kern is correct to point out the potentially unifying aspect of it. Instead, as Will Hanley more recently argues, in the Ottoman realms and in Egypt for ordinary Ottomans what had a practical impact was the application of the 1869 law in the latter half of the century: through control of mobility, identity documents, the census, taxation, military service and access to law courts.[12] The law did not grant political rights of citizenship nor did it totally transform the conception of Ottoman subjecthood. The Ottoman citizenship law of 1869 did, however, come into being at the same time as intellectuals in Greater Syria started to theorise about the meaning of concepts such as the nation and patriotism. This confluence, I argue, shapes the turn-of-the-century and post-1918 discursive context of 'citizenship' and 'nationality' in the Arab Levant. It put a conceptual foundation into place but the active behaviours of citizenship and nationality came through other civic practices and processes explained below.

Hanley has noted that, in 1798, an Egyptian chronicler of Napoleon transliterated citizenship into Arabic as *sitwayan*.[13] Prior to that, the Ottomans used the word for genus (in reference to kind, type or category), *jinsiyya* in Arabic (or *cisiyya* in Ottoman Turkish) to refer to nationality.[14] By the late nineteenth century, the Western European concept of nationality was in fact translated into Ottoman Turkish and Arabic as *jinsiyya*, a translation that the British and French continued to use in legislation in the mandate period. This concept of *jinsiyya* did not correspond to the rights-bearing, liberal version of citizenship or to the term used more frequently for 'citizen' after 1918, *muwatin*.[15] Rather, subjecthood had a far more stable meaning in Ottoman and Arab vocabulary and in common usage: *tabiiyet* or *ra'iya*, translated as 'flock', in reference to the population's collective status within the empire as subjects to the Ottoman sultan, as a shepherd figure. Importantly, this relationship of subject to sultan was based on the traditional notions of protection in exchange for loyalty – *not* political sovereignty and allegiance.[16] Subjects paid taxes but the elements of political identity or rights to the state through subjecthood and, after 1869, nationality, was non-existent. Yet changes underway in Europe and in a number of colonial possessions before the outbreak of war in 1914 re-calibrated subjecthood as based on allegiance (by the collectivity of subjects) to a state or ruler, and subjects, territory and resources came under the sovereign control of that state or ruler. For the Arab inhabitants of southern Syria, the creation of an entirely new geographical entity under foreign (British) sovereignty after 1918 meant that the traditional Ottoman concept of membership in a polity, conceived as membership through the exchange of loyalty for protection, could no longer be sustained.

The pre-1900 Tanzimat reforms triggered important changes in the territorial administration of southern Syria and, as a result, historians can trace the growth of the inhabitants' multiple levels of belonging. The *sanjaks* of Jerusalem, Nablus and Acre all came under the control of the governor of Acre, an official appointed by Istanbul until 1841.[17] After that, Jerusalem became the administrative centre of southern Palestine. The empire reorganised its *vilayets* (provinces) into larger units in the 1860s and introduced general provincial assemblies and administrative councils alongside appointed governors (*valis*). The reorganisation of territory and the new elected provincial councils fostered the distinct notion of a separate 'Syria' within a larger Ottoman system.[18] The administrative changes were conducive to the development of territorial patriotism by Ottoman and Egyptian intellectuals. Egyptian writer Rifa'a Badawi al-Tahtawi first used the word *'watan'* to refer to the fatherland or homeland (influenced by French ideas of *patrie*) as the focus of identity, belonging and duties.[19] The concept of *watan* in its civic sense can be understood as a signifier of patriotic identity that laid the groundwork for actions and behaviours in cultural and social spheres that forged new notions of political identity and participation in the nation. Although Nawaf Salam argues that citizenship in the Islamic world emerged out of ideas on the nation and was modelled on the liberal idea of individual membership in the Ottoman political community, this argument in favour of Arabs' mimicking the European concept of citizenship does not entirely hold up to scrutiny.[20] The concept of citizenship to emerge in the Levant during the interwar period had little to do with individual claims to rights from the state. Instead, and as the book traces for the case of Palestine, claims to citizenship rights came out of the interpretation that membership in the Arab community on the basis of nationality and culture granted that particular community the rights *to* the nation-state.

The genesis of the post-1918 intellectual discussions of Arab nationality and communitarian citizenship can be traced in large part to the writings of the Syrian scholar and educator Boutrus al-Bustani starting in the year 1860. Ussama Makdisi concludes that local debates, such as those initiated by al-Bustani on the place of secular politics in the Empire immediately following the 1860 violence through Syria, helped foster modern concepts of civic identity.[21] This is particularly evident in a series of pamphlets written and distributed by al-Bustani in support of Ottoman nationalism and Syrian Arab patriotism. Bustani urged his fellow patriots (*abna' al-watan*), primarily other Ottoman intellectuals, to actively work toward a secular citizenship that could be 'developed, taught, and embraced simultaneously at an imperial and local level'. Importantly, he wrote that Syrians were bound together as one nationality (*jinsiyya*) within the larger Ottoman state. He stressed that all Syrian nationals as part of a specific community and as Ottoman

citizens must 'sacrifice for the nation' so that the empire could protect their rights in exchange.[22] In his pamphlets al-Bustani referred
to civil rights such as the freedoms of thought and speech but he did
not advocate political rights for members of the Arab and Ottoman
polities.[23]

Representation and participatory government in a very limited
measure began with the introduction of administrative and provincial councils in the Tanzimat era. Al-Bustani's writings combined
with Ottoman reforms are evidence that early steps towards active
civic engagement developed alongside structures of participatory
government and those civil rights listed in the Ottoman constitution. Promulgated in 1876, the constitution listed the further rights
of Ottoman nationals, including a reaffirmation that all Ottomans
had personal liberties and freedoms.[24] It is at this point that we can
find the influence of European liberal citizenship: at the time of
the promulgation of the constitution, a pamphlet translated from
French appeared in Istanbul. Titled *Le Droit des gens* (The Law of
Nations), the tract popularised the idea of the 'natural rights' of men,
which included elected representative democracy. The appearance of
the pamphlet is evidence of the spread of Western European liberal
thought on citizenship rights, natural rights and constitutional government in the Ottoman Empire.[25] However, Arab intellectuals in
Greater Syria continued to understand the concept of natural rights
as stemming from primordial membership in the Arab cultural and
social nation.

In the years before the First World War Ottoman Arab intellectuals in the provinces promoted the transition from passive to active
imperial subjecthood. The Young Turk Revolution of 1908 ushered
in changes to the meaning of citizenship, framed by the nation-
building project of the second constitutional era. As Erol Ülker suggests, the policy of Turkification was meant to construct a national,
Turkish core to the empire and the Ottomanism that stemmed from
the 1869 citizenship law and other reforms was reinterpreted in line
with the ideology of a dominant Turkish nationality.[26] As a result,
the conceptualisation of rights as a function of membership in the
Arab cultural and social community became more important for
Syria's politically aware intellectuals and Arab nationalists. Thus,
nationality came to be linguistically synthesised with *muwātana* (a
member of the nation) in the Arabic context. *Muwātana* took on a
more political connotation when used in written pamphlets and the
press and it often appeared in in reference to the term for regional or

Arab nationalism, 'qawmiyya'. At the same time in Syria, as Waten-paugh showed in his study of constructions of modernity at the end of the Ottoman era, the new middle-class often ambiguously started to lay claim to 'rights' (huquq) voiced in the press, civic associations and in the Ottoman representative councils.[27] Meanwhile, public and civic gatherings and social clubs created spaces for the lower classes to join an emerging political community that exposed them to debates surrounding key events like the 1908 revolution, parliament and the constitution and the dissolution of the empire after the First World War.[28]

These processes and the emergence of new institutions and spaces that accompanied them in Syria and what became Palestine took place on a global scale in the early twentieth century. The formulation of a communitarian concept of citizenship in the Arab Levant is also not unique: Rocco argues that alongside such new institutions, spaces and civic behaviours, rights are conceptualised as a function of membership in a historically specific society or community. He emphasises the formative role that cultural context plays in defining the nature and significance of claims to rights. It is only within the context of specific configurations of social relations, institutions and culture – such as that just before the First World War in the Ottoman Arab provinces and once the British and French assumed sovereignty over the provinces after 1918 – that the idea of rights can be understood and realised.[29] In Palestine, the changing nature of civic and political belonging within the territorial space itself, alongside the mandate's institutions that prevented self-government after the war ended and the mandate charter's provision for Jewish immigration contributed to a new understanding by nationalists of a specifically *Arab* communitarian identity and certain natural, civil and political rights for the Arab inhabitants. The following sections of the chapter continue to use Rocco's theory of communitarian citizenship: I argue that in the years immediately after the end of the Ottoman regime, civic associations that strengthened a Palestinian Arab solidarity and sense of community did not necessarily constitute citizenship claims in and of themselves but these associations and the civic engagement of their members were a 'vital factor' that led to activities and behaviours that did constitute citizenship claims. This is because the civic associations that supported a strong Palestinian Arab identity promoted 'a stronger sense of participatory rights and responsibilities' in traditionally non-political arenas, which allow conditions for citizenship claims to emerge.[30]

Post-war Palestine and the Development of a Political Community, 1918–1921

The rise of mass politics in the final years of the Ottoman administration reshaped the relationships of power within the Arab political community and inched them slowly towards a more horizontal rather than vertical structure. James Gelvin has shown that after 1918 civil society in Syria became separate from the realm of the state and was prominent over the state.[31] It is undeniable that the press, alongside civic associations, played a crucial part in the political development of the Ottoman Empire's Arab provinces. In the territory that became Palestine after 1918, the political and civic community that emerged articulated a mixture of new and old definitions and notions of nationality and citizenship rights, and both included the fundamental component of primordial membership within the Arab community. Of equal importance, the development of this political community from 1918 to 1920 depended upon the role played by the middle-class leaders in spoiling dominant, traditional politics.

Newspaper editors and journalists, educated in Western-style national schools, were situated firmly in the new middle-class and presented themselves and their work as at the vanguard of national modernity. For example, Mustafa Kabha cites in his illuminative study of the press and public opinion that periodicals such as Haifa's *al-Karmil* claimed in 1909 that newspapers were dedicated to the service of the people and 'inform[ed] citizens of their rights and obligations in this country'.[32] Similarly in 1913 the editor of *Filastīn* delivered free copies of his newspaper to many of the villages in the Jaffa district with the aim to 'teach the peasants their rights'.[33] The importance of the press cannot be understated: it helped to create public opinion and familiarised readers with political discussions, legislation, voting regulations, nationalist ideologies and other affairs. It also cultivated public opinion. Palestinian periodicals had a considerable circulation: newspapers made their way into the villages where the literate men would read aloud the week's international, regional and local news during public gatherings. Chris Bayly has called late colonial north India a 'literacy aware society'. The same condition existed in Palestine before and throughout the interwar years.[34] As a result, few inhabitants were left completely unaware of the most significant political issues and events and most could take on for themselves the ready-made opinions of a particular newspaper on any given subject.[35]

The press also used a colourful, often alarming, rhetorical style to describe events at the end of the war and their implications for Palestine – the language forced newspaper readers to pay attention. After the British occupation of Palestine in late 1917 the press liberally printed article after article defining the military occupation as British 'colonialism' (*āsta'mār*). Members of the emerging Palestinian Arab national movement and civic organisations used a similar language in written demands presented to Great Britain and the League of Nations that were replete with references to anti-colonialism and 'natural', national and civil rights. This language shaped a new 'national' discursive field that incorporated symbols and often-ambiguous rhetoric of nationality and citizenship. Thus began the language of demands for Arab national rights on the basis that Ottoman nationality warranted such rights to be granted to the 'native' (usually in reference to the Arabic-speaking former Ottoman subjects) population who would then assume administrative and political control over the territory.[36]

One of the first and most significant associations to form after the war with specifically Palestinian nationalist as well as political inclinations was the Muslim–Christian Association, or MCA (*al-jam'iyya al-islamiyya al-massihiyya*), established in 1918 in both Jaffa and Jerusalem. The popularity of the MCA was evident in the fact that branches were soon opened by its leaders in every major town in Palestine. With slogans that endorsed civic ideals of Muslim–Christian unity, the MCA attracted a large following as a secular and inclusive association that also advocated that the Arabs have the political right to govern Palestine. The MCA touted itself in petitions and letters to the British authorities as representative of all Palestinian Arabs, and used stamps and a flag that combined 'Palestinian' images such as the Holy Sepulcher and the Dome of the Rock.[37] The association was instrumental in organising the first Palestinian Arab Congress in early 1919 and continued to convene it in the following years. Members of the congress went on to form the Arab Executive Committee (*al-lajna al-tanafīdhiyya al-'arabiyya*), or the Executive, of the Palestinian Arab Congress in 1920. This committee grew in importance and assumed the MCA's role as the political and civic representative body of the Palestinian people.

From 1918, nationalists in Palestine identified as members of the wider community (*umma*) and national movement (*al-haraka al-wataniyya*) but political allegiances and ideologies often shifted. One large bloc of self-professed nationalists included those who adhered to the ideology of pan-Arab nationalism. The ideology of pan-Arabism did not influence the politics of the traditional leadership to the great extent that it did in the case of the middle-class and younger nationalists. These pan-Arab populist leaders, such as intellectuals, writers, lawyers and teachers, mobilised and attempted to reach out to the population at large. For example, a number of urban intellectuals publicised the perceived threat to the peasants (*fellahin*) posed by the Zionist project and land issues became topics of discussion in national conferences and associations. Editorials in the early 1920s likened all Palestinians to the symbol of the peasant farmer as the embodiment of the nation. The appeal to certain symbols in order to cultivate civic and national unity, while not always genuine (as in the case of some notables who actively sold land to Zionist groups) nonetheless obscured the more conciliatory activities of the notables in favour of a presentation of national unity as the means to resist British Administration over all of Palestine. As Gelvin has shown in the case of Syria, protests, slogans and public demonstrations expressed unity and instilled a civic model of the nation based on the bonds of a common Arab nationality and citizenship.[38]

Integral to the growth of the nationalist political community in Palestine was the transformation of the traditional public sphere and its institutions, which occurred alongside the imposition of the mandate administration. Nationalist leaders and associations such as the MCA and the Executive used the public sphere, including the press, schools, religious institutions and other public areas, as a site of civic expression and to show opposition to the mandate and Zionism. As early as 1918, significant demonstrations and marches took place in the urban centres of Jerusalem and Jaffa. The several written protests addressed to the military administration in 1919 can also be understood as active political practices as well as civic engagement – in particular, groups gave written protests to British officials during demonstrations.[39] Local popular committees in Palestine's large towns staged demonstrations and claimed to represent the 'will of the nation'. Similarly, the MCA organised one of the first political gatherings in the name of the nation in January and February 1919, the First Palestinian Arab Congress. Delegates attended from all regions of Palestine, and the congress claimed to speak on behalf of all Palestinians when it passed resolutions in support of independent representative democracy and unity with Syria.[40] The congress was not united politically, however: a definite separation existed between the pro-British and the pan-Arab blocs of delegates especially in terms of tactics necessary to achieve independence.[41] Soon after, the

British appointment in 1921 of the young Hajj Mohammed Amin al-Husayni as both the Grand Mufti of Jerusalem and the head of the newly created Supreme Muslim Council (SMC) formed by the British to manage Muslim religious affairs represented the willingness of some elite Arabs to work alongside the mandatory government.

During the years immediately after the war, other Palestinians continued a number of Committee of Union and Progress-era traditions of direct political participation. The MCA and the Arab Executive of the congresses voiced new demands for rights in petitions, strikes and boycotts – actions that had been performed in Ottoman times as civic, although not expressly citizenship, behaviours. In the words of Michelle Campos, boycotts were 'an echo of a republican understanding of citizenship, where every individual has to contribute to the public good' and an example of popular participation in politics. She cites the example of an empire-wide boycott led by Palestine's port cities in 1908 against Austrian and German products to protest the annexation of Bosnia-Herzegovina.[42] The act of boycott in support of the Muslim population of Bosnia-Herzegovina, however, can also be characterised as indicative of a more social, communal and cultural, rather than an explicitly republican, understanding of identity belonging.

Similarly, petitions had long been used by the Arab population to address the local Ottoman administration and the central government in Istanbul. While Gelvin notes that by virtue of their signatures the masses held a stake in their own political affairs and defined their power of negotiation with the authorities, the subject–sultan relationship of protection and loyalty did not traditionally involve demands of a political nature.[43] The language of the written petitions, newspaper editorials and protest demonstrations reflected the changing concepts of national belonging to a polity as well as the newer concept of the relationship between the sovereign and the Arabs in the Levantine mandates. In Palestine, the early public activities of the pan-Arab nationalists helped to create a link between the identity of the Arab population as 'nationals' and the need for these nationals to demand their 'natural rights'. Gelvin has shown that in this atmosphere 'a new *political* public was both created and mobilized'.[44] For example, on the first anniversary of the British occupation of Jaffa, that city's MCA wrote a letter that stressed the relationship between the status of the Arabs and their rights in British-administered Palestine and reminded the British that the nationality of the country and its people was Arab.[45] The idea of a relationship between 'the Arab nation' and an Arab commonwealth nationality (*qawmiyya*) with the concept of rights cropped up frequently in newspaper editorials and in letters by local politicians and members of the Executive to the British Administration and to the League.

In the years before the official ratification of the mandates system, Palestinian writers and MCA leaders offered explanations and definitions of nationality in light of the phrase coined by Great Britain, that of a 'Jewish national home' (al-watan al-qawmī al-yahudiyya). An editorial published in November 1918 by the newspaper Filastīn surmised that the application of nationality in Palestine meant that the national status of the Arabs and Jews who lived in the territory surely must be equal before the law. The editorial stressed that this concept of nationality dated back to the Ottoman period as imperial legislation had conferred the same 'rights' to all of the empire's inhabitants. The writer feared that this meaning of nationality could not be reconciled with the intentions set out for Palestine in the Balfour Declaration and he warned British officials that the Arab citizens would not accept a Palestinian nationality that privileged the political standing of the Jewish immigrants within the wider 'Arab nation'.[46] In fact, a number of newspaper articles published in 1919 voiced the complaint that the then-military administration gave certain rights to the immigrants as if these immigrants were 'nationals of Palestine'. 'National' (watanī or qawmī) became equated with 'native' (ibn al-balad). Certain 'rights' were thus equated with the Arab population's native origin in the territory. Importantly, both nationalist writers and members of the Executive understood the Arabs as the natives of Palestine either by birth or descent. As part of this understanding, both birth and descent entitled them to nationality and national, civil and political rights (huquq midaniyya and huquq siyāsiya).[47]

The conflation of terminology for the native, the national and the citizen used in editorials and in statements by the middle-class leaders in the Executive is an important element in the analysis of the evolution of citizenship in Mandate Palestine. During the early mandate period the word 'jinsiyya' referred to nationality in the context of a territorial nation-state. In the late Ottoman era the word that later came to refer to the citizen, 'muwātin', was based on the Arabic word 'watan' (homeland) and denoted a native as opposed to a foreigner. Both terms came into more frequent use in the interwar years as nationality evolved to connote membership in the Arab nation as political and civil rights became attached to the status of belonging.[48] The plural for citizens, 'muwātinīn', was rarely used within Palestine in documents or articles in the early 1920s. However, the term is not entirely absent: for example, leaders in the cities of Nablus and Tulkarm signed petitions to the 1919 Paris Peace Conference 'on behalf of our citizens' (*nīāba 'an muwātinīnā*).[49] The national leadership explained terms like 'nationality' and civil and political rights in a language that the Arab public identified with.

The use of symbols accompanied the civic language and featured in Arab nationalist and local leaders' discussions and writings that urged the creation of a greater civic identification between different social groups in Palestinian society. In particular, the symbol of the Arab peasant (*fellah*) continued to have a prominent role in the burgeoning Palestinian Arab political community as a link to the traditional past and a reminder of the threats posed by the Jewish national home policy of Britain. Local and populist (or otherwise non-traditionally elite) Arab nationalists challenged the British Administration's failure to protect what they explicitly called the citizenship rights of Arab cultivators and peasants. Leaders stressed the importance of what they depicted as the civil rights to land ownership and use. For example, when the 1920 Land Transfer Ordinance amended the 1910 Ottoman law that had restricted land ownership to Ottoman national corporate entities, editorials decried the new threat posed to the civil rights of the peasants with regard to land ownership and agricultural tenancy on land acquired by foreign Jews.[50] The amendment meant that Jewish immigrants and Zionist entrepreneurs could purchase land in Palestine without holding provisional Palestinian nationality. The implication of the Land Transfer Ordinance was that the British no longer upheld the customary law that protected and favoured the practice of communal land ownership. As a result, peasants were evicted from the land they farmed when they could not produce titles of ownership.[51] In one particular case in which residents of Beisan faced eviction, the Arab lawyer W. F. Boustany pointed out to the government in 1922 that the residents were 'bona fide citizens' whose 'civil rights' must be maintained as part of mandate policy.[52] Palestinian peasants and villagers alike formed their own elected associations that started out as apolitical and often for mutual aid, and soon after became institutions meant to protect the interests of rural Arabs who were increasingly drawn into the new political community.[53]

Since its founding in late 1920, the Executive stressed the concept of civil rights in the new language of internationalism when rendering appeals against the Balfour Declaration and the Jewish national home to the League, Great Britain and the Palestine Administration. The Executive argued the incompatibility of British policy with the principles of international rights and the 'natural rights' of the

Palestinian people, and noted that such policy 'violated the sanctity of civil laws'.[54] The Third Palestinian Arab Congress of 1920 stated its goal to achieve 'international human rights, civil rights, historical, and social rights', including representative government in Palestine.[55] Thus, the Executive seized upon the growing awareness of rhetoric of political nationality that stemmed from historical membership in the Arab community, and the body also increasingly illustrated this rhetoric with examples of national, political and civil rights that were applicable to both urban and rural Palestinians.

The Concept of Palestinian Nationality and the Evolution of Citizenship Practices

Several months after the appointment of Herbert Samuel as high commissioner in mid-1920, the Arab Executive elected the recently deposed mayor of Jerusalem Musa Kazim al-Husayni as its president. Musa Kazim, who was then in his late sixties, came from the prominent al-Husayni family of Jerusalem. He opposed the British administration and his politics came to be respected by all sectors of Palestinian society. Until his death in 1934, Musa Kazim supported equal civil and political rights for all former Ottoman citizens and he was the first Executive leader to question the nationality legislation of 1925 after emigrants in the Americas sent him numerous letters asking his help to induce the British authorities to offer Palestinian citizenship to the emigrants. This section traces how various leaders including Musa Kazim discussed concepts and behaviours of a uniquely Palestinian nationality and citizenship prior to 1925. The populist leaders and the traditional politicians formulated an understanding that civil and political rights for the population came out of membership and participation in the Arab and Ottoman community prior to the end of the war. The Arabic press acknowledged this understanding as civic associations at the local and national level discussed it in the public sphere.

Musa Kazim, as Executive president, addressed a letter to Colonial Secretary Winston Churchill in 1921 and pointed out that before the war the Jews of Palestine enjoyed what he referred to as the privileges and rights of citizenship in the Ottoman Empire. Musa Kazim expressed the belief that 'countries with their civil and other rights and privileges are the property of their inhabitants and constitute an heirloom of the nation'. He emphasised that the Jewish, Christian and Muslim natives of Palestine (*abnā' filastīn*) had ultimate control over their country, and their affiliation with Arab *qawmiyya* (nationalism) meant that they must be granted certain rights and duties. In the letter, Musa Kazim also questioned the status of the British Jews who served in the Palestine Administration, such as High Commissioner Herbert Samuel. He asked Churchill whether they were Jewish or British nationals, arguing that 'it is obvious they cannot be both at the same time'. Musa Kazim wondered if 'Jew-ism' was in fact a nationality, and, if so, he pondered the 'English-ism' of men like Samuel while in Palestine. It was clear to him that 'one -ism must be sacrificed for the other, but which for which?'[56] The idea that the Jewish immigrants constituted their own nationality group in Palestine posed a clear problem to Arab nationalists like Musa Kazim who understood nationality along ethnic lines. This conflation of ethnicity and nationality confused Arab nationalists who could not fathom how the British could confer the same *Palestinian* nationality on Jewish immigrants as they did on the Arabs. At the same time, press reports of Musa Kazim's letter influenced Arab public opinion that European Jews had an ethnic nationality directly linked to their religious identity.

In reference to the Balfour Declaration's promise to maintain the civil and religious rights of the Arab population, Musa Kazim argued that the idea of civil rights 'mean nothing more than equality and justice before the law and obviously no privilege is contained in this'. According to him, the civil rights of the Palestinians as Ottoman subjects unquestionably included representation in a parliament, provincial government and native councils, as well as Arab employment in the highest judicial and civil servant positions, and all the civic freedoms associated with it.[57] Kazim's statements are illustrative of a particular understanding of civil and political rights by some Arab national leaders very early in the British administration of Palestine. Kazim stressed to the Colonial Office that such rights were inalienable for all citizens and could not be granted or taken away by the mandate administration. He suggested that the inherent nature of these rights made their mention in the Balfour Declaration unnecessary. With the text of the Balfour Declaration in mind, he and his colleagues accused the British of conflating civil rights with religious rights.[58] The development of this language normalised a link between nationality (*jinsiyya*) based on birth and descent in a territory and various types of rights (*huquq*) *to* that territory.

Local Arab leaders and intellectuals in villages and urban areas alike contributed to this discussion. They wrote editorials or letters for newspapers and held meetings under the auspices of a number of civic associations, and offered support to the Arab Executive. For example, an editorial in the Jerusalem newspaper *Mir'at al-Sharq* posed the question of 'what [would be] left of our political or civil rights' if the Jews established a homeland in Palestine for Jewish nationals.[59] The dialogue on primordial political and civil rights both *to* and fully within the territory and its government resonated with the Arab public when linked in practical terms with threats posed by Zionism and the Balfour Declaration. In this period, the Palestinian Arab population came to understand civil rights as unrestricted access to land ownership, livelihood, the control of immigration and the local and national economy. Press reports and the MCA increasingly demanded of the British administration that every Arab in Palestine be granted civil rights to equal employment in all private and public spheres following the Zionist Organisation's foundational policy of the conquest of labour (*kibosh avoda*).[60] By the early 1920s, a number of active local leaders focused their attention on the appeal for a proportional representative government and an elected parliament. These nationalists pointedly noted that a parliamentary system with a French or North American-style bill of rights would ensure the protection of the nation's minorities (*huquq aqaliyyāt*) as well as other political and civil rights for the entire population of Palestine.[61]

In 1921 the first Palestinian Arab Delegation (*wafd*) composed of Arab Executive Committee members, including Musa Kazim, travelled to London to meet with Winston Churchill at the Colonial Office. The delegation raised the issue of the national status of the Jewish immigrants. This was the first time that the Arab leadership directly addressed Great Britain on issues of nationality. In a conversation between members of the *wafd*, Churchill and Hubert Young of the Middle East Department in London, the delegation's secretary Shibli Jamal questioned Churchill over the plan to establish a national home for the Jews in Palestine. The meaning of 'national' in the Balfour Declaration concerned the delegation. Jamal asked if those he called 'the Hebrews [*sic*]' became nationals of Palestine by virtue of the Balfour Declaration. At the time of the meeting the draft nationality order was already circulating among mandate administrators and Zionist leaders such as Weizmann. Churchill answered that the Jewish immigrants would become Palestinians. The delegation expressed anxiety over the seemingly unconditional nature of nationality for any immigrant, and sought assurance that certain provisions and greater residency requirements would be necessary for naturalisation.[62] This exchange is telling, and crucial to the understanding of the Arabs' concept of nationality in the early 1920s. The delegation feared the loss of future sovereignty to immigrants on the basis of their perceived ethnic (*qawm*) nationality. In turn, immigrants would become political equals with the Arabs and thus threaten Arab control over an independent Palestine.

At the time of the delegation's visit, the Foreign and Colonial offices and members of the League held ongoing debates over the appropriate body able to grant the nationality of inhabitants of an international mandate. Aware of these wider debates, Jamal questioned what authority would grant Palestinian nationality. Young surmised that the British as the mandatory would do so, but did not mention provisions for state succession or succession of nationality as detailed in the Treaty of Sèvres. The officials offered very little information on nationality despite the queries of the Palestinian delegation. In fact, the Palestinian Arabs heard of (but did not read) the draft nationality law for the first time in London. Colonial officials evaded the direct question of whether a legislative body in Palestine could have a say in the draft nationality law.[63] At no point did the British Government offer to involve the Arab leadership in the official discussions of nationality regulations as they had done for the Zionist Organisation. The Arabs expected a measure of involvement as part of the obligation that the mandatory foster self-government. Shortly after this meeting the delegation sent a report to the president of the League of Nations Commission in Geneva. The report expressed regret that the British did not grant the delegation, representatives of the Palestinian Arabs, the opportunity to scrutinise the provisions to regulate nationality. The report lamented that the mandate administration would deprive the Palestinians of self-government and noted that Great Britain did not have the authority to prepare a nationality law. Instead, the delegation argued that 'this legislative capacity lies within the sphere of the national government set up by the people'.[64]

After the delegation's trip to London, the Arab members of Samuel's Advisory Council gained some knowledge of the draft nationality order. After hearing an illustration of the proposed constitution and nationality laws, council spokesman Turkan Bey declared to the British members of the council that it was obvious the nationality law benefited the Zionist immigrants. He voiced the Arab opposition to the two-year residency period required before an individual could be naturalised as a citizen. He argued (not entirely accurately) that in every other country the residency requirement for naturalisation was at least five years. After consultation with the council's other Arab members, Turkan suggested the swift enactment of the nationality law to help Palestinian Arabs who lived abroad and had lost Ottoman nationality.[65] He was the first to express concern for these stateless emigrants.

The Arabic press reports on the activities of the delegation reached a wide audience. They were instrumental in fashioning and popularising a terminology of civil, political and national rights and nationality.[66] Editorials and articles put forward alternative interpretations of Palestinian nationality, giving it further meaning and form. The English section of the newspaper *Mir'at al-Sharq* stated in 1921 that the question of a 'unity of citizenship between the countries of the Arabic world is one of paramount importance'. The editor asked if the mandates' classification of the Arab world under different colonial administrations inherently clashed with such a 'unity of citizenship'. In answering, '[W]e think not,' he went on to stress that the mandates had 'absolutely nothing to do with questions of nationality or citizenship' and should not attempt to deal 'with [these] fundamental questions of race, nationality, or citizenship'. The ideology of a common citizenship in the Arab world was presented as a benefit for all Arabs and a necessity for the Palestinians.[67] This ideology appeared in opposition to the Palestinian nationality provisions proposed by the British Administration as the Palestinian Arabs formulated their own definition of nationality. Writers, alongside the Arab delegation to London, were quick to point out that the draft nationality provisions did not mirror those in place in the Ottoman provinces since 1869. Criticism of the provisions swiftly emanated from Arab political circles even before the Arab leadership could read the text of the draft law. After the delegation failed to gain any concessions from colonial officials in London and once it returned to Palestine, the ideological clash between the more subaltern, nontraditional and the dominant political movements deepened.

A group of younger nationalists, along with the well-respected Musa Kazim al-Husayni, began to articulate more forcefully the position that if the mandate authorities would not leave the administration of Palestine to its Arab inhabitants the former needed to fulfil various duties as provisional sovereigns. These Palestinians requested a type of colonial paternalism that the French practiced in Syria and Lebanon. As Elizabeth Thompson has argued, the French administrations justified their control of Syria and Lebanon by their use of an ideology of social relief, not unlike a welfare state.[68] In the 1920s, the French significantly expanded benefits to their colonial citizens, supported by a hierarchy of citizenship based on class, religion and location. In Palestine, the dual system of administration limited the role of the British as paternal guardians.[69] Even so, the British constructed an image of democracy in their colonial territories that influenced the younger nationalists' call for protection, aid and assistance for the population. In a study on the development of citizenship in colonial Hong Kong, Agnes Shuk-mei Ku criticises the British practice of 'governance without democracy' through the facade of political rights given to Hong Kong colonial subjects. In Palestine, the proposal for the non-direct election by the religious community for members of a legislative council that would have no power to pass laws illustrates such a practice. The British used democracy 'as a means to achieve political legitimacy and state goals', rather than to foster civic participation and state-building.[70] In Palestine, for instance, younger members of the Arab Executive in 1921 pressed for local communities to support or open their own national schools since the administration had failed in its 'duty' to expand the educational system to teach young people 'how to grow up good citizens of Palestine'.[71] In the early 1920s newspapers published editorials that expanded upon these duties, and writers asked that the Arabs themselves undertake to provide assistance and welfare for the wider population.[72] These suggested actions were referred to as sacred and exemplary civic duties and civic activism.[73]

The administration's refusal to acknowledge the Arab Executive, Musa Kazim, or groups like the MCA as representative of the Palestinian Arabs triggered an increase in public displays of dissatisfaction in the early 1920s. The Executive along with civil society groups launched campaigns to demonstrate the people's endorsement of the Executive as the official representative body of the Palestinian Arabs.[74] Organisations such as the MCA as well as young people handed notes of protest to British colonial officials whenever they visited cities and towns in Palestine. Yet, in large part, these organisation and their members represented local interests and concerns although they worked for causes with broad national appeal. While the urban-based Jaffa MCA protested the police action taken against unarmed demonstrators or press censorship, nationalists in the rural Galilee demanded that the government protect the villages and peasants of Nazareth from land dispossession and establish an agricultural bank. At the same time, the MCA in 1921 sent a letter to the Colonial Office to report that all classes in 'town, village, factory and farm' comprised the nation and had the same demands.[75] In the early 1920s, the accuracy of such a statement is rather in doubt. Yet the canvassing and propaganda of the MCA and younger activists in rural areas was evident. For example, the Haycraft Commission, which was sent to Palestine in 1921 to investigate disturbances between Arab and Jewish communities, reported that the villagers of Tulkarm were 'more politically minded than a small English country town'.[76] The use of civic activism became more evident in 1922 during the boycott of the elections for the legislative council, which featured widespread involvement by urban and rural Palestinians and marked an important step in the politicisation of the Arab citizens of Palestine.

After the mandate administration published the Electoral Order-in-Council in 1922 and made known High Commissioner Samuel's plans for a partially elected legislative body, the Arab Executive decided to focus on an Arab boycott of the elections. The practice of boycotting government-convened committees was not new but it grew in importance once presented in the press explicitly as a tactic of civil disobedience (al-'asiyan al-madaniyya). One year earlier, Musa Kazim al-Husayni had convinced the Arab members of Samuel's consultative committee in Jerusalem to boycott its meetings on the basis that the Arab Executive alone could discuss constitutional and other matters with the British Government.[77] The Fifth Palestinian Arab Congress held in the summer of 1922 resolved to support the boycott of the Legislative Council elections. This decision received widespread endorsement by nationalist associations who touted the boycott as a civic duty. In a statement to the chief secretary in Palestine immediately after the congress, the Nablus MCA argued that the 1922 Electoral Order was based on the terms of the mandate and therefore harmful to the nation's interests especially since members could not pass any ordinance deemed inconsistent with the terms of the charter.[78]

The MCA's claims (published in the press) that the legislative council would threaten the civil and political rights of Arab Palestinians prompted a wide, general boycott. The boycott was a testament of the Arab leadership's displeasure over the lack of political rights and their ability to mobilise their communities. Palestinians were informed of the boycott not only by statements of the MCA and Arab Executive in the press but also by village mukhtars at large demonstrations and in mosques and churches. However, neither the Mufti nor the Supreme Muslim Council supported the boycott – a stance that firmly separated these traditional religious leaders from their middle-class and more secular counterparts. In Jaffa and Jerusalem, the crowds that demonstrated in support of the boycott numbered in the thousands. The elections took place, but out of a planned 809 secondary electors, only 134 Arabs were actually elected – mainly by Jewish voters. Wasserstein refers to the attempt by the government to hold elections as 'a fiasco, and . . . a humiliating setback for Samuel's policy'.[79] The British could not create a legislative council in 1922, and soon after the boycott, seven of ten nominated Arab members of the High Commissioner's Advisory Council withdrew their candidacy.

After 1922, the middle-class activists began to praise non-violent tactics of disobedience against the mandate administration and referred to such acts as national duties. This cultivated the ideology that the population had participatory responsibilities vis-à-vis the nation. Non-cooperation in the early 1920s demonstrated the effective agency of popular leaders to urge fellow Palestinian Arabs to confront the mandatory in order for the nation 'to achieve its legitimate rights' in association with citizenship.[80] At the ever-growing public demonstrations, nationalist leaders and associations explicitly stated their intent to exercise what they termed as the civil rights of free speech and assembly. The MCA branches held meetings and encouraged the involvement of other groups to explain and publicise such tactics throughout Palestine. As early as 1921, activists touted strikes as an individual civic activism in working-class, urban areas. Upon the return of the Palestinian Arab delegation in 1922, national groups held the first two-day strike in support of an independent Palestine. Nationalist leader Omar Bittar wrote that all classes of people in Palestine went on strike to demand their 'natural right' (al-haqq al-tabī'ayyī) of independence.[81] The deliberations of the Sixth Palestinian Arab Congress in 1923 included a plan to study the effectiveness of a boycott of land and property taxes. The congress also decided to encourage citizens not to associate or work with any Arab who accepted membership to British-managed councils.[82] Activists depicted such behaviours as duties that would force Great Britain to rescind the Balfour Declaration and give control of Palestine to the Arabs.[83]

The Immediate Reactions to the 1925 Palestine Citizenship Order-in-Council

In mid-1925, H. E. Field Marshal Lord Plumer replaced Herbert Samuel as Palestine's high commissioner. Arabic newspapers were quick to address the issue of nationality since changes to the citizenship order came after his term of office began. One open letter published in August 1925 in Sawt al-Sha'b lamented that a number of

Jewish immigrants 'should never be allowed to become [Palestinian] nationals and citizens'. The letter pointed out that under a national parliament in Palestine, the Arabs would declare that Jewish citizens would enjoy equal political rights with the Arabs.[84] The focus on nationality legislation was a new one for the press: in the year before the British Government ratified the 1925 Palestine Citizenship Order-in-Council, leaders within Palestine offered few comments on nationality legislation but instead focused on national rights.

When the administration announced changes to the citizenship order in November 1925, to bring it in line with the Treaty of Lausanne, newspapers prominently featured articles on the meaning of Palestinian nationality. The negative impact of these changes on Palestinian Arab emigrants brought the issue of citizenship and nationality to the front pages of newspapers. The changes, which gave emigrants less than nine months to return permanently to Palestine to opt for their nationality, caused an outcry first from several emigrant groups in Latin America. The order itself confirmed what leaders like Musa Kazim had earlier opposed: new Jewish immigrants would receive Palestinian citizenship with few restrictions apart from residence in the country for two years prior to their naturalisation. The Arabic press seized on this point of contention and portrayed it as a glaring example of the unfairness of the British colonial policy of privileging a foreign group over the Arab population of the region. Newspaper articles noted the ease with which immigrants could become full citizens, and writers predicted this as the final blow to hope for the cancellation of the Jewish national home policy. Meanwhile, Palestinian (provisional) nationality, according to one journalist, 'can be obtained by every Jew who sets foot in Palestine and this is not an apparent assault on the highest of our civil rights?' Harking back to the 1921 delegation to London, articles concluded that the denial of the Palestinian voice in nationality legislation stood as another example that the British refused to take the rights of the Arabs into account.[85]

In the summer of 1925, *Mir'at al-Sharq* published two articles that questioned the meaning of nationality in the context of the mandate and the Jewish national home policy. In the light of the high commissioner's announcement of the impending publication of the citizenship order, the paper argued that contradictions existed between the nationality legislation and the meaning of national in the Balfour Declaration and in accordance with the Jewish national home policy. The articles reflected the long-standing confusion among the Arab nationalists and national bodies over the term 'national' (*qawmī*) in the Declaration.[86] As previously noted, the Arabs understood 'national' in ethnic terms and envisioned themselves as part of an ethnic group separate from immigrant Jews. Their confusion was framed around a clash of interest, namely how the citizenship order could grant equal nationality for separate ethnicities. Similarly themed articles published through the end of 1925 pointed out that the Arabic term for nationality (*'jinsiyya'*) began to take on a more territorial and legal – and less cultural and communitarian – meaning, akin to *wantaniyya* (territorial nationalism). The territorial aspect added to the confusion over its explanation in the press. One writer questioned what nationality meant for Jewish communities in Eastern Europe, the birthplace of the majority of the immigrants. He claimed that thousands of Jewish people scattered over the world did not all have the same nationality in the sense of ethnic affiliation in their different countries. If these immigrant (mainly Orthodox) Jews were to be given a separate Palestinian nationality not on par with the Arabs but rather as members of a Jewish national home, then the Arab Palestinians would have an unequal status vis-à-vis the Jewish community. The article also discussed the term 'national' and its translation into Western European languages as 'subject' (*'ra'iyya'*, from the term 'flock').[87] For the Arabs, the meaning of 'subject' took on the same meaning as 'citizen' in terms of being under the jurisdiction of a particular state. Herein was the difference between national and citizen for the Palestinian Arab writers. While nationality was nearly the same as ethnicity, citizenship denoted a status of being under the jurisdiction of a state or administration.

The previous article also made an important point about the text of the Balfour Declaration. The implementation of the Declaration's terms specifically could not alter the rights and status enjoyed by Jews in other countries, and so the status of immigrant Jews who became Palestinian nationals would not be affected. They would remain nationals of their country of origin *and* become nationals of Palestine. The writer asked 'whether this text [Balfour Declaration] is inconsistent with the phrase "Jewish national homeland"'' in terms of national status. Would nationals of Britain, France or America who were Jewish and settled in Palestine as members of the Jewish national home be forced to become Palestinians to the exclusion of their original nationality?[88] Ironically, the query mirrored questions posed by British statesmen only two years prior to this. The Palestinian Arabs wondered whether all Jewish immigrants could hold more than one nationality. Such questions demonstrate that the notions of nationality and nation-state citizenship differed. Only at the end of July 1925 did a brief Arabic article clarify to readers that the existence of a Jewish national home in Palestine did not mean that 'Jewish nationality' would be imposed upon the inhabitants of Palestine.[89]

With the publication of the Citizenship Order-in-Council in the Arabic press and the *Palestine Gazette* (the administration's official periodical) in September 1925 some Palestinian Arabs had the opportunity to become familiar with the order's provisions. Newspapers published the full text of the order but some, such as Tulkarm's *al-Ittihad al-'Arabi*, relegated it to the last page. Every Arabic newspaper titled the legislation as the 'Nationality Law' (*al-qanun al-jinsiyya* or *al-haqq al-jinsiyya*) rather than as the Citizenship Order. The official Arabic translation of the order in the *Palestine Gazette* used the term '*jinsiyya*'.[90] Two months after the administration published the citizenship order the editor of *Sawt al-Sha'b*, 'Isa Bandak, took on the task of explaining on a civic level the dangers posed by the law. Bandak had established and edited the newspaper as a weekly since 1922 and he served as a popular politician in Bethlehem, where he founded the city's Literary Club and another pan-Arab periodical (*Bayt Laham*). The Literary Club and the press in Bethlehem under Bandak's supervision devoted attention to the Palestinian diaspora since a large number of emigrants came from Bethlehem and its environs.[91] Bandak's immediate reactions to the citizenship order, as apparent from the pages of *Sawt al-Sha'b*, were in fact the first ones to address the emigrants' political status – a shift from previous social commentary on the diaspora. In an article titled 'The law prejudices the rights of the Arabs' he expressed anger at the harm done by the order to the interests of the nation since the legislation did not grant any rights for the Arabs on the basis of Palestinian nationality. First and foremost, he critiqued the reason for the law: Great Britain enacted it to facilitate Zionist immigration and meet the terms of the Balfour Declaration within the mandate. The critique fitted in well with the nationalist, anti-Zionist discourse and for good reason. Indeed, the British worked with the Zionist leaders to draft the favourable provisions of the order concerning the acquisition of nationality by Jewish immigrants.[92]

Bandak compared the Palestinian order with citizenship legislation in the United States and found that immigrants to America had to meet several provisions, including five years of permanent residence, in order to be granted a certificate of legal residency. He also explained to the readers the residency laws throughout Europe and reported – as the Arab delegation alluded to in 1921 – that all countries required no less than five years of residency before an immigrant could apply for citizenship. Bandak was the first editor to accuse the administration of unfairly placing no restrictions on whether Jewish immigrants could live full- or part-time in Palestine in order to retain their nationality. The situation, Bandak surmised, created 'a wide crater in the roof of Palestinian nationality' as it allowed any Jew in the world to acquire Palestinian citizenship rights. His main points all related back to the favouritism of Great Britain for the Zionist Organisation's aims.[93] Bandak's arguments echoed those of the Palestinian delegation but the publication of the 1925 order led to the re-emergence of vocal opposition to British legislation in Palestine. This opposition to citizenship provisions was symptomatic of the wider anger over the lack of consultation between the Arabs and the administration.

A number of other reasons for the Arab opposition to the citizenship provisions can be gleaned from editorials by Bandak and others. One reason is the claim that the order was detrimental to the country, which was not economically sound, and that unemployed foreign arrivals to Palestine would not be obliged to contribute to the welfare of the country. Rather, their loyalties would be to the Jewish national home project. Furthermore, the supposed illegality of the order – since a parliament of elected representatives did not create it – was another theme constantly stressed in 1925. Bandak concluded that the establishment of a Jewish national home supported by the nationality order would obstruct Arab national control over the country's resources, allow land to be requisitioned and deplete Arab financial wealth by taking over businesses. These early reactions to the citizenship order are also important because of the readership of Arabic periodicals such as *Sawt al-Sha'b*. This readership included those most impacted by the citizenship order, families of the Palestinian Arab diaspora.

Conclusion

Although the 1925 Citizenship Order-in-Council was published in Arabic in Palestinian periodicals and in the official gazette, the change made to put its timeframe for option for citizenship in line with the Treaty of Lausanne in November was not immediately noted by the press. In December, Palestine's Department of Immigration and Passports issued an official statement to the effect that due to difficulties, the department could not accept requests from Palestinians abroad for passports and documentary certificates of nationality.[94] The publication of the provisions of the order that effectively denied access to legally recognised citizenship to thousands of native born Palestinians who lived abroad galvanised the popular leaders. 'Isa Bandak and others poured their energy into lobbying the administration for the repeal of the order and the implementation of new legislation by a national assembly.

The concept of citizenship and the practices, behaviours, rights and the political identity assumed to be connected to it diverged widely between the British colonial officials and the Palestinian nationalist leaders and associations. Members of the latter group clearly understood elements of this divergence as early as 1921 when the Arab Executive delegation travelled to London and addressed the topic of nationality. The development of a political identity, out of a civic and cultural community in Palestine did not happen overnight or only through the activities of the Executive, the press and the late Ottoman era initiative of civic organisation. However, the early years of the mandate era and the new institutions that came along with the change in government, territorial space, demographics and Arab politics, combined with the public perception that Great Britain would promote democratic ideas and self-government made conditions ripe for claims to political rights of a communitarian formulation of Palestinian citizenship. On the discursive side of this history, the term 'jinsiyya' was used in writings and discussions by Arab nationalists during the time period under study in the current chapter and continued to be favoured over 'muwātana'. The Arabic translation of the citizenship order in the press and in Palestine's official gazette further standardised the use of the term 'nationality' to refer to the legislation on citizenship. However, 'citizen' ('muwatin') was used in petitions and letters signed by Arab communities and forwarded to the administration, Great Britain and the League of Nations. Editorials and printed requests to the Arab population by the Arab Executive and other national bodies referred to the collective Palestinian Arab population in more rhetorical and nationalist language as abna' or ahl Filastīn, natives or people of Palestine, respectively.

At the same time, because the Arabs only had unofficial representation and delegations to Great Britain and to the Palestine Administration, nationalist leaders were given very little information on the draft nationality legislation. Thus, the reaction to the 1925 Palestine Citizenship Order-in-Council was one of confusion

and uncertainty on the part of the Arab elite and middle-class leadership, and Arab emigrants. In this climate, rumours spread that
the Mandate administration deliberately made citizenship provisions favourable for Jewish immigrants to the detriment of the Arab
natives. However, the Executive was limited in its opposition tactics
to the proposed nationality provisions. In the first place, colonial
officials denied permission to the Arabs to scrutinise the law. In
the interim period from 1921 to the order's publication in 1925,
the Executive as a body devoted very little attention to nationality
legislation as the issue seemed less pressing. Second, the growth of
civic associations with localised claims and concerns rendered the
national movement unable to offer a united front against legislation
that changed Ottoman nationality precedents. The development of
civic activism and the discussion of rights and duties played a major
role in this alternative definition of Palestinian citizenship. Although
the activities of the Executive body had slowed down considerably
by 1925, ordinary Palestinians continued to express their 'national
rights' with tactics that were meant to draw the attention of the
British. The successful boycott of the 1922 elections, public demonstrations and petitions were important means through which the
population expressed a sense of civic activism and duty. That sense
of activism and duty can also be attributed to a historical legacy of
citizenship that went back to the late Ottoman Empire. In 1922,
Mir'at al-Sharq published an editorial that posed the question of
what would become of the former traditions of the country and
whether the British wanted the Palestinians 'to forget the honor of
their Arab nationality?'[95] That anxiety did not disappear by 1925,
when the citizenship order-in-council provided the mandate administration with the legal instrument to define Palestinian citizenship
as different from Arab nationality. This differentiation had the most
spectacular impact on Palestinian emigrants, particularly those who
had maintained Ottoman nationality but were unable to return to
Palestine immediately in order to claim their new citizenship.

4

The Diaspora and the Meanings of Palestinian Citizenship, 1925–1931

In 1927, the British Legation at La Paz, Bolivia rejected the cases of Palestinian Arab Sari Ismael and others who applied for recognition of their Palestinian citizenship under Article 2 of the 1925 Citizenship Order-in-Council. The rejection was based on the legation's assessment that they did not intend to return to Palestine because their lengthy absence (seven years in Ismael's case) supposedly indicated that connections with their native homeland were severed. In an attempt to prove his case, Ismael even produced a *laissez-passer* from the Military Governor of Jerusalem that proved he was in Palestine as recently as 1920. The legation assumed that the applicants were former Ottoman citizens and held Turkish nationality by default given that they were not resident in Palestine. Without a Turkish representative to confirm or deny this, the British authorities in Bolivia could not grant visas to these Arabs to return to Palestine.[1] As a result of the provisions of the citizenship legislation in Mandate Palestine, they remained in Bolivia as stateless individuals. Without any identity documentation they could not (and many emigrants did not wish to) naturalise as citizens of their host country.

In the first half of the 1920s, Great Britain's administration of Palestine combined precedents of colonial citizenship with British legislation and international regulations to produce a set of provisions that effectively created an entirely new Palestinian citizenship. As a response to legal realities on the ground, Palestinian Arabs articulated different ideas of what it meant to be a citizen in a local context. Only after the enforcement of the 1925 Palestine Citizenship Order-in-Council did clearer notions of citizenship emerge out of the discursive field of 'the nation'. The primary factor that helped local Arabs to clarify the meaning of nationality, citizenship and rights for the wider public was the situation of Palestinian Arab emigrants. The purpose of this chapter is to show how the question of the status of the emigrants (*al-muhajarīn*) actively created a space for the discussion of citizenship. It argues that emigrants acted out civic and political behaviours that linked citizenship with the concept of nationality as the Arabs of the former Ottoman provinces understood it.[2] This chapter sheds light on the new role taken by the Palestinian diaspora, or *mahjar*, after 1925 in the development of Palestinian civic identity. Despite this new civic identity and the subsequent increased grievances of emigrants who opposed the citizenship legislation, internal and external factors hindered the ability of the mandate administration to resolve these grievances.

Two months before the 1925 Palestine Citizenship Order-in-Council was published, a Foreign Office official noticed a 'possibly incorrect part of Article 2' of the order. The article gave Ottoman subjects born in Palestine and resident abroad just two years to exercise the right to claim Palestinian citizenship once the order-in-council came into force in August 1925. The problem, as the official noted, was that Article 34 of the internationally recognised Lausanne Treaty conflicted with Article 2 of the mandate's citizenship order. Article 34 gave Ottoman nationals (who resided abroad) the right to take on the nationality of their successor state within two years after the treaty came into effect in August 1924. The Lausanne Treaty gave these former Ottomans until August 1926 to return to Palestine and take on citizenship, while the citizenship order-in-council gave the same individuals until August 1927 to do so. Former Ottoman natives living abroad who wished to acquire Palestinian nationality on the basis of their birth were required to return to Palestine six months prior to claiming their status with the intention to reside in the territory permanently. If they did not do so, they automatically received Turkish nationality – although the means through which this took place were not elaborated upon – and were required to reside within the boundaries of the new Turkish republic. The Foreign Office ultimately took no policy decision on the conflicting time limits before the ratification of the citizenship order-in-council. Members doubted the necessity for an amendment, believing it was 'unlikely that there will be many applicants falling under Article 2 of the Order'.[3] Article 2 actually caused many years of controversy, problems and constant protests by the Palestinian Arab *mahjar* and their supporters at home. The history of this controversy, from the beginning of the British administration to 1931, is the subject of the current chapter.

First, it must be recalled that the 1925 Citizenship Order-in-Council was indeed modified by the high commissioner four months *after* its announcement in order to bring Article 2 in line with Article 34 of the Lausanne Treaty. The time period given to Ottoman nationals living abroad to opt for Palestinian nationality was shortened from two years to one. Furthermore, because these nationals were required to return to Palestine and reside there for six months before they could apply, and had to remain in Palestine as permanent residents, they had less than a year to put their affairs in order and return from abroad. Despite the implications of the amendment, the immediate reactions among the *mahjar* communities were quite limited since British consuls failed to publicise the change. Most of the Arab population in Palestine was also initially unaware of the consequences of the order since Arabs born and resident in Palestine were granted citizenship automatically. The earliest reactions to the order can be found in the Arabic press in 1925 when a small number of articles started to call attention to some of its provisions.

The Arab diaspora maintained a connection to *Bilād al-Shām* (Greater Syria) through the press. In the years before 1914, the Syrian diaspora consisted of Arabs from the territories that later became Syria, Palestine, Lebanon and Transjordan. Those emigrants from Palestine who lived in the United States and Latin America received copies of periodicals published in Palestine and printed their own newspapers. Akram Khater has shown that from 1892 to 1907, a total of twenty-one new Syrian Arab dailies, weeklies and monthlies appeared in the US. The Arabic press grew in importance for emigrants, who themselves were exposed to at least one newspaper by the outbreak of the First World War. The *mahjar* press published commentary on the political, social and economic situation in the Levant, and shaped the self-perception as well as more worldly perceptions of Arab emigrant communities in North America.[4] The same can be presumed for Central and South American *Turcos*, or Arabic-speaking émigré communities. Through discussions and editorials in newspapers, the diaspora localised ideas of liberal or republican citizenship as related to Ottoman identity and nationality. At the same time, editors and journalists within Palestine who belonged to the educated middle-class nationalist stratum of society corresponded with relatives, colleagues and friends in the diaspora and encouraged the emigrants to write letters to newspapers. By 1919, these letters included stories about Palestinian communities abroad as well as commentaries on the mandate system and Zionism.

The connection between these communities and nationalist leaders in Palestine assisted the diaspora in crafting its own definition of Palestinian citizenship. The present chapter draws on the argument made

by Engin Isin that citizens are actively 'made' through certain practices and expressions of belonging that mark individuals as part of the
political, social, civic and cultural make-up of a nation.[5] Citizenship,
then, is transformed from an abstract concept to an active and negotiated behaviour. The men and women born in Palestine who moved
outside of the territory in the years before and during the first decade
of British administration were 'made' into Palestinian émigré citizens
in the years before and after the 1925 order-in-council through social,
political, cultural and symbolic associations shared between the *mahjar* and the Arab population of Palestine. Still even before the dissolution of the Ottoman Empire Palestinians abroad retained a sense of
identification with their homeland not only through the Arabic press
but also as their communities formed mutual aid societies and charities, elected leaders for community associations and supported the
national movement in Palestine.

The narrative of the Palestinian Arab diaspora is often lumped
together with the general migration movements from the Levant
that began in earnest in the last two decades of the nineteenth
century.[6] Arabs from the Ottoman province of Greater Syria and
the *Mutasarrifiyya* of Mount Lebanon began to emigrate in large
numbers in those decades. From 1860 to 1914, between 600,000
and one million, as estimates vary, Arabic-speaking Ottomans born
in Greater Syria left for the Americas. Despite this large number,
about one-third returned home and did not permanently settle
abroad. According to Kemal Karpat, the Ottoman Government
often financed the return and re-settlement of emigrants and only
those who *acquired* a foreign nationality lost their Ottoman nationality.[7] The Americas attracted Arab migrants from southern Syria
in the late nineteenth century and a large majority of these travellers came from the environs of Bethlehem and Jerusalem. By the
turn of the century, records show that Palestinian communities in
the diaspora created clubs and associations for cultural exchange
and mutual support and to govern their affairs. Immigration to
the Americas intensified at the turn of the twentieth century. Latin
America was particularly attractive due to lenient immigration policies of states such as Argentina, Brazil and Honduras.[8] Emigrants
from both urban and rural areas of Syria took up work in business
and commerce and some arrived to the Americas with enough capital to set up their own businesses.

However, the situation in South and Central America, as well as
Mexico, Cuba and Haiti, was often fraught with tension for immigrants. Like the Ottoman Empire's provinces, a number of former

colonial territories of Latin America had recently achieved independence and were often sites of both nationalist movements and
conflict. Tensions between socialist reformers and military-based dic-
tatorships turned violent in certain republics in the 1910s and 1920s.
Some governments, including that of Haiti, did not maintain relations
with the Ottoman Empire and anti-Arab sentiment was common.[9]
The situation also meant that in Central and South America emigrants were more exposed to anti-colonial ideologies given the recent
history of these countries. In the Americas, upheavals and changes
in leadership did not always bode well with the Arabs' own changing international statuses. With the end of the First World War and
the dissolution of the Ottoman Empire, the Arabs lost consular and
diplomatic protection since their documentary identity as Ottoman
nationals ceased to be internationally acceptable. The British were
reluctant to offer diplomatic protection to Palestinian Arabs or other
Syrians who resided abroad. It is in this international context and in
the political system of newly created nation-states across the globe
that the discussions and definitions of Palestinian nationality and
citizenship can be situated.

The Palestinian Arab *Mahjar* and Civic Identity, 1918–1925

From the onset of the Palestine Administration, a large number of
Arabs who had emigrated in the years prior to 1920 but who wished
to travel elsewhere or return to either reside or visit their homeland
confronted practical problems. Their loss of Ottoman nationality,
since they were not *physically* present in the Ottoman realms, meant
that they did not have valid passports after 1918 and thus they could
not claim consular protection. Significantly, they were also denied
entry to Palestine as members of its indigenous population. As a
result, despite birth in Palestine and the fact that many emigrants paid
taxes upon land and property they held in the territory's urban and
rural districts, they could not take part in elections. From the start of
the British military occupation in 1918 these Arabs identified themselves as 'Palestinians' and former Ottoman subjects in letters of protest sent to the military government and to newspapers in Palestine.
This section explores when and how the emigrants acquired awareness as Palestinian citizens. Constant networks and links with Syria
allowed emigrants to hold on to, or in some cases enhance, national
and nationalist identities with their place of birth. These links and the
discussions and notions of identity that allowed Palestinian Arabs to

maintain their connections to the territory of Palestine did not stay static but rather shifted and changed in response to the political situations both in the diaspora and within the mandate borders.

A clear theme in the earliest correspondence between the diaspora communities and individuals and nationalist organisations in Palestine, such as the Muslim–Christian Association (MCA) and the Arab Executive was the idea that the Palestinians formed part of a larger Arab nation. The basis for the ideological Arab nation was an awareness of a common ethnicity. With the formation of national associations that advocated the abrogation of the Jewish national home policy immediately after the Paris Peace Conference of 1919, groups and individuals in Palestine began to refer to themselves as sons or natives of Palestine (*abnā' Filastīn*). The émigré associations, often formed as religious or mutual aid societies, developed a marked nationalist outlook. Intellectuals, journalists and political activists, and also ordinary men and women in the diaspora who embraced Arab nationalism prior to 1914 contributed to the formation of national clubs and associations.[10] Once the alarming news of the terms of the war settlement and the threat posed by the Jewish national home policy reached these communities, their organisations became increasingly political in nature. Despite a growing social and economic stratification within Arab emigrant communities in places such as Brazil, Maria del Mar Logrono Narbona argues quite rightly that the migrant Arab intellectuals in such dynamic transnational communities mobilised political support from afar when needed during the early post-war years of British and French colonialism in the Levant.[11]

In the years after the war, the evolution of the new international world system created a stark separation between imperial and post-colonial nation-states. The Arab emigrants in the United States would certainly have been exposed to the rhetoric of President Wilson's Fourteen Points for self-determination and they possibly experienced the practical application of concepts like democracy, political representation, and sovereignty of government. Throughout 1918, numerous clubs sent letters and signed petitions to the MCA in Palestine, Emir Faisal in Damascus, King George V, the military administration in Palestine and the League of Nations that expressed their support for an independent Syrian nation and their opposition to the Balfour Declaration. Petition-writers usually identified themselves as part of 'the Palestinian Colony' of their host country. For example, in November 1918, the Palestinian community of San Salvador signed a protest addressed to King George that stated its opposition to the

Zionist ambitions in Palestine. Significantly, they signed the protest as 'the Palestinians' suggesting that in only a short period of time the community's awareness changed from that of Syrian Arab to specifically Palestinian. Alongside the assertion of their growing recognition of a political identity as a group, emigrants expressed new concerns for their status vis-à-vis Great Britain. In 1919 the signatories of a letter to Prime Minister Lloyd George asked if the Palestinian Arabs came under the diplomatic protection of Great Britain.[12] The shift in identity that was partly prompted by the British occupation of the territory that became the Palestine Mandate led diaspora communities to question their national, as well as diplomatic, allegiances.

By the early 1920s, the émigré organisations had started to voice the concept of national 'duties' as an important element in the definition of modern civic identity. These duties referred to actions of other members of the community that would benefit the community as a whole. Traditionally, mutual aid and welfare societies existed in the Arab diaspora and offered support and assistance to emigrants from the same regions of Palestine. Members also often supported Arabs at home: a number of clubs in places like San Salvador and Monterrey sent money to help refugees, the poor and the needy of or in certain Palestinian towns and villages. After the end of the war, the emigrant members of mutual aid societies increasingly discussed and emphasised that the organisations and their members had political duties as well: they elected representatives in their own societies and gave support to candidates for local urban and village government in Palestine and for particular nationalist politicians.[13] Palestinians in El Salto, Mexico publicised elections for their local society by stating that the society was committed to continuing the defence of Palestinian rights from abroad.[14] Candidates portrayed themselves as supportive of the anti-Zionist actions undertaken by notable nationalist leaders in Jerusalem, Bethlehem and Jaffa. The groups advocated that their members support other types of active duties. For instance, the Palestine Renaissance Society in New York appealed in 1923 for continued support of the jihad (struggle) against colonialism in Palestine. The use of the term 'jihad' mirrored the rhetoric used in Palestine by the MCA and the Arab Executive and in newspaper articles, and it contributed to the horizontal acculturation of a specifically Palestinian civic identity, and the notion that all social classes struggled towards the greater good of ending British colonialism and Zionism.[15]

Prior to the publication of the Palestine Citizenship Order-in-Council in 1925, newspapers, national congresses and delegations to

London paid little attention to potential troubles for the emigrants. The middle-class Arab nationalists initially viewed this varied and large group as a branch of the national movement similarly opposed to Britain's support for Zionism. In the years before the ratification of the Treaty of Lausanne in 1924, the Mandate administration had not yet differentiated between residents abroad and permanent residents, and thus emigrants who kept Ottoman nationality faced no explicit threat to their status as Palestinian Arabs. Rather, the Palestinian press published letters and commentary from the general public that described the nationalism of their brothers in the diaspora and their continued service to the nation. Even so, some of these same pieces of commentary stressed that the emigrants return home to Palestine, noting with alarm the increasing number of Jewish immigrants in the country.[16] Only with the official implementation of the Lausanne Treaty and the subsequent citizenship order did the legal status of the emigrants become more tenuous and ambiguous.

By the mid-1920s the emigrants' difficulties with regard to travel and identification became clear to their families in Palestine. Individuals who wished to return to Palestine or to travel outside their host country needed a passport or *laissez-passer* as verification of their identity. In order to receive temporary travel documents, they needed to prove that they were born in Palestine and had been Ottoman nationals. The frequent inability of emigrants to produce such documentation is evidenced in letters sent to newspapers in Palestine. In September 1920 an editorial in Jerusalem's Arabic newspaper *Mir'at al-Sharq* criticised the hesitation of the immigration department of the civil administration to assist travellers or to approve their applications for travel documents. It also condemned the failure of the authorities to provide necessary facilities for Palestinians in transit.[17]

At that time, British consuls lacked experience or standard advice on the treatment of Palestinians who lived abroad but retained Ottoman nationality and identity documents. By the latter half of 1922 the Colonial Office reported several cases that attested to the confusion of consuls. The District Officer in Bethlehem received a letter from a native of that town describing how a British consul refused his application for a passport in order to leave South America to return to Palestine. The author explained that he was forced to apply for a French passport as an Ottoman national born in Syria, and travelled to Palestine with it. Shortly after, a Palestinian in Chile wrote a letter to his mother and explained that he, too, was unable to leave Chile for Palestine on British travel documents and instead received a passport from the French consul. In a third case, the British consul in Mexico stated that he had no instructions to issue passports to Palestinians.[18]

Although Palestinian emigrants and travellers voiced their grievances to the Mandate authorities and to newspapers they received little assistance as the international position of Palestine before 1922 remained ambiguous. After the dissolution of the Ottoman Empire in 1918, many emigrants expressed their desire to be under British protection but not necessarily to return home. The question of diplomatic protection came to the fore in 1924 when revolutionary violence broke out in Honduras, a country then home to a large Palestinian community. A number of military-backed coups and uprisings took place against the government after the 1919 civil war. The country's second civil war that broke out in 1924 led to more than 5,000 deaths and the destruction of millions of dollars' worth of property. The Palestinian community in La Ceiba was directly affected. Its members reported that all of their shops and homes were damaged or destroyed in 'the guerilla insurgency of the country'. The threat to the Palestinian Arabs combined with the assumption of the community as constituted of Palestinian citizens led inhabitants to appeal to British consular officials in Honduras. However, the community received no financial or political assistance from the consuls and found that Great Britain expressed no interest in providing diplomatic protection to the native Palestinians. Community members addressed the British Government through letters sent to the press in Palestine, arguing that the 'international and humanitarian duty of the English state [was] to defend the rights of the natives of Palestine who have no one to defend them'.[19] They wrote to the Palestine Administration and the League of Nations that the duty of the British Government was to protect and assist individuals from the territories it administered. As a result, the Palestinians asked the League to put pressure on Great Britain to extend its protection to the Palestinians living abroad.

Back in Palestine, Bethlehem's newspaper *Sawt al-Sha'b*, commenting on the events in Honduras, stated that Great Britain had a major role to protect all Palestinian citizens.[20] The Arabic press in Palestine claimed the emigrants to be British subjects, which further reinforced the way the emigrants viewed themselves as citizens of the mandate. On that basis, it came as a surprise to Arab observers when Great Britain did not offer to support the Palestinians who demanded compensation from the Honduran Government.[21] When a similar situation took place in Brazil after uprisings in August 1924, *Sawt al-Sha'b* stressed again the British responsibility to protect Palestinian lives and property, and to safeguard the rights of 'the citizens' in the diaspora. The threats faced by emigrants in Latin America led to the placement of discussions on the meaning of Palestinian nationality squarely on the front pages of newspapers, which stressed the citizenship of these emigrant Palestinian Arabs with increasing frequency.[22]

The problems the emigrants faced in terms of both consular protection and re-entry to Palestine remained unsolved by the end of 1924. Members of the diaspora, the press in Palestine and national leaders juxtaposed the rights of Arab emigrants with those of their Jewish counterparts. Journalists and local leaders found it difficult to accept the denial by the administration to allow emigrants to return to Palestine. Press reports explained to readers that elsewhere in the world individuals were not forbidden to return to their homelands simply because they temporarily resided elsewhere. One writer, arguing that the purpose of the newspaper is to enlighten and guide the people to their rights, instructed Palestinian emigrants to report to their nearest British consul to prove their Ottoman nationality in order to receive travel papers. The author added the advice that if an emigrant found that the consul was not satisfied with the documents he or she possessed, relatives in Palestine could request that the administration allow that emigrant to enter mandated territory.[23] Great Britain, on the other hand, first and foremost lacked the facilities to grant diplomatic protection to individual Arabs who did not carry any passport, or carried an expired Ottoman identity document and little else. The mandate administration could only address certain issues with consular protection since the task to actually provide regulations and guidelines on British protection fell upon the Foreign Office. The Foreign Office did not necessarily have consular offices or staff in certain parts of Latin America and neither it nor the administration held records of resident Palestinians.

Despite this, Palestinians placed the blame for the emigrants' situation squarely upon the Mandate Government. In late 1924 before the final drafts of the nationality order became known to Palestinian leaders, some writers published articles detailing what they knew about the situation of the emigrants in terms of consular protection and documentary identity. A common theme in Jerusalem's newspapers was the contrast between the refusal by the administration to recognise the nationality of the Arab emigrants as Palestinian and the facilities available for every Jewish immigrant to obtain provisional Palestinian nationality. One Arab writer asked if such provisions were 'not an apparent assault on the highest of our rights'.[24] Prior to the issuance of the citizenship order, nationalist journalists and activists viewed the emigrants not as *former* Ottomans (the British classification of these individuals) but as Palestinian natives entitled to the same status as any other Arab born in Palestine. Writers continued to blame British officials in the absence of any official attempt to address the problems caused by immigration and provisional citizenship legislation prior to the late 1920s.

In 1925, British consuls received instructions from the mandate administration in connection with the Honduras affair: the administration asked that nationality certificates not be granted to non-permanent residents of Palestine.[25] The impact of the instruction was limited. The Foreign Office failed to apply the policy in a uniform manner as even its permanent officials disagreed on the diplomatic approach towards the Palestinian diaspora. The case of Palestinian textile merchants normally resident in Port-au-Prince, Haiti serves to illustrate the failure to standardise policy on former Ottoman nationals who resided in the newly mandated territories granted by the League of Nations to Great Britain. In the early summer of 1925 a group of merchants requested certificates to enable them to travel as Palestinians to Great Britain and the US for business purposes. Initially, the Foreign Office allowed for travel on the basis of their Ottoman nationality but warned that no further protection could be given by British consulates until the merchants could prove that they held Palestinian citizenship as opposed to only expired Ottoman identity papers. One Palestinian merchant in Port-au-Prince expressed the feeling of the victimisation of Palestinians who worked abroad with no acceptable identity documents, arguing that the Jewish national home policy was 'an attempt . . . to force [Arabs] to surrender their Palestinian citizenship'. He added, in a letter to the Foreign Office, that provisional certificates of nationality held by some former Ottomans posed practical problems in that they did not guarantee diplomatic protection by Britain or France.[26] In response to the merchants, the mandate administration continued to stress its opposition, and that of the Foreign Office, to granting Palestinian provisional nationality to individuals deemed to want that status only in order to receive the protection of Great Britain. The specifics of the merchants' situation and request to travel on valid passports did not receive further attention by the authorities.

The claims by Palestinians in Honduras remained unresolved by the end of 1925. The British Foreign Office stood by their own policy that did not permit Arabs to claim British protection unless they had proof of Palestinian citizenship. Natives in consular districts could only obtain Palestinian citizenship if they proved their birth in Palestine rather than elsewhere in the Ottoman provinces and if they had not given up Ottoman nationality during their residence abroad. As the citizenship order required, these individuals could only claim their right to Palestinian citizenship if they complied with the residency provision, meaning permanent residence in that territory. To enter Palestine, emigrants had to possess emergency certificates approved by the Chief Secretary of the Permit Section of the Palestine Government. Upon arrival to Palestine's shores, these natives were often treated as immigrants rather than as indigenous to the territory.[27] Meanwhile in Great Britain, the Foreign Office officially decided that every applicant must demonstrate that it would be 'reasonable and proper for him to be under British rather than Turkish protection'.[28] Such a subjective policy placed yet another obstacle before the emigrants.

The impact of British policies concerning the nationality of native Palestinians living outside of Palestine was as negative as it was unclear. From 1918 to 1925, the confusion grew as to the proper international status of the emigrants, to whom these Arabs could turn to for consular assistance, and how to travel with invalid Ottoman documents. As British officials drafted nationality legislation for Palestine, the practical impact of their legislation upon the émigré communities was not thoroughly considered. Mandate officials were also somewhat oblivious of that fact that the members of diaspora communities believed themselves to be citizens of Palestine. In the years before 1925 in spite of the distance that separated the *mahjar* from the *mashriq*, the émigré communities grasped the awareness of a specifically Palestinian national and civic identity.

Nationality as Citizenship: Ideological Concepts and Active Practices in the Diaspora and at Home, 1925–1931

Once the provisions of the 1925 Citizenship Order-in-Council became known, the denial of *jus sanguinis* and *jus soli* citizenship to Arab emigrants became a story reported in Palestine's Arabic newspapers. In published letters to friends, family, newspaper editors and the mandate administration, emigrants criticised what they argued to be the administration's failure to grant them ipso facto citizenship. Importantly, émigré Palestinian Arabs depicted nationality as a right connected to birth in Palestine and Arab ethnicity. In often strong language, some emigrants argued that the citizenship order was tantamount to the removal of Arab ethnicity from Palestine, a notion that newspapers picked up fairly quickly. The debates over the situation of the emigrants led to a particular discussion on, and demand for, what the emigrants and their supporters termed 'the right to return' (*haqq al-'awda*).

Only a few months before the Treaty of Lausanne timeframe passed for the former Ottoman subjects to opt for the nationality of their new territories in the middle of 1926, 'Isa Bandak, the populist, anti-colonial editor of Bethlehem's *Sawt al-Sha'b*, wrote that no less than 20,000 Palestinian Arabs living or travelling abroad had no one to defend their interests. Since they did not have valid nationality documents, these Arabs could not obtain consular protection.[29] Bandak, like others such as Arab Executive President Musa Kazim al-Husayni, a number of middle-class nationalists and members of diaspora associations, were baffled by the situation. They found it difficult to reconcile their idea of citizenship as based on an understanding of nationality as rooted in both Arab ethnicity and Ottoman imperial subjecthood with the definition of citizenship provided by the 1925 Order-in-Council. To Bandak and Musa Kazim, it seemed natural that the thousands of emigrants could do nothing but keep their Ottoman nationality after the end of the First World War. On the basis of that former nationality, it further seemed reasonable and proper that Arabs born under the Ottoman Empire would automatically receive the citizenship of their new mandate administrations.

The pages of *Sawt al-Sha'b* by early 1926 contained numerous explanations for the restrictions created by the citizenship order. Prominently, the newspaper's articles expressed the growing fear that the order constituted a ploy to increase Jewish immigration at the expense of the citizenship of Arabs born in Palestine. With the expiration of the citizenship order's retroactive two-year timeframe in August 1926, Bandak confronted the administration in his editorials over the limited measures taken to facilitate the naturalisation of Ottoman subjects absent from their homes in August 1924, and of those whose applications had been refused. He wondered if orders had been uniformly distributed to all British consuls and whether the orders were intended to deprive emigrants from 'the right to return to their country and enjoy [British] political and consular protection'. Bandak urged action: he implored the emigrants 'to rush off to the [British] consul to review the means for understanding nationality' and to write back to families detailing the obstacles they faced.[30] He stressed that emigrants should not lose their 'right' to citizenship (*haqq al-jinsiyya*) and reported that many emigrants failed to register as Ottoman nationals in British consulates. He urged them to notify consuls that they were Palestinian natives.[31] Thus, Bandak's newspaper set in motion a discourse that came to circulate in Palestine and the diaspora, which blamed Great Britain for deliberate discrimination against the Arabs in favour of their support for the aims of the Zionist Organisation in Palestine.

Bandak's efforts to bring attention to the citizenship order's provisions made headway among Arab communities in Latin America. This is probably due to Bandak's outspoken presence in Bethlehem, a town that had been a historical centre of migration and that retained a strong connection with émigré communities. New social organisations such as youth, sport and local patriotic clubs played a role as well in that members explained the situation of the emigrants to interested individuals. Local leaders and residents lobbied the government to extend the August 1926 deadline set to apply for citizenship. Like Bandak, these lobbyists came primarily from the area around Bethlehem, Jerusalem and Ramallah, and they used their position as middle-class nationalists – newspaper editors, municipal council leaders, lawyers and members of prominent families – to publicise the situation of the diaspora in public meetings. These local leaders closely scrutinised citizenship legislation in both Great Britain and in Palestine and they appealed to the rest of the population through manifestos and open letters.

Among the Arabic periodicals, it was *Sawt al-Sha'b* that solicited the largest number of letters from Palestinians in the Republic of El Salvador, Honduras and Brazil throughout 1926. The Palestinian community in El Salvador had especially strong ties to Bethlehem. The author of one of these letters noted that emigrants from Bethlehem did not want to go through the process of naturalisation in other countries. Instead, they wanted what he termed automatic 'rightful nationality'. He added that the British consul refused to give citizenship documents to the children of Palestinian residents of El Salvador on the pretext that they were natives of their country of birth – El Salvador.[32] Another letter stressed that '[one] does not lose nationality' as the Ottoman nationality law provided for the transmission of nationality through descent.[33] This letter demonstrates the expectation that mandate citizenship legislation would be in line with familiar Ottoman precedents.

Other newspapers took the lead from Bandak and referred to his editorials on the citizenship order and also printed letters from the diaspora. Articles, often on the front pages of newspapers, urged citizens to hold meetings to study the citizenship law and its implications for emigrants, and to review those orders that the Foreign Office circulated to consuls. In mid-May 1926, the Bethlehem Nationalist Society planned to hold a meeting with the notables and village leaders of Jerusalem municipality in order to discuss the status and treatment of children born outside of Palestine.[34] Bandak and other local leaders then wrote open letters to High Commissioner Plumer. This dialogue between the press, the emigrants and nationalists in Palestine reinforced ideas of ethno-nationality as it developed in relation to *jus sanguinis* acquisition of citizenship and in opposition to the colonial-style citizenship imposed by the mandate administration.

As the press and political and social organisations received letters from emigrants, a number of assumptions associated with provisions of the citizenship order came to the fore. The most common to emerge was, as noted previously, the British favouritism for Jewish immigration to Palestine. One journalist wrote that the Palestine Government realised the Jews were not applying in large numbers for Palestinian nationality because of their lack of confidence in the national homeland. He claimed that in response, 'the English put in place a deliberately strange plan which is more evidence of favouritism toward the Jews and their interests'. As part of that strange plan, he continued, the administration allowed for immigrants to unofficially hold dual nationality.[35] The accusation of favouritism had a profound impact on Arab society, which had been inundated with anti-Zionist propaganda. The citizenship legislation was touted as hard proof of a future takeover of the mandate government by the Zionist leaders. The press noted the irony of the policy that restricted any stateless former Ottoman national from Palestinian citizenship if he held another nationality, whereas Jewish immigrants could hold dual nationality.

Another theme stressed in light of the emigrants' situation was that of colonial 'injustice' embodied by the citizenship order. One writer asked whether justice meant that 'the government [can] deprive the Arab natives of Palestine the entitlement to their native nationality . . . [of] parents and grandparents while [the government makes] it easy for outsiders to obtain Palestinian nationality?' The sensational and outraged tone of many letters sometimes warranted responses from officials in Palestine and Great Britain. *Sawt al-Sha'b* printed these replies as well. In one response, the colonial secretary expressed confidence that a large segment of the diaspora undoubtedly applied for nationality in the time allotted to do so. As the press pointed out, and as records demonstrate, the mandate did not publish estimates of the number of emigrants who returned to Palestine to claim citizenship.[36]

The public assertion that Ottoman nationality translated into Palestinian citizenship struck a chord with members of the Arab Executive. Musa Kazim met with Colonial Secretary Leopold Amery in the summer of 1926 to discuss the issues of consular protection and the status of Palestinians abroad. During the meeting, Musa Kazim pointedly told Amery that the public held the British responsible for having transformed Palestinian emigrants into 'orphans from the government'.[37] At the same time, Bandak and other local leaders in Bethlehem arranged a meeting with the secretary of the Executive, Jamal al-Husayni, to discuss the situation of the Palestinians during the Honduras crisis as they were threatened with anti-Arab sentiment and expulsion as a result of Honduran immigration legislation.[38]

At the end of August 1926, Bandak joined Musa Kazim and others in another meeting with colonial officials in Jerusalem to discuss the obligations of the mandatory to the emigrants and to ask for an extension of the deadline for natives to claim citizenship. Secretary Amery refused to discuss changes to the order or increase assistance for the emigrants. Musa Kazim then drafted an open letter to the administration to ask that the timeframe of the citizenship order be extended one year and to stress that some emigrants were not informed of the order as many had never received notice of it. In addition, he pointed out that these individuals faced the difficult task of arranging to leave their countries of residence permanently in the short time span envisaged by the legislation. The law itself, Musa Kazim added, was difficult to understand for even competent legal authorities.[39]

The émigré communities in Latin America followed reports of the meetings on citizenship legislation between national leaders and colonial officials. They noted the lobbyist efforts on their behalf, as these efforts elicited important debates on the so-called right to return. In 1926, the United Palestinian Society in Honduras submitted a petition to the Executive asking that its members hold the government to their 'duty to protect' the emigrants' property and lives.[40] Several months later as debates continued over the refusal by immigration authorities in Palestine to allow natives to enter the territory without recognised citizenship, Jerusalem's *al-Jamiyya al-'Arabiyya* included an article that equated the denial of travel facilities to a negation of the Palestinians' right to return to their original homeland.[41] By early 1927, the emigrants' supporters in Palestine had appropriated the phrase. In fact, as the Palestine immigration authorities routinely denied visas and entry to returning emigrants, the 'right to return' became a loaded phrase. It brought to light the key argument in support of the emigrants' rights to citizenship, namely that the order's provisions should account for both *jus sanguinis* and *jus soli* nationality. Conversations on the right to return emphasised a birth-right to not only nationality but of belonging to a particular nation.

As the country began to experience economic problems in the latter 1920s, local leaders appealed to the mandate administration using economic arguments in an attempt to convince officials of the financial benefits offered by the return of emigrants. These leaders tried to convince the administration that Palestine could only achieve independence if the Arab community had the same economic opportunities as the Jewish immigrant community. The local Arab leadership explained that the future economic independence of the Palestinian Arab community would be hampered if the British government denied the emigrants' right to return to Palestine as citizens. These emigrants, they noted, would return with expertise in business and commerce. A group of local leaders in Bethlehem wrote to the high commissioner that the town's emigrants, who had long been a source of prosperity, faced not only the deprivation of their 'civil, political and social rights through no fault of their own' but that their lack of citizenship potentially meant a future of 'urban decay' for Bethlehem and other towns in the country.[42] Letters urged the government to be aware that 'Arab emigrants in all corners of the globe' will protest to Great Britain and the League of Nations against the citizenship order-in-council on economic and political grounds.[43] Musa Kazim advocated action, telling Palestinians that each had the duty to 'stand up in order to defend [the emigrants'] rights, which are our rights'.[44] In the two years after the citizenship order-in-council, the slogan 'the right to nationality' became synonymous with the 'right to return'. Lawyers, writers and other leaders urged concerned citizens to begin grassroots, civil-society-based initiatives to organise delegations to lobby certain officials and the British public, and to begin a letter-writing campaign.

In parallel to events within Palestine, emigrants started similar grassroots-style campaigns to protest the citizenship order-in-council. In the summer of 1927 'Isa al-'Isa, the editor of Jaffa's *Filastīn*, published a communiqué from Mexico's Society for Palestinian Unity. After protests sent to the mandate government and to Great Britain by Mexico's Palestinian community went unanswered, the Society sent a delegation to Mexico City to meet with the British ambassador and discuss citizenship issues. The delegation included members of other Arab groups throughout Mexico.[45] D. V. Kelly, the ambassador, promised to do all he possibly could but complained to the delegation that his own government denied his request to print the notice of the amendment of the citizenship order issued in November 1925 because it was too expensive.[46] The Society for Palestinian Unity succeeded in attracting greater attention in Mexico to the problems posed by the citizenship order. Its members used rhetorical tones, for instance stating that 'every one of us is willing to sacrifice ourselves to raise this injustice and to receive our legitimate rights given to us by nature itself and approved by our birth . . . [it is] this nationality which the English are trying to remove from us to implement Zionism'.[47] Ambassador Kelly forwarded Palestinian grievances to the Foreign Office, and explained that the delegation represented 3,000 to 4,000 Palestinians in Mexico alone – not an insignificant number.[48]

The tone of the emigrants' complaints became more angry and anxious. *Al-Jamiyya al-'Arabiyya* published a letter from the same group, which accused the British authorities of creating the law on citizenship in order to 'lessen the Arab race and strengthen the Jewish race'. The writers' citation of the administration's immigration policy bolstered this claim of ethnic discrimination. The letter of protest added that 'there is not a force in this world which can remove our rights . . . for us, it is the blood in our veins and we have the right to nationality and naturalisation in the beloved homeland'. Its tone alone drew attention, and informed the views of Palestinian national leaders and activists on nationality as an ancestral right.[49] It was indeed powerful rhetoric: sensational, political and easily understood on a popular level.

The tone of the petitions, however, varied. Reading through these petitions, the writing of some demonstrates the willingness of members of the diaspora to negotiate with Jewish land brokers in the case of denials to return to Palestine. For instance, in the summer of 1927, the Permanent Mandates Commission received a petition from Palestinian Arabs in Honduras signed by men who owned land in Palestine. The signatories, all Palestinian by birth, protested collectively 'as a result of the High Commissioner's refusal to recognise us as citizens of Palestine'. Yet, as they owned thousands of acres in their homeland, they asked to be informed of Jewish bankers and financiers who were willing to buy land from Palestinians who lived abroad. The signatories requested that they be told of their citizenship status, when they would receive permission to return to their 'beloved homeland' and to which flag they owed their allegiance.[50] From these statements it is clear that two years after the publication of the citizenship order-in-council, emigrant communities remained unsure of their nationality and their status in relation to Great Britain.

Finally, the actions of Palestinians in the Americas inspired protests by the diaspora in other areas such as in Egypt. In early 1928, twenty Palestinian students at Cairo's al-Azhar University wrote to High Commissioner Plumer to explain that the situation of Palestinians in Egypt resembled that of those in Latin America. Many students had been unable to give up their studies and return to reside permanently in Palestine at the time of the citizenship order. They could not renew their passports or receive new passports to return to Palestine. The students asked the high commissioner if they should change their nationality 'so that the Jews replace us in our homeland?'[51] The students, like the Arab emigrants in Latin America, argued that the citizenship order discriminated against them on the basis of their Arab nationality. By the end of the 1920s the lack of a concrete response from British officials over problems posed by the citizenship order did little to dispel the claims by the emigrants and their supporters that the mandate laws favoured Jewish immigrants. The lack of a resolution helped refine the meaning of the 'right' to citizenship in the Palestinian Arab context. Ottoman nationality and the *jus sanguinis* and *jus soli* means of its acquisition set the obvious precedent for Palestine's leaders in their conceptualisation of the two statuses. In the mid-1920s, this particular rhetorical language aided the emigrants' sense of identification as Palestinians, as suggested by their writings to family and supporters at home. The links between associations and the Arabic press in Palestine with the diaspora galvanised concerned nationalists into action. Alongside these requests by emigrants to meet with consular officials were telegrams and letters of protest and appeals to the mandate administration. By 1927, administrators in Palestine and in London had little choice but to address the citizenship order's restrictions.

The Committee for the Defence of Arab Emigrant Rights to Palestinian Citizenship

The work of 'Isa Bandak, the most active lobbyist for the emigrants, was not only confined to writing editorials and presenting grievances to colonial officials. Bandak's other contribution to resolve the emigrant situation was the formation of an association of citizens in Bethlehem that aimed to educate Palestinian Arabs about the citizenship order. The first mention of the Committee for the Defence of Arab Emigrant Rights to Palestinian Nationality (*al-lajna li-ladifā' 'an huquq al-muhājarīn al-'arab ala al-jinsiyya al-filastīniyya*), or the DAER, appears in *Sawt al-Sha'b* just after the formation of the committee in 1927. The committee's role in shaping concepts of nationality and citizenship is the focus of this section. The DAER committee was instrumental for three reasons. First, DAER emerged as the central organisation through which the opinions, protests and demands of the emigrants could be voiced. As embodied in this role, the committee aimed to become the leading representative of the Palestinians on nationality issues and a mediator between the emigrants and both the London and Palestine administrations. It lobbied for changes to the citizenship legislation to benefit all native-born Palestinians. Second, the DAER committee made a point to address the British public in its appeals, using a grassroots approach to lobbyist efforts. Finally, aside from appealing to Great Britain, the committee crafted an internationalist rhetoric on the right to nationality and the larger problems posed by the administration's legislation in Palestine.

The DAER committee members saw their organisation as the 'expert' on Palestinian nationality legislation. The secretary, Khalil 'Isa Muqas, explained the duty of the committee as to provide the necessary facilities and guidance on the subject of nationality.[52] Although the committee billed itself as the voice of the emigrants, its leaders initially did not represent a wide variety of Palestinians as they were elected by the inhabitants of Bethlehem, Beit Jala and Beit Sahour. Soon after its formation, however, the committee proposed to hold a conference of Palestinian intellectuals who would discuss the seriousness of the emigrant question and lobby the government in a representative capacity. The DAER committee recruited its members in municipalities from which large numbers of emigrants originally came. The membership seems to have been mostly representative of the nationalist middle-class and included local political and religious leaders, writers and lawyers.[53] The committee relied on reports of émigré associations in order to compile its figures of the total numbers of Palestinians living abroad. Since none of DAER's listed members held an official position in the administration or in the Department of Migration and Statistics, these figures do not match the British totals of emigrants or even the totals printed in Arab newspapers. Despite the discrepancies, the sizeable figures reported made an impression upon the Palestinian Arab public. By mid-1927, DAER claimed to represent the (over-estimated) figure of 50,000 Palestinian natives who were denied their nationality.[54]

After its formation, the committee first lobbied High Commissioner Plumer and other officials in the Mandate administration. Claiming to speak for all emigrant Arabs, its leaders offered aims and demands in a memorandum sent to the high commissioner in early 1928. The document was not anti-British: it condemned citizenship legislation, but hinted that the committee believed that the British did not intend to deprive the majority of emigrants from 'their natural civil rights'. The lobbyists stressed the economic component of the emigrant situation as they reminded Plumer that most emigrants owned immovable property and real estate in Palestine that was subject to taxation.[55] The committee started out with cautious appeals to the economic necessity of granting citizenship to the emigrants in its first memorandum, and its leaders became increasingly vocal.

The initial response by the Colonial Office to DAER's claims was not an encouraging one. Colonial Secretary Amery stated his belief that the Palestinian communities in South America had no connection with Palestine and no intention to return to settle. On these grounds he thought that the principles to decide on nationality applications were 'quite fair and equitable'.[56] Other colonial officials responded to the committee differently and in contrast to Amery some took note of the economic aspect of the demands. One official wrote to Under-Secretary Ormsby-Gore that the committee's memorandum brought up very important questions that affected the nationality of those Arabs abroad who had 'very considerable material interests in Palestine'. He suggested that a general grant of citizenship would not merely be an act of fairness in order to solve the problem of Palestinian Arab statelessness, but the favourable extension of citizenship meant 'considerable advantage to British interests'. These responses show the differences of opinion within the British Government over the impact of DAER activities. In fact, the Colonial Office admitted that Arab sentiment had been stirred by the committee to protest over what was an arbitrary denial of rights.[57]

In February 1928, the committee accused the Palestine Administration of obstructing what it referred to as the right to enjoy nationality by descent. That right had been removed by the mandatory, DAER claimed, in order to facilitate Jewish immigration. It produced a document stating that approximately 9,000 Palestinian emigrants, out of a total of approximately 30,000 in the Americas and Europe, requested citizenship by the end of 1927.[58] The small number of applicants offered the proof, according to the committee, that the blame for the emigrants' situation was to be placed squarely on the British support for a Jewish national home in Palestine. Prior to the accusation, Sir Steward Symes, the government's Chief Secretary, voiced his satisfaction in the summer of 1927 'that fairly regular connection is maintained between the individuals of "colonies" . . . in the Americas and their country of origin'. In contrast to the Foreign Office stance, Symes recommended that the Palestine Administration reconsider applications for citizenship made by Palestinian Arabs from abroad. Although many of these applicants intended to continue to live outside Palestine, his recommendation indicates the willingness of the administration to acknowledge the situation. Symes even asked for a Foreign Office enquiry into Palestinian diaspora communities, especially those in Chile and Mexico, to discover whether it would be possible to grant them financial and diplomatic protection.[59] Indeed, the DAER committee by early 1928 succeeded in shifting the discourse on the emigrants in official government circles.

In early 1928, the DAER preparatory committee printed a forty-page entreaty titled 'Appeal to the Noble British People' that was widely publicised in the Arab press. With this, the committee attempted to address the public in Great Britain rather than the government. The significance of this document was that it was evidence of the grassroots civic activism that informed the activities of DAER. None of the noted Arab political leaders in Palestine – the Mufti, the various political factions or the Arab Executive – contributed to it. The appeal catered to the emotions of people of Great Britain and called upon them to pressure the Parliament to consider the demands of the Palestinian Arab emigrants.[60] In forty pages, the committee endeavoured to offer its definition of Palestinian nationality. It asked that nationality be granted through *jus sanguinis* and *jus soli* provisions. It also advocated a general extension of citizenship to all Palestinian natives based on Great Britain's own citizenship legislation.[61]

The committee sought to incorporate internationalist rhetoric of nationality in its appeals. Importantly, it outlined an understanding of the place of nationality in the international system. It noted that nationality laws connected an individual with his or her nation of origin and that certain nationality principles were recognised by every 'modern and civilised' nation. The committee envisioned an international right to nationality that mandated that individuals had diplomatic protection from their nation's government; thus, the alienation of emigrants from their nationality could not be internationally sanctioned. Ideas of nationality as linked to citizenship were expressed not only by Palestinian Arabs but they were part of a larger debate on the place of citizenship in the context of the post-1918 dominance of the nation-state. The DAER appeal to the British people evoked the text of Article 34 of the Treaty of Lausanne to demonstrate the need to conform Mandate legislation to international regulations.[62] It can be assumed that the appeal did not achieve the aims that the committee had hoped for.

It is unclear how many emigrants wrote to the defence committee with specific queries. Even so, it can be surmised that families near Bethlehem and Jerusalem knew of its raison d'être and its agency in connection with local nationalist associations. Certainly the literate Arab population with family in the diaspora read its frequent reports published in the newspapers. One cannot deny, however, that a certain anti-Zionist rhetoric can be drawn out of these reports and appeals; however, this rhetoric is not at all new. Rather, it helped DAER to link the mandatory's support for a Jewish national home in Palestine with the denial of the Arab emigrants' rights to citizenship and to return to their homeland.

Consuls, Emigrants and the British Government: Miscommunication and Divergent Practices

The work of the emigrants and their lobbyists, as detailed in the preceding section, meant that the wider Palestinian Arab population could more easily understand the reasons for opposition to the 1925 citizenship legislation. However, the conflict of opinion within the Foreign Office over the treatment of Arabs who lived outside of mandate territory hindered any immediate resolution of the Arabs' grievances. In October 1927, the British Foreign Office sent to its consul in San Salvador a draft copy of instructions regarding an amendment to the Palestine Immigration Ordinance. The document explained that ordinary British emergency certificates for travel to the mandate territory could be issued only to individuals who possessed Palestinian nationality. The draft instructions also contained a clause stating that if applicants for travel visas to Palestine were unable to obtain a Turkish passport or Turkish travel documents from their state of residence, they could apply for an emergency certificate valid for three months that allowed holders to undertake a single journey to Palestine in order to naturalise.[63] The draft contradicted Foreign Office policy detailed in earlier circulars that allowed for emergency travel certificates to be given to stateless Palestinian Arabs. This portrait of conflicting correspondence and governmental circulars demonstrates the general confusion and miscommunication between the British consulates and the Foreign Office.

Foreign Secretary Austen Chamberlain continued to hold the Foreign Office line that it was not desirable to issue travel certificates to 'former Turkish nationals' to visit Palestine if those individuals had not acquired Palestinian nationality. In fact, he maintained that non-citizen Palestinian Arabs who arrived at Palestinian ports with single-journey visas were liable to be '[suspected of] an attempt to evade the law and the Immigration authorities are . . . justified, in refusing permission to land'. Emigrants born in Palestine but without Palestinian citizenship by 1927 were treated as suspect by the immigration authorities upon arrival to Palestine.[64] However, Jewish immigrants to Palestine were granted permission by the same immigration authorities to settle and take provisional nationality, on the advice of the Zionist Organisation. British consuls, however, did not interpret the instructions consistently in all cases. Palestinian natives throughout Latin America, for instance, experienced different treatments by British consuls. The Palestine Administration had the option to refuse entry of emigrants on arbitrary grounds, such as the doubt that emigrants would remain in Palestine as permanent residents and instead use their citizenship to claim British protection.[65] According to British Secretary Chamberlain, consular officers could not issue any travel documents endorsed by Great Britain except for Arab individuals to return to reside permanently in Palestine, since such individuals abroad were neither British subjects nor British-protected persons. As for those Arabs whose applications for citizenship had been rejected, some consuls believed that they acquired Turkish nationality by default. Yet the emigrants did not hold Turkish passports nor pledge allegiance to Turkey. The default acquisition of Turkish nationality had no basis in international law. Therefore, it is difficult to explain how Great Britain could assign Turkish citizenship to individuals without their consent and without the agreement of Turkey, simply on the basis that these individuals' Palestinian citizenship applications had been rejected.[66]

The Palestine Administration and the British Cabinet in London attempted in 1927 to address the growing number of grievances by Palestinian Arabs against the citizenship legislation. In the first place, the Colonial Office insisted that the British Government could not extend the order-in-council's stated timeframe (within which natives could claim nationality) without the consent of the Turkish Government. Evidence of British correspondence with the Turkish Government on this issue does not exist in the archives. In fact, the

Colonial Office advised against contact with Turkey, believing the latter would be reluctant to become involved.[67] Meanwhile, High Commissioner Plumer wrote in mid-1927 that Palestinian natives must show 'genuine desire to resume their connection with Palestine' to travel to the territory to naturalise. This did not guarantee that their naturalisation would be approved.[68] Plumer's statement side-stepped the issue at the heart of the Palestinian grievances: namely, that the Arabs found naturalisation to be unacceptable as a negation of their right to nationality.

Palestine's attorney-general, Norman Bentwich, addressed the situation as well. He stated his intent to reconsider applications from people 'who by birth, race and sentiment are genuinely attached to Palestine' despite their likelihood to be resident abroad for an indefinite period. However, the Foreign Office disagreed and one official recommended that grants for citizenship be done on the basis of merit. If individuals were not judged to want citizenship enough to return to Palestine in the time allotted for them to do so, the official deemed them to 'never have been Palestinian, [and] . . . remain Ottoman subjects'.[69] The office failed to explain the existence of Ottoman subjects in the absence of an Ottoman Empire. It also offered little understanding of the principles of state succession introduced by the Treaty of Sevres in 1920 and the Treaty of Lausanne in 1923. The League of Nations had long worked to eliminate instances of statelessness in the post-war period, but the British Foreign and Colonial Offices neglected these ongoing debates on nationality.

The Foreign and Colonial Offices discussed complaints together, including those addressed to the League of Nations. One such letter from the Sociedad Fraternidad Palestina of San Salvador, written in September 1927, claimed to speak on behalf of more than a thousand Palestinian natives employed in trade who professed that they had 'no subversive aims' and accepted the international mandate assigned to Palestine. But, it continued, the natives were bound to Palestine 'by the strongest moral, social and political ties . . . like every human being who has . . . a feeling of attachment to his native land'. The Society felt the mandatory power seemed determined to destroy what it termed as fundamental rights to nationality by preventing natives from returning to their own country while it allowed foreign elements to enter.[70] After viewing other strongly worded complaints, William Ormsby-Gore suggested reconsideration of claims to citizenship made in due time by individuals who returned to Palestine at some point after they left the territory prior to 1920. These claims had initially been rejected by the administration.

His suggestion meant that any Palestinian by birth and resident abroad with Turkish nationalitywould 'be freely granted permission to visit or settle in Palestine with his family' but would need to naturalise to become an official citizen. Ormsby-Gore wrote that the extent to which the communities in the diaspora took advantage of the concession, if the administration put it into place, would be regarded as a measure of their genuine attachment to their homeland.[71]

In early 1929, the DAER committee reminded the colonial secretary that the false belief that emigrants severed their connections with their homeland 'paralysed to an unimaginable degree' an estimated 30,000 natives who had no recognised nationality.[72] One ray of hope for emigrants came in April 1929 with the news that an Arab native of Ramleh filed a lawsuit against the Palestine's high commissioner and director of immigration after authorities refused him citizenship upon return to Palestine. The legal proceedings had a favourable outcome for the complainant, who aimed for the recognition of his citizenship. The High Court of Justice in Palestine also required the government to pay the expenses of the lawsuit.[73] Despite this outcome of the challenge to the citizenship order, many Arabs resident in the diaspora who did not intend to immediately return to Palestine began to face increasingly hostile and anti-Arab host governments. The El Salvador Palestinian Unity Committee wrote a letter in 1929 detailing the expulsion of Arabs from El Salvador as a 'painful catastrophe [*nakba*]' and broadcast an appeal to Palestinians at home to help. 'Isa Bandak wrote a lengthy memo to Plumer's replacement, High Commissioner John Chancellor, to urge the Palestine Government to repeal the 'unjust aggression' in El Salvador against the country's approximately 2,000 Palestinian residents.[74] Other countries also refused to readmit any resident without nationality who had left the country's borders.[75] By the late 1920s, the all-important official nationality documents meant that emigrants had a chance to maintain their livelihoods.

This paralysis noted by DAER was as much economic as it was political. The committee continued to lobby High Commissioner Chancellor, with evidence that the emigrants kept their relations with Palestine through ownership of property and land and through the payment of taxes.[76] On the point of the financial situation of a number of emigrants, the mandate administration maintained an interesting position. Although it denied return and ipso facto citizenship to emigrants from all social classes, the administration continued to collect the tax revenues on the immoveable property and land owned by these individuals. By 1929, the tide of Jewish immigration to Palestine had again risen, while bankruptcy threatened the administration. Yet, even appeals to the economic benefits of a blanket grant of citizenship to all natives living abroad fell on deaf – or otherwise uninterested – ears.[77] Complicating matters, the Wailing Wall riots of 1929 forced the administration to focus on the perceived religious strife rather than economic tensions between the Jewish and Arab communities in Palestine. Although commissions of inquiry in the aftermath focused on Jewish immigration, they did not recognise demands of the Palestinian emigrants.

Conclusion

Despite the controversy over the changes to the 1925 Citizenship Order-in-Council, the British Government did not ratify an amended order until July 1931. The amendment had a very limited effect and did not reflect the demands of the emigrants and their lobbyists. Rather, it was aimed at Palestinians resident abroad between 1924 and 1925 only, and provided them with 'treaty nationality' ipso facto. Meanwhile, the Home Office debated the inclusion of a clause in the amended order stating that periodic visits made to Palestine by natives were not enough to signify maintenance of a 'substantial connection' with the country. The issue of substantial connections between the diaspora and the mandate territory continued to be a point of conflict. In early 1933, *Sawt al-Sha'b* reported that a very large number of Palestinian natives went to Turkish consuls to take Turkish citizenship in order to have consular protection and to travel to Palestine on a recognised passport.[78] It is important to note that from 1927 to 1937, the stated number of Palestinians registered as resident abroad rose by approximately 10,000 persons, up to in the region of 40,000.[79]

The Palestinian Arabs crafted their own – often multiple – meanings of citizenship in the 1920s in response to the situation in Palestine after the implementation of legislation. As the chapter has shown, these meanings were expressed most prominently by the emigrants once they returned to Palestine and once their hope to acquire citizenship came under threat. They defined rights and protections associated with citizenship in letters sent home and reprinted by individuals in Palestine who knew of their situation. These emigrants always connected their arguments in support of citizenship with their understanding of Palestine as an Arab nation (*al-umma al-'arabiyya*) creating a link between Ottoman nationality and Palestinian citizen-ship rights.

The reactions in Palestine to the situation of the emigrants can be used to chart the changing terminology of nationality and citi-zenship as well as the changing expressions of citizenship. Until the issue of the citizenship order the use of the term '*jinsiyya*' in the sense of citizenship was reinforced by a number of factors. The first was the Ottoman legislative precedent that termed the population of the Arab provinces as Ottoman nationals. The middle-class Arab nationalists focused upon the language used in the Ottoman law as they became increasingly alarmed by rumours and reports of the new Palestine citizenship order. Another factor was that citizenship was translated as *jinsiyya* in the Arabic publication of the Citizenship Order-in-Council in the mandate's official gazette, in the order-in-council itself and in the press reports written shortly after its provi-sions were made known.

The Palestinian Arab *mahjar* also factored in as a driving force for the changing discourse of nationality and citizenship after 1925. Discussions of citizenship and contentions over it were activated by the emigrants' situation as affected by legislation. The outcry over the denial of the 'right of return' and ipso facto citizenship for native Palestinians who resided outside of Palestine shaped the vocabulary and language associated with citizenship and the rights to that citi-zenship. The main impact of mandate law upon this changing termi-nology was that nationality and citizenship began to be perceived as separate statuses as the emigrants argued that their Ottoman Arab nationality entitled them to Palestinian citizenship. In conclusion, the Palestinian Arab emigrant featured prominently in Arab demands to the administration after the mid-1920s. The situation of the diaspora was constantly re-assessed in the Arabic press and by lobbyists such as 'Isa Bandak.

The arguments developed by the emigrants and DAER lobbyists in the mid- to late 1920s greatly impacted the Arab population's general conceptualisation of their nationality and identity as Pales-tinian. In the absence of a right to return to Palestine as citizens, the emigrants nonetheless practised citizenship through the formation of émigré civil societies, elections for national leaders and aid for Palestinians at home. This in turn forced the local authorities and the government in London to reconsider citizenship legislation as a response to the anger over the order's perceived injustices. This reconsideration was a long time coming, as officials in London and Jerusalem were not in agreement over the proper resolution for

Arab natives who resided abroad and wished to return to Palestine as citizens. The Jewish national home policy continued to guide the administration in legislation, including legislation that impacted only the Arab population. The advocacy of the DAER committee did not stop. Rather, the late 1920s and early 1930s witnessed a rise in the tactics of the populist leaders to protest against British policy.

5

Institutionalising Citizenship: Creating Distinctions between Arab and Jewish Palestinian Citizens, 1926–1934

[The Palestine Citizenship Order-in-Council] termed as an 'Instruction' is just the sort of enterprise from the mind of Bentwich who loves the loose generalities of International Law.
Sir J. Risley, Colonial Office memo (May 1929)

In 1930 the Colonial Office in London received a notice of the 'borderline case' of a Jewish Palestinian citizen who faced the revocation of his naturalisation due to his residence outside Palestine. Certificates of naturalisation could be annulled if their holders were absent from Palestine for three years and could not offer an explanation for their residence elsewhere. In large part the Colonial and Foreign Offices followed this policy because they feared that Palestinian citizenship could be used by individuals to claim 'un-entitled' British imperial protection. The two offices also stressed that any citizen absent for more than three years could not possibly maintain a 'connection' – or indeed loyalty – to Palestine and that they thus forfeited their rights of residence, citizenship, British protection and passport facilities. Since the mid-1920s, both offices knew of these risks even as each continually emphasised that 'Palestinian citizenship [carried] with it the right to British protection in foreign countries'. As to the case at hand, which had been passed to the Colonial Office for further advice, the officials who scrutinised the Jewish citizen's claims focused on the accusation that the individual retained his Palestinian citizenship simply to enjoy British protection while resident abroad. In the end, Colonial Office Under-Secretary John Shuckerberg decided that 'it would be better, at this juncture, not to risk a further squabble with the Jewish Agency' over the revocation of citizenship.[1]

Had his naturalisation certificate and passport been revoked, the Jewish man would likely have become stateless, and the blame for that position would have been heaped on to the Foreign Office. The individual remained a Palestine citizen despite his residence outside of the mandate's borders.

The incident was not unusual and it also represents one way in which various administrators involved in the Mandate bureaucracy applied the provisions of Palestinian citizenship differently for Jews as opposed to Arabs. The Arabs frequently suspected and accused the administration of favouritism for Jewish immigrants in the application of citizenship provisions but the historical reality was not so clear cut. Individual officials in the Palestine Administration did not always apply provisions in the ways set out by the government in London, nor did the local immigration and administration departments display consistent favouritism towards the immigrants in matters of naturalisation, passport control or entry to Palestine. Instead, local actions were often done to manage relations between Jews and Arabs in a way favourable to the conduct of British administration. As detailed in the previous chapter, the mandate's immigration officials did not accept as valid most claims by émigré Palestinian Arabs of their loyalty and wishes to return to Palestine as citizens at a future date. The Mandate archives contain handfuls of cases of Jewish citizens absent from Palestine for three or more years who received warning notices about the potential revocation of their citizenship and passports. Even so, the mandate immigration department was obliged to offer these addressees the chance to refute claims that they lost their connection with Palestine before the official revocation of their citizenship. In contrast with most Arab emigrants, almost all of the Jewish citizens who left Palestine possessed Palestine passports. In many cases these passports were renewed for periods of time if the warning letters were answered with promises of return from the Palestinian Jewish émigré.[2] As the following chapter addresses, the British Foreign Office instructed consuls to classify Arab Palestinian emigrants as (defunct) Ottoman citizens even by the 1930s since these emigrants did not possess Palestine passports.[3] At other times, detailed below, the British Government seemed largely disinterested in the ways in which citizenship policy exacerbated volatile communal relations.

The procedures used by the local government in Palestine and the government in Great Britain to change and approve provisions for further citizenship and nationality legislation depended not only upon the local situation for Jewish and Arab citizens and émigrés, but also on the obligation that legislation stay in-line with wider imperial legislation. Legislation needed to accommodate the ever-increasing number of citizenship certificates given to immigrants to Palestine. At the same time, by the early 1930s, Great Britain began to tightly regulate the movement of people into its imperial domains, including Palestine, as both the fear of communist agitation and the entrance of 'undesirables' into these territories heightened social and political tensions. In Palestine the British controlled the process of naturalisation in order to efficiently uphold the terms of the mandate and the obligations to the Jewish national home policy. In other words, the control of citizenship legislation by a number of local and imperial departments became a bureaucratic technique to enforce mandate policy – a policy that simply had to pay particular attention to Jewish immigration and naturalisation. Different departments of the administration and the Colonial Office in London established procedures to deal with the implementation of legislation and to arbitrate over applications for both naturalisation and citizenship. In reality, the division of control over legislation reflects the complex and blurred natures of citizenship and nationality, and precedents of indirect rule elsewhere within the British Empire. This blurring of lines between the nature of citizenship and nationality in Palestine by governmental departments resulted in a non-standardised and uneven application of certain provisions of citizenship legislation.

The present chapter analyses the ways Palestinian citizenship became bureaucratised after the 1925 Citizenship Order-in-Council through the early 1930s. This process of bureaucratisation allowed local and imperial officials to use nationality and citizenship as tools to classify, categorise and discipline the citizenry, immigrants and non-habitual residents. These tools served different purposes for the British officials in London, for those in Jerusalem and for the leadership of the Zionist Organisation in relation to its activities in Palestine. The division of control between Whitehall and the Palestine Administration meant that, overall, the creation of legislation was de-centralised in nature. The division of control was not always balanced, however: within Whitehall the Foreign and Colonial Offices disagreed over the application of policy and so too did local administrators in Palestine. As part of citizenship legislation the differences between administrators' policies toward Jewish immigration, including the fear of subversives, communists and Bolsheviks, resulted in a variety of opinions regarding revocation and grants of citizenship to Jews and Arabs. At the same time, because officials in Jerusalem and London voiced fears of potential conflicts of interest with the Jewish Agency and Zionist Organisation, these policies ultimately favoured a smooth and swift naturalisation process for Jewish immigrants. As time went by, colonial officials noted a desire for a specific type of Jewish immigrant: one Europeanised, white, entrepreneurial and self-sufficient, and with the potential to be loyal to Palestine and, by extension, Great Britain.[4] The classification and categorisation of individuals served to create a 'politics of distinction' between Arab and Jewish Palestinians in the application of nationality and citizenship. The Department for Migration and Statistics did not classify the Jewish immigrants as one monolithic group and, indeed, the immigrants were far from uniform. Palestine was unique as a quasi-colonial possession in the 1920s and 1930s in the internationalisation of the citizenship question: the Jewish national home policy meant that immigrants and potential citizens arrived to Palestine from a range of countries and colonies and frequently travelled back and forth between them.

The British and French based their legislation of colonial citizenship and nationality, not only in the Levantine mandates but also in India and African mandates and colonies, upon ideas of 'whiteness', 'the native', communalism, perceptions of minority and an absence of the political, social and civil rights of citizenship that became more widespread in the metropole during the interwar period. As Emma Hunter has shown for the case of British-mandated Tanganyika, colonial officials supported a model of 'good' civic citizenship based on involvement in the public sphere in social and cultural contexts and as opposed to political citizenship. Elsewhere in East and Central Africa British colonial officials debated through the 1920s and 1930s whether the 'native' and 'non-native' should be partly defined by cultural standards that supposedly determined assimilation into the realm of good citizenship. Hunter terms the British conceptualisation of the relationship between the mandate inhabitants and the British as a 'liberalism without liberties' founded on 'an understanding of citizenship based on duties rather than rights'.[5] The notion of apolitical 'good citizens' fit into interwar thinking in Palestine as well, as will be shown below. With the inauguration of the Mandate, colonial officials based the Jewish national home policy on a racial hierarchy between Jews and Arabs, and looked toward the Jewish immigrants as the non-native, civilising influence in Palestine.[6]

These distinctions enhanced by the citizenship legislation were very much a part of the wider colonial experience and colonial perceptions of the 'character' of whites, natives and settlers. As Ann Stoler has aptly shown, this categorisation by colonial administrators was a method of control based on privileging the identities of certain inhabitants as that of 'citizens'.[7] Thus, in matters of naturalisation, immigrants received separate treatment from that applied to natives. Birth in a territory (*jus soli*) did not always automatically confer citizenship, as demonstrated in the previous chapter. Social and cultural practices also came to signify that an individual was modern or European and thus able to become a citizen. Indeed, the language used by colonial officials in reference to the population of Palestine reflected this ideology. For example, Palestinian Arabs and Palestinian Jews were viewed as separate races in the colonial vocabulary of cultural and national identity.[8] The need to adhere to policy to facilitate a Jewish national home while at the same time preventing immigrants of a certain unsavoury character from acquiring citizenship convinced the imperial and the local governments of the importance of colonial-style nationality legislation. Along with the 1925 Citizenship Order-in-Council, the 1922 Electoral Order-in-Council and the text of the mandate underlined a differential treatment of the two communities implying that the application of citizenship would discriminate between both in order to uphold the mandate charter. Out of these imperial perceptions of matters such as race, culture and a certain European-ness came the treatment of Jewish Palestinian citizens as more akin to British subjects in matters of immigration and documentary identity.

The bureaucratisation (and categorisation) of citizenship in Palestine from the mid-1920s to the mid-1930s as officials interpreted the Citizenship Order-in-Council and its amendments can be studied in light of the concept of citizenship in the British Empire. The case study of Mandate Palestine demonstrates the different administrative tiers for colonial statuses in British territories. The tiers represented those inhabitants restricted from travel, or those with the privilege to enter the United Kingdom and its overseas possessions. During the interwar period, many states experienced confusion over boundaries, the sovereignty of territorial possessions, the classification of nationals and legal provisions affecting increased immigration and travel. All of these factors played an important role in the interpretation of Palestinian citizenship and the issue of further legislation that regulated it.

The Politics of Distinction: Palestinian Jewish and Arab Citizenships

Distinctive practices in the application of citizenship provisions for the Jewish, as opposed to Arab, population emerged before the passage of the 1925 Palestine Citizenship Order-in-Council. The primary difference can be traced back to the method by which Jewish immigrants to Palestine acquired provisional nationality in accordance with the 1922 Legislative Council Election Order. Prior to the 1922 order, officials were aware that they would need to implement Article 7 of the Palestine Mandate, which required Great Britain to issue a law that regulated the acquisition of Palestinian nationality for Jewish immigrants. The article, which did not mention the Arab population, foreshadowed the future separate routes to the acquisition of citizenship and naturalisation in Palestine. The distinctions can perhaps be traced further back, to the British colonial experience of creating legislation to delineate the statuses of the native, the European and the settler in other imperial possessions.

Administrators in territories of the British Empire, similar to Dutch, French and other colonial officials, included a number of assumptions about the cultural aptitude of 'the native' in colonial legislation that marked national status prior to the outbreak of the First World War. Distinguishing between the subject statuses of the indigenous populations in imperial realms also allowed colonial powers to 'order' colonial societies in order to preserve the hegemony of the local British administrators even in the era of indirect rule.[9] It can be argued that in the case of the Palestine Mandate after 1920, the local and imperial governments selectively applied these colonial precedents to create order and manage the Arab indigenous and Jewish immigrant populations through delineating identity statuses and bureaucratising citizenship and nationality. Drawing on the historical anthropology of Stoler, historians can view colonial discussions and ideas on citizenship, nationality and sovereignty during the interwar period as sites of production of European power as well as reflections of new developments of nation-state nationality and citizenship in the imperial metropole.[10] A number of imperial debates on race and culture within Europe and Great Britain prior to the outbreak of the First World War were translated into particular socio-cultural practices in the colonies and possessions that remained after the war.[11] The immigration regulations in support of the Jewish national home plan specifically stated that potential citizens had to be of a good character. The markers of character and the

nativist ideologies behind them permeated debates over immigration restrictions and the restrictions themselves.[12] To again reference
Stoler's argument, character did not derive from abstract or universal values but rather it centred on the concept of being European,
which indicated a particular standard of living, a set of cultural
competencies and social practices.[13] France provides one example
for multi-layered subjecthoods that Great Britain mimicked. In the
one hundred years before the end of the Second World War, French
political theory rationalised that French citizenship was a status for
inhabitants of metropolitan France. Inhabitants of French colonies
or overseas territories were French nationals or French subjects but
not French citizens – the difference was often blurred but the latter
referred to individuals with an inherent set of educational, social,
cultural and political criteria for 'being French'.[14]

To fast-forward to the immediate post-war years, the 1922 Legislative Council Election Order defined the Palestinian citizenry for
the purpose of enfranchisement for elections to a proposed (and
ultimately un-realised) legislative council. The order codified a distinction between two types of citizens in Palestine: former Ottoman
nationals resident in Palestine, and non-Ottoman habitual residents
of Palestine. Jewish immigrants in the latter group received provisional certificates of nationality upon arrival to Palestine. Habitual
residence in Palestine remained undefined and essentially any Jewish
arrivals were considered immediately as citizens for electoral purposes. Significantly, the order did not stipulate that these immigrants
had to give up their birth-nationalities or passports. This omission
mainly benefited immigrants, since the Ottoman administration had
prohibited the possession of dual nationality and mandate immigration officials and British consuls treated Palestinian Arabs who
acquired other passports strictly as nationals of the territory indicated by their passport. These Arabs – likely very few in number –
could not immigrate back to Palestine. The 1925 Citizenship Order
required that all applicants for naturalisation prove they met the two-
year residence in Palestine requirement. In order for native but non-
resident Ottoman nationals to claim Palestinian citizenship, Article
2 of the 1925 order required they return to Palestine and reside in
that territory for a period of six months. These former Ottomans
had to prove that their return would be permanent.[15] The return and
period of residency had to be prior to 1 August 1926, the deadline
given to so-called natives to claim their citizenship. Since Jewish provisional citizens came from a variety of backgrounds, administrative
and legal advisors placed emphasis on the need to accommodate for

the entire world-wide Jewish community in Palestine especially in immigration regulations.

The nature of the provisions for Jewish immigrants faced increasing challenges by the end of the 1920s. After the August 1929 Wailing Wall riots and amidst Arab demands to suspend immigration to Palestine, the British Government and Colonial Secretary Lord Passfield sent to Palestine the Shaw Commission headed by Judge Walter Shaw and composed of four Members of Parliament to investigate the causes of the riots. Sir John Chancellor, the high commissioner at the time, was notably less enthusiastic than his predecessors about the Zionist Organisation and the commission reflected his attitude, and increasingly that of other local officials immediately after the riots. It recommended suspension of Jewish land purchases and the imposition of a quota on Jewish immigration. These recommendations were then examined by John Hope-Simpson, whose report stated that the capacity for absorption of more immigrants had been reached in Palestine and that further immigration would severely impact the *fellahin* through the further dispossession of their land. Unfortunately for the Arabs, the home government had a different attitude. In February 1931 British Prime Minister Ramsey MacDonald wrote a letter to Chaim Weizmann in which MacDonald retracted the recommendations and reaffirmed the Balfour Declaration as the guide to British policy in Palestine. Consequently, the administration made no drastic changes to immigration or naturalisation policies.[16]

The tense political situation after 1929, along with the MacDonald letter, suggests that Great Britain had rightly been fearful that numerous revocations of Palestinian citizenship held by Jews could lead to disagreement with international Zionist and Jewish Agency leaders. The Zionist Organisation and its representative to Great Britain, the Jewish Agency, significantly influenced the application, or non-application, of citizenship requirements and practices for Jewish immigrants. Zionist involvement in citizenship legislation dated back to 1919 when Chaim Weizmann's suggestions on the proposals were sent to the Colonial Office in the form of 'official observations'.[17] More than a decade later in correspondence between the Colonial Office and the Palestine Government in 1933, officials noted the influence of the Zionist Organisation on immigration and citizenship and stated that it had become 'difficult for the Palestine Government to treat one set of Palestinian citizens differently from the rest and to subject them to immigration restrictions which at present apply solely to persons who are not Palestinian citizens'.[18]

The memo referred to those new arrivals that had not naturalised as citizens – a not uncommon situation for Jewish immigrants habitually resident in Palestine.

Also in the early 1930s the Palestine Administration noted the introduction in Parliament of a bill to extend Palestinian citizenship to any and all Jews without nationality. The Member of Parliament who submitted the bill surely had been unaware of the practical problems its approval would pose. The mandatory government opposed the measure and reacted by declaring that the MP in question did not realise 'the obvious': that if the estimated 200,000 Jews around the globe who had lost their nationality thus acquired Palestinian citizenship, they could automatically enter Palestine by right. Officials in Palestine added that this was not what the bill intended. One colonial official wrote:

> If the bill was to confer upon a certain class of aliens Palestinian citizenship in a way which did not carry with it the rights to be enjoyed in Palestine . . . attached to that status, they would nevertheless appear to have a claim to be treated as British-protected persons outside Palestine.

It appears that the local government realised that it needed to maintain a balance between offering Palestinian citizenship in the legal and political sense to immigrants who resided in Palestine with downplaying its resistance to allowing unrestricted immigration and a place of safe haven for European stateless Jews who had not yet immigrated to Palestine. The Arab press criticised the MP's proposal and mentioned that neither the mandate government nor the League of Nations charters contained any provision to allow for such an action. The Colonial Office, on the same footing as the Palestine Administration, wrote to High Commissioner Wauchope that if the bill meant anything 'presumably it seems that the whole of German Jewry should be granted Palestinian citizenship!'[19] As tensions over Germany's Adolf Hitler grew, the bill did not advance in Parliament but it did popularise the idea in official circles that Palestinian citizenship could simply be given to Jews as a 'natural' right without preconditions such as residency.

Despite its nullification, the bill demonstrates the differing attitudes and proposals within Whitehall from those of the local administration with respect to the application of citizenship for Jewish immigrants. Parliament was far more conciliatory towards privileges at an imperial-level for Jewish immigrants than the local administration.

The proposed bill further demonstrates the growing opinion in Great Britain that Jewish citizens could be accorded separate treatment from their Arab counterparts in Palestine on the basis of not only culture and socio-economic standing – hardly a new approach imperially – but also in accordance with international concerns. Just before the proposal of an extension of citizenship to a large number of European Jews, Colonial Office Secretary William Ormsby-Gore expressed the view that it was the 'quality' of Jews who entered Palestine that mattered. Officials in both the Palestine and London administrations perceived the immigrants as not only potential citizens but as a civilising influence.[20] Despite this view, no quotas were set on the type of Jewish immigrants deemed of the right quality for entrance to Palestine but officials continued to unofficially endorse the imperial practice of cultivating good citizenship through allowing Europeanised non-natives to naturalise with relative ease. On a similar note, prior to Ormsby-Gore's expression of opinion, a confidante of Colonial Secretary Leopold Amery reported that Blanche Dugdale, the niece of Arthur Balfour and a close friend of Weizmann, expressed hope that Jewish immigrants would become more English and despaired that despite possession of Palestine passports that entitled British protection these Jews were treated as foreigners in England. She urged Amery, without success, to simply change this legislative status.[21]

Internationalising Citizenship in the Palestinian Context: Enforcing Passports and Visas

The increased need for documentary identity between the two world wars meant that governments were increasingly forced to classify inhabitants as nationals, subjects or citizens, and offer them identification papers. The Palestine Mandate was remarkable in the internationalisation of citizenship, meaning that it brought together numerous ethno-national groups living throughout the world as Palestinian citizens. This placed it in a unique position in the wider British Empire. Although only briefly mentioned here, Palestine also presents an excellent case study on transnational migrations of both Jews and Arabs in the early twentieth century across numerous – and new – borders. The Jewish national home policy allowed for the acquisition of citizenship by Jews who came from a wide range of countries and colonies. This range of ethno-nationalities held by Palestine's Jewish population did not compare to any other single colonial population in the British Empire except for similarities with the composition (although not religion) of migrants to South Africa.

By the late 1920s mandate officials and numerous other actors involved in crafting entry, immigration and citizenship policies had not standardised the provisions that were to regulate the application for, or the issuing of, passports. Great Britain's 1920 Aliens Restriction Order – one of the amendments to the 1914 and 1919 British Nationality and Status of Aliens Acts upon which the Palestine's nationality and immigration legislation was modelled – required anyone who entered or left the United Kingdom to have a passport with a photo. With this act, the passport became the most important document to verify and legitimise identity and it allowed for registration and monitoring of the movements of aliens in the United Kingdom and the empire.[22] However, the same order did not immediately or readily translate to British colonies, possessions and mandates.

In 1926 the Colonial Office noted that both Jewish and Arab Palestinian citizens 'may be placed in an awkward position if they want to travel' to or from Palestine. The office proposed to issue emergency travel documents to individuals without passports. Palestinian passports were largely unavailable at the time of the citizenship order-in-council. Although Great Britain initially printed temporary passports in 1920, only official persons used them and they did not resemble the Palestine passport issued from 1924 onwards. The regular printing of passports did not begin until 1926.[23] Instead, emergency certificates were used for one-way travel for mainly *Jewish* provisional citizens and some residents of Palestine, but these were susceptible to abuse since their holders were under no obligation to live in Palestine. British consuls monitored their use by ensuring that holders only presented them once and did so only for one-way journeys. Despite not fulfilling the residency obligation required for Palestinian citizenship, theoretically holders could be treated, even in their countries of birth, as British-protected persons. The *laissez-passer* helped make up for the lack of passports, since it was treated like an emergency travel certificate until after 1926 when the Palestine passport became more common. The passport looked similar to its British counterpart: it was brown with the words 'British Passport' on the cover above the seal of the Palestine Government but 'Palestine' appeared under the seal.[24]

By the time of the citizenship order, the passport translated into documentary proof of nationality, citizenship and diplomatic protection.[25] Statelessness was measured by the lack of a passport. As the nation-state in the early twentieth century became a more intense network of institutions, passport and immigration controls aided the widespread institutionalisation of nationality and citizenship.[26] A passport proved not only national belonging but according to historian John Torpey, it was also part of a profusion of bureaucratic techniques in order to administer the boundaries of a nation. Its importance after the First World War forced the League of Nations to pay attention to the plight of individuals who did not hold a passport or identity documents, including Arabs and some minority ethnic groups left outside of any recognised nation-state after 1918. In the light of the Russian refugee crisis the League's High Commissioner for Refugees, Fridtjof Nansen, instituted the Nansen Passport after 1922. Governments could accept the Nansen Passport as proof of identity without the need to grant citizenship rights to its bearer.[27]

With the widespread imperial usage of passports came the increased need for efficient travel facilities for emigrants, immigrants and travellers from and to Palestine. The responsibility for this initially fell to the British Foreign and Home Offices in the metropole, in charge of consular and diplomatic facilities, and immigration and passport controls, respectively. Before the standard issue of Palestine passports, Jewish and Arab *inhabitants* could travel and prove their identity but, as the previous chapter has demonstrated, British consuls and local immigration authorities did not always follow or even have centralised procedures with respect to these travellers' identities. Prior to 1925, the category of 'provisional' Palestinian citizenship confused consuls who were unsure of its international acceptance and whether both Arabs and Jews could declare it as their non-documentary national identity. Mandate officials and consuls generally granted *laissez-passer* to Palestinian Arabs on the basis of their Ottoman passport. Jewish immigrants could travel on their certificates of provisional Palestinian nationality but, as the chapter will demonstrate later, faced difficulties returning to their home countries if the British revoked their certificates or their eventual passports once residents' absences came to be recorded and monitored. The Arabs faced a disadvantage if they carried Ottoman identity documents: they could be refused *laissez-passer* by British consuls. Furthermore, many former Ottoman subjects including Sephardic Jews were still regarded as enemies before ratification of the 1924 Treaty of Lausanne. European Jewish residents with provisional certificates of Palestinian nationality did not face the same problems but Jews who had been Ottoman subjects often did.[28]

At the end of 1925 the Colonial Office requested that for the case of Palestine, certain procedures for travellers be clarified including the standard treatment given by British foreign consuls to applicants for entry into Palestine. Disagreements between the Colonial and Foreign Offices over how to treat native Palestinians who lived abroad hindered any type of joint resolution as the Foreign Office continued to argue that these Palestinians had no right to claim British diplomatic protection. The history of this bureaucratisation of immigration and nationality documentation must account for an analysis of the differences of opinion and tensions between and within government departments as well as with local authorities in Palestine. For example, High Commissioner Plumer in 1927 believed that a more inclusive permission to settle in Palestine could be offered to individuals born in there but without citizenship, against the opinion of the Foreign Office. At the same time, the local government faced the on-the-ground implications of these differences of opinion. Palestine's Attorney-General, Norman Bentwich, announced that he would reconsider sympathetically applicants from people 'who by birth, race and sentiment are genuinely attached to Palestine' despite residence abroad and the unlikelihood of their return for an indefinite period. J. H. Lloyd in the Colonial Office came out against this announcement. He argued that the office had little doubt that many of these people wanted British protection in order to make claims against the governments in their states of residence – in line with the long-standing objection of the Foreign Office to the same issue.[29]

The Colonial Office's official stance found the reconsideration of applicants contrary 'to the general rule' set by the Foreign Office to avoid the creation of a class of people entitled to British protection although they did not live in a British-administered territory. Such groups of people were 'a nuisance to the Consuls and no credit to the Empire'. The present system that did not support the grant of citizenship or travel facilities to natives of Palestine who resided abroad prior to the 1925 order-in-council, or who had not lived in the territory for the minimum three years avoided creating this nuisance, and colonial officials in London deemed it 'absolutely fair and equitable'. Little emigration had taken place in 1919 or before 1920, the Colonial Office claimed, and people not resident in Palestine since 1920 had no legitimate claim to be considered as Palestinian nationals. Furthermore, the Colonial Secretary argued that people who could not afford to take the time to qualify for naturalisation (which meant returning to Palestine to reside) had no reason to be granted citizenship status.[30] Natives who applied to travel to Palestine could not always obtain a Turkish passport or travel documents – despite British opinion these individuals were considered to be Turkish citizens by the government in Ankara. Emigrants who resided in countries without a Turkish consulate found it impossible to attempt to request Turkish travel documents before and after 1925.[31] Their naturalisation as Turkish citizens, however, was grounds for refusal of Palestinian citizenship since mandate practice prohibited Arabs from holding dual Palestinian and any other nationality.

Another problem that plagued attempts to enforce passport and travel document policies was the expiration of the provisional certificates of Palestinian nationality. This affected both Arab natives who lived abroad and Jewish immigrants who were granted provisional nationality but who did not permanently live in Palestine. Certificates given to Jewish immigrants from 1920 to 1925 as proof of provisional nationality had been issued on the understanding that these immigrants would acquire Palestinian citizenship and settle within the boundaries of the mandate territory. Because many Jews continued to use provisional certificates rather than claim citizenship, the Palestine Government was forced to extend the validity of the provisional certificates until the end of 1926. The Foreign Office decided to stop endorsing *laissez-passer* after March 1927 in another attempt to force Jewish immigrants to apply for a passport to prove their citizenship. Those who could not prove that they were Palestinian citizens under the residency provisions of the citizenship order would theoretically be unable to travel on British-issued documents.[32]

The passport linked Palestinian citizenship to variations of British consular and diplomatic protection. Once the Palestine passport came into regular circulation in 1926, High Commissioner Plumer noted that it did not entitle bearers the right to enter the United Kingdom or any British protectorate, dominion, colony or mandate.[33] In October 1925, the Secretary of State for Home Affairs confirmed that Palestinian passports would offer no privileges for travel throughout the Empire or exemption from immigration and visa regulations.[34] Despite the Home Office statement, Palestinian Arabs and Jews, as well as individual officials in Whitehall, referred to Palestinians as imperial subjects. Of course, Great Britain did not treat Palestinian citizens as British imperial subjects but the hierarchy of administration meant that approval of all legislation had to come directly from Whitehall since Great

Britain ruled Palestine directly. The application of immigration and citizenship legislation in Palestine, the import of English law and the system of education led to confusion over whether the mandate's inhabitants could be treated in a similar fashion to the inhabitants of outright colonies or of the directly administered mandates in Africa. In practice the mandate government was not in the legal position of providing travel and consular facilities to its own citizens: Palestinian consular officers or embassies did not exist. The duty of protection instead fell upon the government that held the mandate – Great Britain.

Naturalised citizens (mainly Jews, other non-Ottoman nationals and those Arabs who chose to naturalise) absent from Palestine for three years prior to applying for passport renewal would be required to state the reason for the absence to the Controller of Permits in Jerusalem.[35] A five-year validity of Palestine passports was first proposed by the administration but the Colonial Office suggested two years in order to ensure that naturalised citizens could not evade the residency obligation for more than two years without renewing their passports.[36] If they attempted to do so, their citizenship status and diplomatic and consular protection could be called into question when the passport was due for renewal. In November 1926, High Commissioner Plumer authorised the Chief Immigration Officer to limit to two years the validity of Palestinian passports held by naturalised citizens in order to prevent 'a considerable number' of such people from obtaining a passport and then settling abroad while they still came under imperial protection. Plumer, not entirely favourable towards the Zionist movement, referred to the practice of Jewish individuals who acquired citizenship and left Palestine as 'the exploitation of Palestinian nationality'.[37] It can be deduced that debates on passport renewals primarily focused on Jewish citizens since they freely travelled in and out of Palestine, whereas Arab emigrants were frequently denied entry back into Palestine in the first place. Indeed immigration officers mainly processed passport applications and renewals for Jewish residents.

As neither the 1925 citizenship order nor the mandate's immigration legislation provided a definitive and fully accepted standard procedure for the mandate authorities and British consuls to enforce passport and visa controls, the disputes between officials of the Colonial Office and the Palestine Administration exacerbated the disagreement over what procedures to apply to inhabitants of the mandate. Although a variety of governmental bodies attempted to coordinate, the need for each body to control a certain stage of the procedures created divergences of opinion not only in Palestine and Whitehall, but in regions where British consulates dealt with Palestinian Arabs and Jews. The institutional control of Palestinian citizenship came to be linked closely with naturalisation, nationality legislation and imperial control over Palestinians in transit.

Bureaucratising Palestinian Nationality: Naturalisation, Revocation and Amending Citizenship

Following Arab complaints and a multiplicity of positions on the regulations for the acquisition of Palestinian citizenship by emigrant Arab natives, as well as the increased perception by colonial officials of the dangers of Palestine's highly internationalised citizenship, the administration bowed to pressure to consider an amendment of the citizenship order in the latter 1920s. The reform of naturalisation standards became one of the main points of contention over the proposed amendment. The naturalisation process normally applied to Jewish immigrants, although a small number of native-born Palestinian Arabs turned to the option if they found their claims to citizenship refused. Since immigrants had in the first instance to go through the naturalisation process, the administration and the British Government constantly sought to ensure the efficient application of its provisions. In large part, this meant institutionalising the different procedures of naturalisation. In other words, these procedures filtered through various bureaucratic departments in Palestine and Great Britain, becoming set practice with formal rules and differentiations based on an individual's nationality at the time that he or she entered Palestine. The distinctions and differences in the application and acquisition of recognised and legal citizenship between Arabs and Jews emerged from the institutionalisation of naturalisation and are crucial to understanding how each group experienced the loss of citizenship, the denial of naturalisation and instances of dual nationality. Drawing on heightened British colonial perceptions of Eastern European Jews as deviant, disloyal political agitators, this section analyses how the Palestine Administration and Colonial Office determined who was fit to receive citizenship. The hierarchy of citizenship and subjecthood applied in Palestine was far from novel. Rather, it was standard practice in European colonies to maintain imperial hegemony. For similar reasons of maintaining hegemony, during the interwar period the United States codified such a hierarchy based on 'ethnic' or national origin into immigration law and produced the new category of the illegal alien.[38]

Palestinian naturalisation, while following British legislation, was conditional on other factors such as gender, marital status, deportation and the laws of other states. Since encouragement for Jewish immigration to Palestine was a cornerstone of mandate policy, the British officials focused mainly on how these conditions affected the Jewish residents. The Palestine Administration first instituted naturalisation in 1925 in accordance with the provisions of the citizenship order-in-council. On the basis of the 1922 electoral order, Jewish habitual residents with provisional certificates of nationality would not need to naturalise, but new arrivals (including Arabs) needed to do so. As explained in Chapter 2, the stated qualifications for naturalisation were simple: Jewish immigrants needed to have knowledge of Hebrew, English or Arabic, a good 'character' and residence in Palestine for two out of three years prior to their naturalisation. In addition, applicants paid minimal fees and gave an oath of loyalty to the government.[39] The straightforward nature of the procedure suggests that debate over it was initially limited. In fact, the question of *British* naturalisation for Arab, Jewish and other civil servants in the Palestinian Government entered into discussion at the local and imperial levels first. In early 1926 discussions between the Colonial Office and the Palestine Government drew attention to questions of naturalisation procedure, highlighting the questionable status of the Palestine Mandate as part of the British colonial empire. The Colonial Office regarded naturalisation, whether to British or Palestinian citizenship, as a practice to be carried out entirely as provided for in United Kingdom legislation.[40] The debate further demonstrated the unique situation of the mandate – as *not* a traditional colony but under Colonial Office jurisdiction – and Great Britain's obligations toward the Zionist Organisation.

Prior to 1925, the Colonial Office had questioned whether future Palestinian citizens employed in the Mandate Government could be granted British naturalisation. This practice was widespread in British colonies. The status of Palestine as a mandate and not a colony did not impact the decision of the Colonial Office on the issue, and in the final decades of empire subjecthood was often classified along blurred lines.[41] The basic criteria of who could be a 'European' fluctuated in different colonial contexts in the early twentieth century,[42] but colonial officials voiced worries about loyalty of Palestinians, particularly Jewish citizens, to Great Britain.

In certain cases, as one official explained, it would be 'inexpedient' to view Palestinians as subjects of the empire because the British Government '[has] brought into being the "Palestinian Citizen." If we proceed to convert him into a British subject by naturalisation, we shall expose ourselves to criticism.' Such a practice would go against the policy of the government to foster a Jewish (and strictly not British) national home. Palestine was considered a protected state with a local nationality but even so it became mandate practice to allow non-British or non-Palestinian civil servants in Palestine to choose the citizenship of either Great Britain or Palestine, pending the authorisation of the high commissioner.[43] In imperial thinking, this cultivated loyalty to the empire. Any alien to Palestine who obtained (British) imperial naturalisation inside Palestine (such as a civil servant) was to be recognised legally – although not necessarily politically – as a British subject everywhere, including within Palestine.[44] The option for civil servants to naturalise as British subjects seemed an attractive one, but in practice Palestinian citizens had British protection outside of Palestine just as British subjects did, although they had no political rights.

Palestinian naturalisation translated into enfranchisement for Jewish immigrants and only the names of citizens could be added to communal voting registers. Yet, a significant number of immigrants did not actually naturalise as citizens for reasons explained in subsequent chapters. On one level, this led to the administration's reassessment of naturalisation policies.[45] In 1929, Norman Bentwich stressed that naturalisation needed to appeal to as many Jewish immigrants as possible. He initially claimed that fees to naturalise hindered the policy meant 'to encourage settlers to adopt Palestinian citizenship'.[46] In the first instance, the Palestine Administration attempted to ensure that naturalisation procedures for married women and minor children conformed to imperial legislation. Women married to Palestinian citizens took on the nationality of their spouses in line with British Dominions legislation. The citizenship and nationality status of women and children required clarification as cases of marriage and divorce both increased from 1930 and, specifically, officials took marriages and divorces very seriously in light of demands for quotas and restrictions on Jewish immigration. Immigration authorities required proof of legitimate marriages between Jewish Palestinian citizens and foreigners, and obtaining such proof often presented an obstacle to naturalisation of new immigrants.

An additional difference in the practice of naturalisation between Arab and Jewish Palestinians involved minor children. The local administration sought to standardise the two sets of rules through which minor children not born in Palestine received citizenship through parents. The British, through little fault of their own, interacted quite differently with Jewish men who nautralised as citizens and had minor children to add to naturalisation certificates than they did with Arab natives of Palestine who sought to have children who were born abroad granted ipso facto citizenship. As noted elsewhere, the Colonial Office had been especially clear that children born to native Arab parents who resided outside Palestine and did not have *Palestinian* citizenship were not to be considered Palestinian. Additionally, the Colonial and Home Offices agreed that Palestinian *citizens* who lived abroad could not register the birth of their children at British consulates. It seems from reports of consuls in the Americas and the Arab press that Arab citizens tended to be resident abroad more often than Jewish citizens when their children were born. The policy meant that British consuls, especially in Latin America with its population of Arabs in the tens of thousands, did not have exact records on the number of Palestinians by descent resident in their districts. Jewish immigrants to Palestine, or naturalised citizens returned from travels abroad, could add their minor children to their naturalisation certificates even if the children had not been born inside mandate territory.[47] Finally, it should be noted that Arabs (as well as the few Palestinian Jews who migrated) in Latin America, particularly those involved in peddling or trade, often resided far from any consular office and that rendered attempts to register themselves or their children nearly impossible by reason of geographical location. It can be argued that the local administration's stress on the standardisation of provisions for minor children as well as the practice of registering children abroad was done to keep Palestine in line with imperial policy and to ensure consistency in any Foreign Office instructions to consuls who came across natives of Palestine.

Instances of dual nationality plagued both Jewish immigrants and the Palestine Administration and these complicated efforts at regulation. It must be recalled that dual nationality was acceptable *only* for Jewish immigrants in Palestine. Arabs born in Palestine who lived abroad could not return to their homeland as citizens if they acquired any new nationality, including that of Turkey. This official stance against dual nationality was not unusual in emerging nation-states. On the one hand, dual nationality undermined the link between an individual and a sovereign state, while, on the other, it multiplied claims to protections and rights.[48] Dependent on the regulations of the country from which Jewish immigrants came, an application to naturalise in Palestine could lead to the revocation of individual, original nationalities. In these cases, immigrants were stripped of their former nationality and rendered stateless even if they were refused naturalisation in Palestine. Such immigrants faced a similar situation to that of Palestinian Arab emigrants who could not claim Palestinian citizenship: they became stateless, without consular protection and without a valid passport. This was most often the case for the Jewish immigrants from states in Eastern Europe that refused to accept dual nationality of natives. It is perhaps for this reason that by the end of the 1920s many of the early immigrants to Palestine retained their provisional nationality certificates and were reluctant to opt for citizenship.

Palestine and imperial officials devoted significant amounts of energy in their attempts to rectify the problems posed by dual nationality, particularly the deportation of naturalised citizens from Palestine. The mandate administration had the power to deport anyone refused Palestinian citizenship, disloyal to the administration or who carried citizenship while resident abroad. Once a naturalised Jewish citizen was deported by immigration authorities in Palestine, Great Britain and the Palestine Government were under no obligation to offer that former citizen diplomatic protection. Colonial officials such as Gerard Clauson proposed to ask foreign countries not to strip deported or non-naturalised Jewish immigrants of their original nationality in order to avoid instances of statelessness. Even so, by 1930 some European governments forced Jewish emigrants to renounce their nationality before they left for Palestine.[49] Colonial Secretary Leopold Amery advised Assistant Under-Secretary for the Colonies John Shuckburgh that the Jewish immigrants without Palestinian citizenship were liable to be deported for not complying with the provisions of the citizenship and immigration legislation. It is noteworthy that the colonial secretary also tried to induce some foreign governments to accept their former nationals who had been deported from Palestine.[50]

By the end of the 1920s, the remonstrations by a number of Palestinian Arabs against what they perceived as the citizenship order's failure to adequately address the nationality status of emigrants, as explained in the previous chapter, drew the attention of the high commissioner and added to the uncertainties over proposed changes to the 1925 order. Due to the active protest campaign led by the Committee for the Defence of Arab Emigrant Rights to Palestinian Nationality (DAER), beginning in 1927, certain colonial administrators took a greater interest in applications for citizenship by

Palestinian natives who resided outside of Palestine. Yet the opinions in the local administration and the Cabinet varied over how closely connected these individuals were to Palestine, hindering a unanimous resolution. Still, the protests forced the hand of the Colonial Office: it reconsidered rejections of citizenship as a result of the large numbers of petitions received from Palestinian communities in South and Central America from 1925 to 1930. In 1927 Colonial Secretary Amery seemed inclined to support extension of citizenship to emigrants who maintained a connection with their native land.[51] As seemed to be the trend regarding the mandate, the Foreign and Home Offices disagreed and, guided by imperial reasoning, continued to instruct British consular officials not to accept applications from individuals whom they deemed to want citizenship for the purpose of obtaining diplomatic protection. High Commissioner Plumer advised colonial officials that individuals must show a 'genuine desire to resume their connection with Palestine' in order to receive consent to travel to Palestine and naturalise. Still, the Foreign Office declined to stray from its policy on diplomatic and consular protection and it rejected thousands of applicants for citizenship through the latter 1920s, in spite of their possession of Ottoman identity documents.[52]

Colonial officials in Britain initiated serious discussion of an amendment to the Citizenship Order-in-Council in 1929 after the violence and rioting that summer in Palestine and because of the unresolved issues that affected the acquisition and revocation of citizenship for both groups. Even prior to the riots, Colonial Office Legal Advisor J. S. Risley supported the change in certain provisions of the legislation and wrote in a memo that the order-in-council's use of terms and its ambiguities was 'just the sort of enterprise' from the mind of Attorney-General Bentwich who 'loves the loose generalities of International Law'.[53] These loose generalities, such as the meaning of nationality and citizenship in the international context, were not the only stumbling blocks to amending the order. The synthesis of colonial and imperial legislation and the internationalised nature of citizenship in Palestine not only made the mandate legislation unique but also weakened its international standing and recognition. Bentwich, too, complicated matters because of his lack of experience in colonial administration and, according to some colleagues, in English law.[54] Additionally, statements by the Colonial Office suggest a general feeling that because some emigrants had not expressed interest in returning to Palestine, the majority of individuals in the diaspora had the same attitude.

By December 1927, Secretary of State for the Colonies, William Ormsby-Gore, discussed the Palestine Government's proposal to reconsider those rejected claims for citizenship that were made in time by emigrants who were legally Ottoman subjects and left Palestine before, during or after 1920 (and had since returned and resided for at least six months). In opposition to imperial policy, Ormsby-Gore suggested that any Palestinian by birth who resided abroad with the newly created Turkish nationality would be 'freely granted permission to visit or settle in Palestine with his family'. This suggestion did not take into account stateless Palestinians who did not possess Turkish nationality papers but did possess Ottoman identity documents. According to Ormsby-Gore, the extent to which Palestinian communities abroad took advantage of this concession would be regarded as the measurement of the genuine attachment of the entire community to Palestine. These emigrants should find it easy, he continued, to fulfil the conditions to be naturalised 'if their principle interests be in Palestine'.[55] Yet, the key issue for determining the emigrants' eligibility for citizenship was the period of time they resided outside Palestine.

A single amendment to Article 1 of the order came under consideration by 1929. The basis of Article 1 was that former Ottoman subjects habitually resident in Palestine on 6 August 1924 were entitled by the Treaty of Lausanne to Palestinian citizenship.[56] Risley suggested the addition to Article 1 of an amended clause that allowed for 'treaty nationality'. This meant that former Ottoman subjects who were habitually resident in Palestine on the date that the Treaty of Lausanne went into force (6 August 1924) but left before 1 August 1925 and returned anytime after without another nationality would be entitled to make a declaration of the retention of Palestinian citizenship. The Foreign Office called such a provision unnecessary and suggested that the rest of the order should be amended instead of Article 1.[57] However, provisions for treaty nationality would not have affected the vast majority of emigrants who left Palestine before August 1924. Within the Palestine Administration, High Commissioner Plumer recognised the need to make some concessions. He asked the Colonial Office to agree to a consideration of applications for Palestinian citizenship by Ottoman subjects who resided in Palestine until October 1924 – several months after the Treaty of Lausanne came into effect – and then left, returning by 1927 to Palestine.[58] This was only the minimum concession that the emigrants and their lobbyists had campaigned for. The subjective review of applications by the administration and the Foreign Office did little to ease the hardships of emigrants not entitled to citizenship or entry to Palestine.

Another entirely different idea came from Bentwich, representative of the local administration rather than Whitehall. Rather than an amendment to provide treaty nationality, he suggested that individuals resort to the court system. A court's job would be to determine the habitual residency of Palestinian applicants for citizenship. Of course, the practice of obtaining court decisions on applications for citizenship from Palestinians abroad would be logistically difficult and time-consuming. Bentwich proposed other ideas that the Arabs found more favourable to their demands, including one in particular that would allow for any person who left Palestine during 1924 or 1925 and returned within five years to be regarded as a habitual resident according to the citizenship order's Article 1.[59] The implementation of this plan would have entitled these individuals to citizenship and it also offered the longest extension period for natives to choose citizenship as yet suggested by a mandate official. It also allowed returning emigrants to 'be treated as Palestinians as of right and not by naturalisation [which] is a great moment to those involved', meaning the Arab emigrants and their supporters. Bentwich's proposal acknowledged and reflected the argument of the emigrants against naturalisation and supported their demand for citizenship by right of nationality (*haqq al-jinsiyya*). He argued that this would bring the Treaty of Lausanne's provisions and the order-in-council into closer conformity as the treaty gave Ottoman subjects habitually resident in territories detached from the Empire after the war the ipso facto nationality of the state those territories were transferred to, on the conditions of local laws within them.[60] The Foreign Office countered that the period for option for emigrants be changed to four years rather than five.[61]

In a subsequent memo from the Foreign Office to the Colonial Office, the Foreign Secretary wrote in 1929 that the entire citizenship order-in-council should be amended. In other words, he felt that inserting new amendments to articles would not be sufficient. The following year the Colonial Office came to the same conclusion.[62] Although both offices agreed that the British Government should ratify an entirely new order, other governmental departments as well as the Palestine Administration were asked to contribute to drafting the proposed amended order. Almost immediately after this agreement, the Foreign and Home Offices expressed differences of opinion over the draft's new and re-worked provisions.[63] One of the initial disagreements concerned the distribution of power and, by extension, sovereignty, between the Palestine Administration and Whitehall in situations of granting or revoking the naturalisation or citizenship of Palestinian Arabs and Jews.[64] In particular, one provision of the amended order draft gave high commissioners the power to revoke the citizenship from Palestinian natives who resided abroad but returned to Palestine to take citizenship after 1924, as well as from Jews who arrived to Palestine from 1918 to 1925.[65]

In July 1931, the British Government won out over Bentwich and local administrators: it ratified the newly written order, titled as the 1931 Palestine (Amendment) Citizenship Order-in-Council. It incorporated the provision for treaty nationality and gave four years from the date of issue to allow native-born Palestinians to claim citizenship. Ottoman subjects who were habitually resident in Palestine before 1 August 1925 received ipso facto Palestinian citizenship unless they had acquired another nationality prior to the amendment. Yet, the Home Office reaffirmed that native-born Palestinians resident abroad must maintain a substantial connection to Palestine to qualify for ipso facto treaty nationality – periodic visits to the territory were not enough.[66] The administration in Jerusalem benefited from the new amendment. It gave a significant measure of autonomy to the high commissioner, as it granted to his office the explicit power to revoke or annul a certificate of naturalisation for any reason deemed legitimate.[67] This change contrasted with the near-hierarchy of Whitehall over local administrators in immigration and naturalisation legislation. In sum, the amended citizenship order did not radically alter the original order nor allow for a significant number of Palestinian Arab emigrants to return to Palestine as citizens. In fact, only those Arabs who left in the year between the ratification of the Lausanne Treaty and the issue of the 1925 citizenship order qualified to return as such. Colonial administrators drafted the amended order during a time of change with the departure of both High Commissioner Chancellor and the attorney-general. The latter was a significant change. Bentwich, who had become somewhat the resident expert on nationality legislation, was replaced by Harry Trusted in 1931.[68] The secretary, under-secretary and other staff positions in the Colonial Office were also re-shuffled. These administrative changes, plus new developments in the internal political situation in Palestine hampered any general agreement between all departments involved.

The Amended Order, Subversive Citizens and the International Context

In the years immediately after the approval of the 1931 Palestine (Amendment) Citizenship Order-in-Council, the Mandate administration and London were forced to consider the international travel of Palestine's citizens. The citizenship order amendment came during a time period of heightened surveillance over populations and individuals in transit within British – and French – territories. As a result, the distinctions in the application of the order did not necessarily privilege all Jewish immigrants. In the interwar period, the Colonial Office and Palestine's Criminal Investigation Department (CID) increasingly feared a connection between Bolshevism, anarchism and communism with Palestine's urban, secular Jewish population.[69] A quiet, yet persistent, discourse that certain European Jews were subversive, disloyal and international conspirators grew alongside wider imperial apprehension over workers' unions, labour strikes and anti-colonial protests.[70] Such fears within the wider context of Bolshevist and communist anxieties were also prevalent in the Arabic press as well as among those colonial officials who did not fully support the Zionist project in Palestine and their counterparts in Iraq.

By virtue of the 1931 amended citizenship order the high commissioners had the power to grant or revoke any person's citizenship and the latter action was threatened more frequently after 1930 against Jews. Jewish citizens who resided outside of Palestine in contravention of the residency clause faced the possibility of having their citizenship revoked or annulled. Mandate authorities began to place some of these Jews into the category of 'undesirable persons' due to their political beliefs, morals and suspected subversive acts.[71] Still, the action of revoking the naturalisation of these 'undesirables' put Palestine's high commissioners in an awkward position: they faced the British Government's concern – and perhaps guilt – that the removal of Palestinian citizenship rendered certain Jewish immigrants from Eastern Europe stateless and unable to be easily deported.

Throughout the 1920s, immigration authorities in the British Empire and elsewhere tightened controls on the entry of Eastern European immigrants, fearing the spread of Bolshevik as well as anti-colonial propaganda. Prior to the First World War, Great Britain had set up special immigration controls for suspected subversive aliens who may incite political violence or anti-colonial riots.[72] By the interwar period, the international range of Palestine's potential Jewish citizens elicited similar fears among officials and the CID. As discussed above, the British supported a particular type of Jewish immigrant, and so it comes as little surprise that in the late 1920s High Commissioner Chancellor expressed anxiety over Eastern European and Russian Jews who immigrated to Palestine. Certain anticipation existed that the socialist and internationalist affiliations of these immigrants translated into a lack of patriotism and loyalty to Palestine and to Great Britain.[73] Before 1931, the high commissioners recommended the annulment of citizenship of a small number of 'unsavoury' Jewish immigrants. In the metropole, the Foreign Office rather than the local administration faced the repercussions of these annulments and deportations when it attempted to negotiate with other countries to allow their natives to return. Most deportations of Palestine's naturalised citizens did not affect only the deportee. With the removal of the citizenship of an adult male came the revocation of the same status of his wife and children. Although revocations and deportations did in fact happen, they reflected poorly on the facilitation of Jewish immigration and they alarmed the Zionist Organisation.

Three years after the issue of the amended citizenship order, it was evident that the amendment had done little to clarify the intricacies of Palestinian citizenship as it related to imperial policy. Dominions Office member K. O. Roberts-Wray stated that it was an 'indisputable fact' that the legislation, including provisions on the revocation of naturalisation and the annulment of citizenship, was never intended to deny any Palestinian Jew of his citizenship. Roberts-Wray saw no reason for Palestine to be 'guided *strictly*' by the United Kingdom nationality laws and practices in matters of nationality and de-naturalisation, both of which did not always favour the Jewish national home project. Despite increased threats to Great Britain from so-called communist propaganda in overseas territories, Roberts-Wray expressed alarm at proposals to allow the Palestine Government to de-naturalise those long-standing Palestinian Jewish citizens who were believed to have left Palestine and travelled for the purpose of obtaining communist propaganda. He emphasised that individuals who became Jewish citizens by virtue of provisional certificates of nationality granted before 1925 could not be de-naturalised in any circumstance.[74] In fact, implementing such a provision to (as the Foreign Office claimed) allow the Palestine Government to 'keep these dangerous elements outside Palestine', would risk confrontation with Zionist leadership.[75] Other colonial officials suggested withholding travel facilities so that 'indoctrinated' people could not leave Palestine.[76] A memo from the Dominions Office to Sir John Maffey, the Under-secretary of State for the Colonies in 1934, offered support for the proposal to deprive Palestinian citizenship from any Arab or Jew who went to the Soviet Union for what was referred to as a course in communist propaganda. However, many of those accused as subversives had citizenship by virtue of their prior Ottoman nationality or habitual residence in Palestine and the administration had never proposed removing citizenship from these individuals.[77]

Attorney-General Trusted, Bentwich's replacement, noted his wish to minimise conflict with the Zionist Organisation when he wrote in a memo to the Department of Immigration in 1934 that three years' residence abroad for a naturalised Palestinian Jew was 'not enough [cause] to revoke Palestinian citizenship'. He referred to the case of a Jewish immigrant who was given a certificate of naturalisation in 1929 despite his apparent residence in Morocco since 1927. When the individual applied to renew his Palestinian passport in 1934, officials questioned whether he had lost his connection to Palestine due to his seven-year residence abroad. The individual in question gave evidence in favour of retaining citizenship. He claimed that he refused French citizenship in Morocco, owned immovable property in Palestine and that Palestine was his home country. The administration decided to renew his passport for three years on the condition that he returned to Palestine to reside permanently before it expired.[78] In addition, the commissioner for migration and statistics duly posted (often multiple) letters of warning to those Jewish citizens resident outside of Palestine for three or more years that offered them the chance to refute the accusation that they had lost their connection to Palestine and that they forfeited their citizenship and passports. In a number of cases, citizens' justifications of being too poor or ill to return to Palestine in due time to affirm their connection to that territory resulted in leniency by mandate officials and instructions to British consuls to renew the Palestinian passports of these citizens.[79]

The disinterest in (or lack of ability on the part of the administration in Jerusalem) the revocation of Palestine passports *in absentia* often received mention in the Arabic press. Articles and nationalist leaders again accused the immigration officials of biases that allowed for Jewish citizens who settled outside of Palestine for a number of years to retain Palestine passports. A closer understanding of the application of imperial policy sheds light on the Arabs' claims. In 1928 the press reported on a new article to the mandate's immigration law meant to punish, with three months' imprisonment and a fine of 100 lira, any immigrant who lied about his or her birth date or name in his or her passport. In response, an Arab journalist ironically questioned how the government intended to punish the immigrant 'who carries three passports in his pocket for at least three different nationalities'.[80] While emigrants and their supporters within Palestine accused policy-makers of attempting to increase the number of Jewish Palestinian citizens in possession of passports and, as a consequence, diplomatic protection, British actions again make some sense in light of imperial and diplomatic concerns. In 1927, Khalil Marcos, an emigrant and secretary of the Nablus Committee in support of the Palestinian Arab Congress, wrote to the high commissioner that 25,000 Palestinian natives lived in Latin America and were not considered citizens of Palestine. The number alone is significant – the number of Jewish Palestinian citizens who resided abroad was likely well under 1,000 and these citizens had passports. Throughout the entirety of the mandate's existence, the Foreign Office saw these Arab emigrants, most of whom did not have Palestinian passports, as a 'class' that was simply too large, too widespread and too unmanageable. The Foreign Office could not conceive of allowing this number of people to depend upon British diplomatic protection and call upon British consular resources. Furthermore, from the British Government's point of view, British officials were doing as they were obliged to do under the terms of the mandate and the Treaty of Lausanne – that was to treat these emigrants as if they had acquiring ipso facto Turkish nationality after 1926.[81] The fact that the latter process simply could not happen under international law did not impact British reasoning. The Jewish Palestinian émigrés, however, could be easily managed by British consuls in terms of their smaller numbers, residence in European and French North African urban locales, and the ability of consuls to keep tabs on where their passports were used.

At the crux of the governmental disagreements that continued even after the 1931 amended citizenship order was the idea that revocation of citizenship held by Jews reflected poorly on the government's efforts to facilitate a Jewish national home. Still, other colonial administrators believed that certain immigrants had the potential to subvert and behave in a disloyal manner to both the Palestine Administration and Great Britain. Not only were Jewish male immigrants suspect, but in the early 1930s the status of Jewish female immigrants became a contentious one in the light of international politics. For example, in opposition to the opinion by H. F. Downie, the head of the Middle East Department, High Commissioner Chancellor and the Colonial Office did not entirely support the empire-wide regulation that when a man's citizenship was revoked, his wife and children lost theirs as well.[82] One proposed, but unaccepted, amendment to the citizenship order concerned certain 'undesirable' women who sought a Palestinian passport and citizenship. This category included prostitutes, criminals and political offenders who married Palestinian citizens in order to obtain citizenship and British protection. In accordance with the citizenship order's Article 13, alien women who became Palestinian citizens by marriage would not cease to be Palestinians if they divorced their husbands. These women had legal citizenship, but the administration also targeted for deportation the Jewish women who resided illegally in Palestine without citizenship of their own. Colonial officials lobbied before 1931 for the insertion of an amendment in the citizenship order to the effect that an alien woman could not acquire citizenship as a consequence of marriage or if she was faced with a deportation order as an 'undesirable' or otherwise labeled as a 'bad character.'[83] The detailed and lengthy discussions of these particular cases in the archives are perhaps indicative of their frequency by the early 1930s.

The debate over how to grant Palestinian naturalisation was part of an Empire-wide debate over the status of married women and the retention of their original nationality. In 1932, the Home Office (with the support of the Foreign Office) stated that it had no objection in principle to preventing any Jewish immigrant from receiving Palestinian citizenship upon marriage, but noted international standards. Those standards specifically included the progressive 1930 Hague Convention principles that, although unsigned by Great Britain, maintained that all women retained their original nationality upon marriage. In that case, 'undesirable' women would not be stateless in the event of deportation.[84] In reality, few divorced women were classified as undesirable and they kept their Palestinian citizenship. Despite this, Palestine's high commissioner in 1931, Arthur Wauchope, argued that the practice to allow women suspected of coming to Palestine to enter into false marriages and thus acquire citizenship was inconsistent with British nationality laws. He summarised his opinion thus: divorced women stayed in Palestine 'free to continue their objectionable activities . . . with all the privileges of indefeasible Palestinian nationality'. At the same time, officials in Britain suggested that the British nationality law, particularly as it applied to the Dominions, be changed to allow for separate naturalisation of husband and wife. This change, supported in the metropole, would have been complicated and expensive to implement in Palestine, and it threatened to curtail the immigration of Jewish women.[85] Wauchope suggested that future legislation must give Jewish wives the opportunity of separate naturalisation from their husbands 'on very easy terms', to assure women that they could naturalise quickly and easily upon their arrival with their spouses to Palestine.[86]

This debate again emphasises that the Palestine Mandate occupied a unique position in the wider British Empire. Debates over the separate naturalisation for Jewish spouses underscore the distinct bureaucratic measures envisaged by Jerusalem and Whitehall with regards to citizenship where the Jewish community was involved. The implementation of measures upon the Arab community and especially Muslim women was not mentioned, perhaps for fear of not treading upon Islamic family law. In support of the proposal for separate naturalisation for Jewish women, one colonial official wrote that unless the high commissioner and Foreign Office saw 'strong *practical* objections to this (as opposed to objections based merely on principle and on the analogy of British practice), . . . the special circumstances arising in Palestine should prevail'.[87] The debate over separate naturalisation in Palestine extended to the Dominions Office of the British Government in whose interest it was to ensure that nationality legislation was as uniform as possible throughout the Empire.[88]

The Dominions Office, which had considerable influence over wider imperial policy even beyond the management of its territories, held the opposite opinion on female naturalisation. Its comments reflect how by 1933 Palestine came to be perceived in matters of nationality. To the Colonial Office, Assistant Secretary of the Dominions Office C. W. Dixon replied the following:

> It would be rather a pity if so fundamental a change from existing British practice was made in a territory under Mandate of His Majesty, as it might be quoted by some of the Dominions as an argument in favour of the view that the law of nationality as regards married women in relation to nationality of the Dominion concerned need not be the same as that in relation to British nationality. It is not likely that any Dominion would wish to copy Palestine . . . as the Dominions which attach most importance to the idea of separate Dominion nationality are those which are strongest on maintaining uniformity of nationality between husband and wife . . . Our answer would, I suppose, have to be that already suggested to FO, and HO, viz. *that Palestine citizenship is not 'nationality.'*

In suggesting that Palestinian citizenship was not like British nationality, Dixon maintained that nationality legislation in the Dominions would not necessarily effect how Palestinian individuals acquired citizenship, in opposition to the belief of the Palestine Administration. He added that if the matter of independent naturalisation for wives was one of 'first-class importance', the possible embarrassment in the Dominions over policy contradictions should not be sufficient grounds to refuse Wauchope's suggested proposal.[89] The Palestine Administration in

1933 consulted with Whitehall and asked the British Government to opt for separate naturalisation. Great Britain refused to consider the proposal not only since it diverted from Empire-wide policy, but also because the administration had not shown that the situation in Palestine necessitated that a departure from uniformity was justifiable. Defeated when the scheme of separate naturalisations was not implemented, the Colonial Office cautioned that conditions of immigration in Palestine 'rendered abuses of nationality laws more than ordinarily dangerous' in light of the political activities of certain male and female Jewish immigrants.[90]

In the early 1920s, Great Britain had argued that Palestinian citizenship was not a sovereign, internationally recognised nationality in accordance with British nationality law. Furthermore, the law officers of the Empire had previously stated that Palestine was not a foreign state. Since Article 7 of the mandate gave the Palestine Administration the responsibility to enact a nationality law, officials suggested in the early 1930s that it would be difficult 'to contend that the obligation imposed by that Article has not been discharged by the making of the Palestine Citizenship Order of 1925'. Still the Foreign Office argued that Palestinian citizenship was not the same as Palestinian nationality, and that it did 'not think it ought to be so . . . [Officials] do not regard Palestinian citizenship as "nationality." ' In other words, it was possible to claim that Palestinian nationality did not exist since the *Palestine Administration* had not yet enacted a nationality law. Nationality then did not exist in Palestine in a political or ethnic sense. Rather the *British Government* had passed a citizenship order-in-council and the citizenship it created simply conferred a non-political legal subjectivity, and the promise of a Palestine passport that granted imperial diplomatic and consular protection only for those citizens who travelled outside of the mandate's borders. Thus, the Palestine Administration could possibly be charged with *not* carrying out Article 7 of the mandate.[91] Since the administration itself did not pass a nationality law, citizenship could be imposed and manipulated from London and the Colonial Office, making the inhabitants of Palestine akin to colonial citizen-subjects.

Similar to the discussion of independent naturalisation of women, the British Government was reluctant to set precedents of legislation in Palestine even in light of the increased threat of political agitation in Europe and in other British territories. The British Government connected threats of political agitation with the Arab community as well, particularly after Colonial Secretary Passfield recognised the struggle of the Arabs to attain rights as a 'separate race' in Palestine.

Against the constant Jewish immigration, an estimated 30,000 Palestinian Arab emigrants and their children remained without citizenship by the mid-1930s, whether they wished for that status or not. The timing is important: discriminatory immigration quotas and naturalisation policies against Arabs in the United States meant that Palestinians there did not become new American citizens. In Latin American countries, xenophobic immigration policies restricted Arab settlement and access to employment, and stateless Palestinians found themselves threatened with deportation and being unable to take on a new nationality due to lack of identity documents.[92] The Passfield Letter linked the political inferiority and the lack of political rights of the Palestinian Arab citizenry with increased political agitation against British policy and the Zionist movement.[93] For example, Lord Islington, in a speech to Parliament in mid-1934, stated 'though fulfilling the duties of citizenship, [the Arabs] are totally without its rights'.[94] This situation, as he noted, explained the increased political agitation in Palestine and that agitation was a sentiment that administrations in Palestine and London soon echoed.

Conclusion

The policy to facilitate the Jewish national home in Palestine encouraged a kind of settler-colonialism through citizenship legislation and its application. Jewish immigrants who settled in Palestine received naturalisation quickly and alongside of this came British imperial protection in the form of citizenship and passports. The inclusive status of 'the citizen' and the privileges that came with it vis-à-vis British policy benefited immigrants who wished to help with the national home project. Arabs from outside Palestine, of course, did not have the option to take on Palestinian citizenship or settle. The British in Palestine and the Yishuv leadership saw the Jews as belonging to a distinct race that had not mattered for the Jewish community in Palestine prior to the mandate, argues Shira Robinson, while at the same time holding Palestinian citizenship.[95] Efforts by the Yishuv to promote exclusive Jewish land and labour ownership and employment posited the Jewish immigrants, or at least the mainly Ashkenazi immigrants, as more European and white than the 'native' Arabic-speaking population. This characterisation, and the entrepreneurial promise of progress (and the promise of independent *financial* means for this progress) in Palestine through Jewish immigration, also impacted the favourable perception by the British Government of Jewish immigration, settlement and, by extension, citizenship.

In many cases, the application of citizenship provisions and the naturalisation of Jewish immigrants conflicted with Empire-wide nationality laws, and the Palestine Administration and British Government shaped the regulations to fit in with mandate policy but also to ease tensions between departments and officials responsible for different aspects of administration. Favouritism for Jewish immigrants, as some administrators and Arab leaders claimed, was not the driving force behind the application of citizenship and naturalisation policies. At the same time, different approaches by administrators to procedure served to reinforce Britain's rule in Palestine: since standard policy and agreements on even the small details of citizenship legislation were usually hard to come by, complaints by the Arabs over contraventions of policy had little basis. Meanwhile the attempts to institutionalise citizenship reflected the differences between citizenship for Jewish immigrants and citizenship for former Ottoman subjects. The experiences of colonial officials who served elsewhere in British territories prior to their service in Palestine influenced certain nationality, naturalisation and immigration regulations that were implemented in the mandated territory. Indeed, the language used by colonial officials in reference to immigration and the population of Palestine reflected certain colonial ideologies and understandings. For example, Palestinian Arabs and Palestinian Jews were viewed as separate races in the colonial vocabulary of national identity. Jewish Palestinian citizens were treated as more akin to British subjects in matters of immigration and travel by virtue of the fact that since their naturalisation was recorded, they easily received documentary identity in the form of passports and thus could claim diplomatic protection as Palestinian citizens while abroad.

As the chapter demonstrates, the 1931 amended citizenship order came at a time of scrutiny of policy in Palestine by the British Government, but the order itself was not included in the larger scrutiny of policy by investigative commissions or the prime minister. Great Britain exercised power in the Palestine Mandate as if it was a colony and, as such, officials expected inhabitant-subjects to maintain a measure of loyalty to the laws as well as the political beliefs of Great Britain. Consequently, Whitehall ultimately approved or rejected nationality and citizenship proposals, and took into consideration the imperial and the European contexts during the decades after the end of the First World War. In addition, the nature of citizenship legislation as decentralised and constructed amidst competing

agendas and opinions clearly hindered smooth passage of amendments or changes to the legislation. The hindrance can be attributed
to the actions of different governmental departments, official and
unofficial advisers who all played a role in approving or challeng-
ing changes to mandate legislation. In sum, by 1931 the changes to
the order-in-council of 1925 did not grant greater civic, political or
social rights as requested by Arab nationalists – they simply affected
a legal realm. The following two chapters devote specific attention to
the changes in the Arabs' understanding and application of *political*
citizenship and rights during the 1930s. By the end of 1935 the ways
in which the Palestine Administration classified and treated the Arab
citizens began to be dependent upon how volatile the political relationship became between the administration and the majority Arab
population.

6

Whose Rights to Citizenship? Expressions and Variations of Palestinian Mandate Citizenship, 1926–1935

... and when the children ask why no shops are open or salesmen are in the streets, the mother will answer that the Palestinian Arabs are striking to show the amount of dissatisfaction with the government and the Zionist policy . . . [This strike] will be civilised dissent.

'*Iḍrāb ghadān!*' [Strike Tomorrow!],
Mir'at al-Sharq (22 August 1931)

In August 1931 a number of Palestinian Arab populist groups convened a congress in the city of Nablus that subsequently called a general strike throughout the territory to oppose British policy that allowed Jewish settlements to be armed.[1] The main nationalist body in Palestine, the Arab Executive Committee, ultimately issued the official call to strike on 23 August 1931 but the strike and demonstrations would not have attracted the attention that they did without the growth of Palestinian civil society and its general emphasis on a number of demands for political, civil and national rights of the Arab population. Populist leaders, grassroots forums and civic associations converged to play a major role in the political community of Palestine by this time. In the decade after the order-in-council, new ideas of citizenship and what it entailed as a political status emerged out of the context of both civil society and popular politics. At the centre of these new ideas, expressions and vocabularies of Palestinian Arab citizenship was the Arabic press. The growth and popularity of the press allowed it to communicate legal developments and link these developments to the changing notions and the political mobilisation of Palestinian Arab citizenship.[2] In other words, by the early 1930s, the Arab press succeeded in disseminating a new language, vocabulary and ideology of citizenship rights and duties in the political, legal and social spheres in an increasingly easily understood fashion to a larger portion of the Arab population.

After the visit of Lord Balfour to Palestine in 1925, newspapers referred to the rights, duties and practices of Arab citizens with more frequency. However, it was the administration's plan to hold municipal elections in 1926 that galvanised the press to delving into the links between legislation and the changing nature of the political and civil rights, as opposed to the strictly legalistic aspects, of citizenship. Concepts such as rights, justice and legitimacy – heavily used in the press and written statements – were understood in large part through historical experiences of the rule of law in Palestine from the Ottoman Administration. Editors and writers constantly appealed for the reinstatement of a representative parliament, of laws delineating the rights of all citizens vis-à-vis the government, and of a written constitution.[3] They, and others, began to more frequently demand active expressions of discontent through boycotts, strikes, petitions and other non-cooperation measures. By 1926, newspapers took on the task of informing their readers of the citizenship order's provisions and, in particular, general mandate legislation that they argued favoured Jewish immigrants. Periodicals did not always report in precise detail the large amount of legislation issued in Palestine[4] but writers pointedly focused on regulations that privileged the Yishuv. In doing so, a particular journalistic tone became commonplace: legislation that negatively affected the livelihoods and political aspirations of the Arabs was conceived of as a negation of the rights associated with citizenship.

The following historical analysis frames certain vocabularies, expressions and active behaviours of citizenship and national identity in the decade before the 1936 Palestine Revolt as more dominant and others as more subaltern. Importantly, it traces how citizenship became political and rights-based for the Palestinian Arab leadership, despite the insistence by mandate officials that it be legal and apolitical. Citizenship has been described in more theoretical studies as a set of practices and as a bundle of civil, political and social rights and duties that define an individual's membership in his or her polity, and many of these rights come from practices of citizenship that are put into law.[5] From the late 1920s through the mid-1930s, different Arabic-speaking social, political and civic groups in Palestine began to articulate a demand for this bundle of rights that went with membership in what they conceived as the nation-state polity of Palestine and, specifically, for rights *to* this 'state' rather than religious and civil rights within the mandate, as guaranteed by the Balfour Declaration. Certain dominant and certain subaltern groups perceived entitlement to this bundle of rights in different ways. One group that highlighted the argument that rights should be given to all Palestinian natives was the populist Palestinian Arab Istiqlal (Independence) Party. The Istiqlal Party played a prominent, albeit brief, role in the process through which the young middle-class Arab leadership integrated the rhetorical nationalistic language of rights and duties into a repertoire of public and civic action. Their language emphasised the role of the subaltern citizens, such as the Arab workers, students and peasants, in laying claim to rights of political representation, employment and welfare.[6] The rhetorical language and vocabulary used by this cross-section of society further explains a number of distinctions between the British and Arab notions of Palestinian citizenship after 1925.

The middle-class nationalist leadership was guided by pan-Arab and anti-colonial ideologies and attitudes, and many members of this community were urban-based. Some of these remained part of the Arab Executive as they shaped a new framework of populist (sha'bī) politics that idealised all Palestinian Arabs as rights-bearing citizens, including previously non-political groups, under the banner of 'the nation'. The chapter begins with an analysis of the increasingly vocal demands for citizenship rights after the issue of the 1925 Citizenship Order-in-Council and prompted by legislation in the realms of municipal election laws and land and cultivators ordinances. British officials had no intention to offer political rights to the Palestinian Arab citizens; rather, legislation reinforced the apolitical nature of citizenship. The Arabs' reaction to this legislation influenced the changing language and expression of citizenship in the context of popular politics. The Istiqlal Party, which popularised Palestinian citizenship as an inseparable political component of national identity, helped to spur this new approach.

The more inclusive redefinitions of Palestinian citizenship and civil and political rights after 1925 allowed for certain citizens to both have a greater stake in the nationalists' political projects to shape belonging to the nation and to become empowered by identity politics. The empowerment of civic identity politics happens, according to Margaret Somers, when individuals feel that a sense of who they are has been violated, especially in terms of their perceived natural rights. In order to assert claims to political and civil rights the 'politics of citizenship discourse' is mobilised to justify rights through membership in a historically constructed national community. Citizenship rights take on significance as they become a practice rather than simply a noun.[7] In Palestine, the realm of popular politics and its emphasis on Palestinian Arab and pan-Arab identities provided the space in which the Arab community could assert its active opposition to the mandate and Zionism as a key part of citizenship's rights and duties. The legislation – or lack of certain legislation – from the late 1920s increasingly affected working-class and rural Arabs more so than it affected the Jewish community. The Jewish population of Palestine was, in large part, segregated from the Arab community as the Yishuv became more like a state-within-a-state, providing schools, employment and other economic opportunities to the Jewish immigrants. The impact of this policy was most clearly understood by the Arabs in the form of the growing Jewish settlements and the legislation that stimulated Jewish immigration.

The Arabic Press and Mandate Legislation

The 1925 Palestine Citizenship Order-in-Council initially had little impact on the Arabs who resided in mandate territory. This is understandable since their residence guaranteed ipso facto citizenship. Citizenship took on significance as a status once national leaders and newspapers publicised reports on the situation of the thousands of Palestinians in the diaspora who were unable to claim that status. In light of the reported plight of the Arab emigrants (*muhājarīn*) and the statistics on Jewish immigration to Palestine national and local leaders began to draw attention to legislation that negatively impacted all individuals that they termed as Palestinian Arab nationals. These leaders defined Palestinian citizenship first as a status granted by natural right through birth in the territory or descent from Palestinian parents. To this end, by 1927 associations, conferences and Arab Executive members presented a number of demands to the Palestine Administration and the British Government for the recognition of *jus sanguinis* and *jus soli* in citizenship legislation as well as explicit political rights for Arab citizens.

The indigenous press fostered the linkages of global civil society and what Emma Hunter calls the 'globalization of political concepts' that captured the attention of colonised peoples between Latin America, the Middle East, Africa and the Soviet Union by the early 1930s.[8] In Palestine, Arabic periodicals reported the publication of the citizenship order in the autumnn of 1925, but many newspapers focused on other events, particularly the uprising in

Syria's Jabal Druze against the French during 1925 and 1926. News about the anti-colonial revolt in Syria, growing factionalism in the Arab Executive Committee and the conflict between the faction headed by Mufti Hajj Amin al-Husayni (the *Majlisiyun*) and that of the leaders of the opposition in Jerusalem (the *Mu'āridun*) monopolised the news.

Yet after 1926, the rhetorical vocabulary of rights became manifest alongside that of nationality and citizenship. Rachel Sieder's work on Guatemala in the 1930s provides an interesting comparison with the ways that citizenship rights were perceived by non-dominant political groups. Sieder has shown in the context of interwar Latin America that governments tried to create a certain type of subject or citizen through legislation. These same laws that gave or removed political rights provided a medium through which the would-be subjects or citizens resisted or accommodated to their conditions of subordination.[9] As in the Guatemalan case, the Arab leadership frequently challenged the legalities of mandate policies and civil society leaders actively encouraged claims to political and civil rights of citizenship by the Palestinians *as citizens* and as part of a historical trajectory based on their prior experience as Ottoman nationals. The figure of the pre-war Ottoman Arab (and, of course, male) national, embodied with a number of political and civil rights, was used by writers as a rallying point to mobilise individuals to demand that the administration offer similar rights associated with citizenship. In Palestine as elsewhere, the development of citizenship depended on interactions between different understandings of 'rights', 'obligations', and 'justice' that were, in the words of Sieder, constituted by different individuals and groups within particular frameworks.[10] In the case of the Levant generally and Palestine specifically, that framework was of a communitarian understanding of national identity and belonging.

The first citizenship right in the mandate granted to both Jewish and Arab Palestinians, the franchise, came into effect with the Citizenship Order-in-Council. Prior to that, the 1922 Legislative Election Order-in-Council gave the franchise to all residents of Palestine provided they were former Ottoman subjects or Jewish immigrants who pledged to take on citizenship once legislation was passed to that effect. Although citizenship became a requirement for the franchise and to stand for office, by 1926 the mandate administration failed to implement High Commissioner Samuel's proposals for the devolution of local and municipal government functions to the citizens themselves. Therefore, this right to vote did not translate into the Arabs' requested rights *to* the territory of the mandate through self-government. Samuel's successor, Herbert Plumer, stated that the Arabs specifically had too little sense of civic responsibility to even have the right to vote.[11] Even so, in 1926, his administration supported the formation of municipal and local councils (that existed in the Ottoman Empire) to regulate communal affairs as a step toward self-government.[12] The 1926 Municipal Franchise Ordinance ensured proportional representation on municipal councils in accordance with the number of votes from each religious community.[13] Palestinians could vote only for other members of their own religious community. Thus, no sense of a unified civic citizenship factored into the municipal elections because of the separation of citizens into religious groupings.

The Arabic newspapers immediately took issue with the municipal property tax qualification required of all voters for the municipal council elections. Only individuals who paid a fee on immovable property, or paid a standard fee if they did not own immoveable property, in the twelve months prior to the elections could vote. Voters also had to be occupants of recognised premises worth a certain amount of money within the municipal area. Candidates for council positions had to have paid a specific sum (100 piasters) in taxes.[14] The ordinance, according to one Arab journalist in late 1926, was 'contrary to the spirit of true democracy' since its most striking feature was that it did not enable what he referred to as 'all classes of people' the right to vote. Specifically, he argued that certain classes of Arabs were treated 'as if they are enemies and not natives of this country' since the poorer urban Arabs – and their Jewish counterparts – did not meet the financial qualifications for enfranchisement. The author noted that if the reader could imagine the extreme poverty of the people of Palestine, he would know that the majority of the population's rights had been taken away by the qualifications for the franchise. The British constructed the law with their vision of Palestine as divided into religious groups in mind, and the author addressed this as 'the irony in this law . . . which indicates [the government's] consistent policy in this country [to] invest it as three communities for the benefit of colonialism'. He wryly added that the law came about after the Palestinian people asked the government to 'civilise' the nation, and he asked why the British did not put proper civil laws in place in Palestine as they did in Great Britain and elsewhere in the Empire.[15]

The press viewed the elections as an example of the mandate's discriminatory attitude towards the urban lower-class whose members were unable to participate in local politics or hold positions of leadership. The discussion over the municipal elections continued through 1927. The Arab writers and local leaders depicted the right to vote as inalienable and meant to be held by (male) Palestinians by virtue of their nationality.[16] The mandatory's attitude, according to the press, served to negate what nationalists argued to be the most important right of Palestinian citizens: the right to representation. Furthermore, although Clause 3 of the Municipal Franchise Ordinance explicitly stated that electors had to be Palestinian citizens, Attorney-General Bentwich advised the mandate administration that those Jewish immigrants awaiting the outcome of their applications for naturalisation had no reason to be refused and were eligible to vote.[17] This further angered Arab leaders.

For the municipal elections held in 1933, the election ordinance defined a Palestinian citizen for the purpose of the legal franchise as any person who had applied for citizenship before 1 September 1933 as long as their application was not refused. Applicants for citizenship did not need to have been granted that status in order to vote; in fact, Jewish applicants could very well have been denied citizenship after they cast their vote, or could withdraw their applications for naturalisation after voting. The following year, the Permanent Mandates Commission asked the Palestine Administration whether a large proportion of those who voted in 1933 'in virtue of an application' for Palestinian citizenship subsequently failed to secure the citizenship. Chief Secretary Moody responded that as of 1 September 1933, 1,500 applications for citizenship awaited decision and the applicants with a receipt of the fee paid for submitting their application were entitled to exercise the right to vote. Of this number, Moody informed the commission that 20 per cent failed to obtain citizenship. In Haifa, the District Commissioner found that only two out of seventy Jewish voters were actually qualified to vote because only these two individuals had applied for citizenship.[18] These are not insignificant numbers considering that one-fifth of the non-citizens who voted in the 1933 elections were never granted citizenship. Thus, they contributed to increasing the proportional representation of their own religious community on municipal councils in a country that was not yet their legal residence. In the Arabic press, editorials argued that the denial of rights to a large number of poor citizens served only to bolster the political standing of Jewish immigrants (who were generally but not always in better economic positions) within Palestine's municipalities. These criticisms, published and read throughout the country, had some justification as shown by the figures given by Moody to the Permanent Mandates Commission.

Newspapers reacted to legislative changes in land, public works and development with the argument that the Arabs' civil rights were eroded in order to give way to greater rights for Jewish citizens. For example, although Arab merchants, labourers and corporations had few explicit rights, Jewish residents and their companies – whether nationals of Palestine or not – received concessions for public works and development projects. The mandate charter guaranteed this preference, stating as it did that Jewish-run businesses could be offered the rights to construct or operate any public works, services or utilities.[19] The registered 'nationality' of the business or corporation was irrelevant to its right to hold a monopoly in Palestine. Editorials and articles focused on the conditions that this allowance by the administration created for Palestine's Arab citizens. One newspaper article stated in 1928 that the 'citizens of the villages' were neglected because the government and the Jewish companies that operated public works did not take their requests (such as to pave the roads) seriously. That same year, a number of nationalist organisations asked that Arab employees of the Department of Works go on strike in order to force the government to address the most important of their civil rights: the improvement of the economic situation in Arab villages.[20]

Editorials argued frequently that the administration's support for Jewish-run companies limited Arab business ventures and thus rights to a stake in ownership of the economy. Similarly by the latter half of the 1920s the Arabic press, alongside local nationalist leaders like 'Isa Bandak, discussed other pieces of mandate legislation related to citizenship, elections and taxation. Bandak's *Sawt al-Sha'b* invoked the phrase 'no taxation without representation' (*la dara'ib bilā tamthīl*). The first editorial to use the phrase alluded to the notion that until citizens were granted certain rights to the polity, they should not pay taxes to the government – a simple and effectively communicated slogan.[21] Other arguments against the mandate legislation that centred on the negation of Arab citizenship rights extended to the spheres of employment and welfare. Urban workers' associations, often influenced by young anti-mandate activists, referred to the government's duty to ensure equality in employment, wages and benefits pay as well as safe working conditions for all citizens.[22] Civil rights of citizenship also came to be associated with employment especially as the national leadership questioned the lack of government job opportunities for educated Muslim Palestinians. In 1928, a delegation of young men from Jaffa argued that only Palestinian citizens should be entitled to serve in the administration, although it did not go as far as to demand complete control by citizens over all matters of government.[23] This public dialogue and the arguments that arose from it were influenced by the belief that the Arab citizenry deserved a privileged position in Palestine by virtue of their citizenship, their numerical superiority and their Arab nationality. At the pinnacle of these arguments, citizenship was portrayed as an active status that the administration manipulated in order to deny Arab individuals the right to participate in government, the economy and legislation.

Populist civic and national groups portrayed the government legislation that impacted the Arab *fellahin* (peasants) as one of the biggest affronts to Palestinian Arab rights of citizenship. This particular portrayal allowed national and local groups to construe (perhaps largely unknown to the peasants themselves) a notion of civic and political belonging and project it on to this class within Palestinian society. One year after the announcement of the 1925 citizenship order, a news editorial explained the duties of the government toward the peasant citizens of Palestine: the most important was to provide assistance to the *fellah* through favourable land legislation. Despite the deteriorating economic situation of the mid-1920s, the system of taxes and tithes imposed on peasants was so high that the money taken was equivalent to at least a third of the Palestine's yearly budget. On top of their constant debt to money-lenders who charged exorbitant interest rates, peasants were expected to contribute tithes (*werko*) in cash to the government, which alone made up about 32per cent of a family's income by 1930.[24] Newspapers, and in particular the Gaza district's weekly *al-Ittihad al-'Arabī*, gave a great deal of space to the peasants' situation. Although urban Palestinian Arab citizens faced different challenges due to legislation, the activities of a number of writers, students and lawyers effectively challenged land legislation and brought the situation of the peasant to the fore of press reports.

Palestinian Arab populist leaders had long accused the British administration of ratifying land legislation that harmed the peasants' livelihoods and these leaders inserted the vocabulary of rights into their accusations by 1930. Indeed throughout the mandate's existence, rural owner-occupiers, agricultural tenants and labourers were never entitled to legal protection through tenancy rights. For example, when absentee Arab owners sold land to Jewish settlers the tenants often had no choice but to leave the land they farmed. In Ottoman times, tenants farmed land in common and were forced to leave far less frequently when that land changed hands.[25] Further-more, the government did not recognise the Arab village, village land funds or rural development associations as legal entities able to pos-sess immovable property. Zionist companies and the Jewish Agency, on the other hand, could register land in their name, since they were treated legally as if they were individual citizens of Palestine. Accord-ing to the memoirs of the Palestinian land lawyer Hanna Nakkarah, the 1928 Land Settlement Ordinance required the registration of title deeds in order to record taxes, fees and development, and to partition common land. Unclaimed land was held in trust by the high commis-sioner. The problematic issue was that in every Arab village common land was used for public purposes and perceived as being for the ben-efit of all residents.[26]

Arab peasant associations borrowed this language of rights that the more radical, young political leaders and the press employed in order to express their displeasure with mandate legislation. For exam-ple, in 1928 and 1929 agricultural groups in Gaza presented protest letters to High Commissioner John Chancellor in opposition to the Land Settlement Ordinance. The peasant spokesmen, like the press, invoked the idealised notion that Ottoman nationals had previously held the civil right of land ownership. The Muslim Youth Association in Khan Younis stated that the ordinance '[took] away the people's rights of natural ownership of land'.[27] Another appeal written by the Society to Conserve the Land of Gaza alleged that the goal of the Land Settlement Ordinance was to 'remove all that is Arab and erase all traces of the Arab in Palestine'.[28] Influenced by other national bod-ies in Palestine, peasant associations adopted and re-shaped the rhe-torical language that framed access to land as an inalienable right. As a result of increased communication among urban and rural commu-nities by the end of the 1920s larger segments of Palestinian society tailored their reactions to legislation and their specific, often localised demands into a style of language that emphasised the rights-based notion of their civic and political membership in the polity of Pal-estine. The activities of populist leaders and writers publicised legal developments and opened up a space for both the educated and the subaltern to be represented as rights-bearing citizens of Palestine.

Variations and Representations of Mandate Citizens

Awni Abd al-Hadi, a veteran pan-Arab nationalist and Palestinian politician from Nablus, addressed the government's failures to imple-ment beneficial legislation for all Arab inhabitants of the mandate and stated in 1931 that in the Palestinian case, 'it will be the duty of every one of [the] citizens to call upon [the administration] to live up to its duties'.[29] If political rhetoric represented 'every one' of the Palestinian Arabs as monolithic citizens, variations of types of mandate citizens – and who classified certain individuals as citizens – existed in practice. Recent research by Weldon C. Matthews stresses the need to study concepts of identity as contingent on specific circumstances in order to analyse how the different Palestinians defined themselves as part of a nation after a decade of mandate administration.[30] The current section analyses the ways in which the new generation of nationalist political leaders engaged with the representation of the citizen and particularly the subaltern citizen, and the types of rights assumed by these leaders to be entitled to different social groups by virtue of their national identity. Certain groups in Palestine – workers, peasants, women and students – came to be represented as citizens both through their own efforts and through the support of the popular politics movement.

In his study of the ideological and practical processes by which French peasants became full-fledged members of the citizenry after the French Revolution, Eugene Weber notes that national and civic consciousness arises once rural inhabitants become aware of national, as opposed to only local, issues.[31] One way to do this in rural Palestine, according to the Arab leaders, was to appeal to citizens to establish village national schools.[32] By their account, an educated peasant was a peasant who could speak for himself, demand rights as a citizen including the right to vote, own land and access government services. In reference to India, Dipesh Chakrabarty writes that '[t]he peasant did not have to undergo a historical mutation into the industrial worker in order to become the citizen-subject of the nation'.[33] The same is true for Palestine: peasants, as well as other members of the working classes, became *represented* by others as citizens often under the umbrella of the ever-widening populist, middle-class national movement. The ideology of a multiplicity of Arab citizens, with a number of social and political roles, came in large part out of the type of civic education offered by national schools and their teachers who were affiliated with nationalist associations. Civic education placed emphasis on a historical Arab nationality in Palestine and the symbiotic relationship of rights and duties between nationals and their nation. Such an education not only played a role in imparting the concept of civil rights and civic duties to students but by 1928 it also stimulated the formation of Palestinian branches of the Young Men's Muslim Association, or YMMA (*jam'iyyat al-shabān al-muslimīn*), and the Arab Scouts in rural areas as well as in towns. The former association published its own newspaper, *Sawt al-Haqq* (The Voice of Truth), and its outspoken young editor, school-teacher Hamdi al-Husayni, introduced the concerns of Arab urban workers and the importance of civic activities into the platform of the YMMA. For instance, the more rural Gaza branch set up night courses to teach workers how to read.[34] Students' clubs and numerous civic-minded urban associations (that boasted heavy student involvement) formed throughout the late 1920s and worked to organise unions of Arab workers, discussed political issues in public forums, and raised funds to buy agricultural land in trust for Arab peasants.[35]

At the same time a former law student and schoolteacher from Nablus named Akram Zu'aytir began to advocate that the youth lead popular protests and actions of civil disobedience (*al-'asīyan al-madaniyya*). His inspiration came from the actions of Gandhi in India. In 1929, Zu'aytir suggested that the Palestinian Arabs implement a programme of non-cooperation that included the refusal to pay taxes and the resignation of civil servants. Since he wrote for the newspaper *Mir'at al-Sharq*, this and other periodicals promoted the programme.[36] Indeed many of the younger Arab nationalist clan worked as journalists and editors and most were educated, having completed at least secondary school. Full-fledged youth associations in this period were not all political in nature but their structure meant that they promoted civic ideals and a civic identity for their members. As an example, the Youth Club of Bethlehem, established in 1928, claimed that its task was to spread the spirit of patriotism as well as to work for Arab unity. Members also sought to carry out practical work: the club gave attention to women's affairs and especially women's literacy, established a night school and a public library and gave charity aid to the poor.[37] Youth associations used publications, public lectures and teachers to inform the population of their aims. At the January 1932 Youth Conference in Jaffa, delegates debated certain duties to be undertaken by the citizens of Palestine. The conference passed a number of resolutions and formed several civic committees composed of and administered by a variety of Arab citizens, including students, writers and lawyers. The committees, such as that for civic education, called upon the mandate government to establish national schools and include curriculums in agricultural education as part of their duty to the Arab citizens.[38] The emphasis by youth associations and their conference resolutions on civic identity and rights for both the rural peasants and the urban workers meant that the two groups were represented as part of the Palestinian citizenry. The students and middle-class national leaders sought to demonstrate that all classes could claim rights and pressure the administration to give up its obligations to the mandate charter. Prominent was the issue of the protection of the land holdings of the Arab peasants in the face of increased Jewish immigration by the early 1930s. In times of crisis due to the increased debt and poverty of the peasants and the threat posed by the Histadrut, the exclusively Jewish labour union, to the Arab proletariat legitimised specific social demands through participation in civil society and national demonstrations, as Joel Beinin has shown.[39]

However, prior to 1936 the demands for civil and political rights and the representation of subaltern citizenship originated from urban, educated, radical nationalists. Peasants were depicted in newspapers, congress resolutions and handwritten petitions to the government as active participants in politics and anti-mandate activities. Migdal also notes that interdependence between peasants and other classes created a national identity consciousness in the 1930s.[40] Public conferences and their resolutions on behalf of the peasants shaped the perception of the peasant as an equal citizen by the virtue of his native birth in Palestine and his service to the nation. A May 1928 newspaper editorial posed the serious question of whether the peasants knew their rights and their duty to demand them.[41] Charters drawn up by landowning farmers who belonged to rural associations expressed the aims to improve the standard of living for the *fellahin* and to help protect their land rights. Indeed, every adult *fellah* had the 'right' to join most societies and elect their administrative bodies. In the early 1930s, village societies increased in number and in activity. For example, the principles of Acre's Village Cooperative Society stated that its members oppose everything that 'intrud[ed] on [the farmer's] national and political rights'.[42] Not only did the number of letters and petitions to the administration by peasant associations increase through the 1930s, but the administrative surveillance of rural associations that were deemed too political also increased.

Arab urban workers were a significant bloc that drove the expansion of populist political activities by the latter half of the 1920s. The growing workers' movement contested the meaning of citizenship offered by the mandate and, in particular, the failure of citizenship legislation to extend certain social and civil benefits to the Arab working class. To counter the administration's definition of citizenship, leaders of urban unions commonly expressed the belief that the mandatory had a duty to provide Arab workers with rights (of unionisation and shorter work hours) and welfare (housing and health care) equal to that offered to Jewish labourers by the Histadrut. Arab railway workers in Palestine first organised themselves with their Jewish co-workers in Haifa in 1921 but it took several years for a workers' movement to emerge.[43] Once it did come into being, the movement was one of the few in Mandate Palestine that bridged the divide between Arab and Jewish citizens.[44]

At its most basic level, the socialist, anti-colonial principles of the union leadership attracted Arab workers particularly in the impoverished, crowded port cities of Haifa and Jaffa. The membership rolls of Arab workers' societies included farmers, labourers, clerks, masons, drivers and others. Significantly, the spoken and printed rhetoric of the labour leaders – reproduced in the press and at national conferences – employed the same vocabulary as the populist national leadership. The language used depicted the urban, low-income Arab worker as deserving the same treatment as the Jewish worker by virtue of his Arab nationality. The Palestine Arab Workers Society (PAWS) enhanced this image as it aimed to attain benefits for all workers, to promote educational, social and economic improvements, to enact a law to limit work hours and fix salaries, and to provide housing and access to health services.[45]

Palestinian Arab middle-class women differed little from their male counterparts in the national movement with regard to their collective platform and identity. While the politically active women were usually from elite, educated backgrounds, their activities nonetheless contributed to the representation of all Arab women as citizens of Palestine despite legislation that denied them the right to vote. At once subaltern and elite, these women claimed to speak on behalf of the entirety of Palestinian Arab citizenry. The activities of Arab women during the mandate administration have been narrated elsewhere, but these studies lack specific analysis of conceptualisation of Palestinian citizenship.[46] Arab women organised themselves and created their own civil society networks in Palestine and in the *mahjar* just as they did in other Arab mandates and countries. Female newspaper columnists called upon women to educate themselves, to demand their rights to a civic, national education and to fulfil their national 'duties' to the country.[47] As historian Ellen Fleischmann explains, notions of rights were never fully defined but female writers in Palestine, as in other Arab countries, referred to liberal citizenship rights such as participation in the public and political sphere.[48]

The proceedings of women's conferences offer a better explanation of the rights that Palestinian women discussed among themselves, agitated for and hoped to receive. These public gatherings offer a glimpse of the ways in which these women expressed themselves as Palestinian citizens. The first Palestine Arab Women's Congress took place in 1929 organised by a network of societies such as charities, educational associations and the Arab Women's Association (AWA). Attended by more than 200 Palestinian women, the congress' decisions were liberal and supportive of women's efforts to participate in civil society.[49] Petitions and statements by the executive body of the congress mimicked the wording and tone and suggested the same tactics as the male-dominated national associations and conferences. Petitions issued by the Executive of the Women's Congress in 1932 explicitly discussed the issue of citizenship rights. The Executive referred to the unfair administrative practice that allowed non-Palestinian civil servants such as Greeks, Persians, Italians, Egyptians and Syrians to acquire Palestinian citizenship despite retaining the nationality of their native countries. These men, the women argued, could easily be replaced 'by bona-fide Palestinian citizens'. As for civic education, the women emphasised the 'vital importance to the Arabs' to support improvements of the 'intellectual, moral and social standing of future citizens of the country'. The Executive noted that citizens, especially the peasants, had been deprived of constitutional rights and protections despite their standing. In closing their charter of congress resolutions, the signatories (President Wahide El-Khalili and Secretary Matiel Mogannam) demanded the establishment of a democratically elected national government.[50] The politicisation by the press and the nationalist leadership through their forums and conferences of the often poor or disadvantaged situation of unrepresented peasants, young people, workers and women meant that the identity of these groups became politicised as well. As a result, these different groups represented themselves and one another as rights-bearing citizens of Palestine, whose Arab identity translated into their entitlement to rights to the self-government of the territory.

The growing popularity of this representation of 'the citizen' in Palestine came perhaps in part from its similarity to citizens in Western European and American political systems. This concept of citizenship received support not only in the press but through the networks forged between subaltern citizens and the institutions that represented them and whose leaders familiarised themselves with styles of civic belonging common in imperial metropoles. These discourses of rights and the sets of practices of political membership fashioned 'the new man . . . [as] transformed into the citizen of the new state'.[51] It is more difficult to argue that the lower-class or non-affiliated individuals in Palestinian society broadly advocated for citizenship rights with a pure understanding of what those rights entailed in the wider British empire or in sovereign nation-states but this is not the point for the discussion here. Rather, it is that multiple meanings of citizenship were often imposed upon different socio-economic and political classes in Mandate Palestine by the populist national leadership as a means to achieving an end: that of full, sovereign rights to both citizenship and national representation to participate in government and legislative processes.

Transitioning into the Second Decade of the Mandate: The Istiqlal Party

In order to understand the parameters of the internal Arab political situation in Palestine by the end of the 1920s it is necessary to note events of 1923. That year, the Sixth Palestinian Arab Congress made a demand for complete independence of Palestine – for the last time. In fact, the Arab Executive Committee felt it unnecessary to hold any further national congresses after the sixth meeting until early 1928. The seventh (and last) congress offered even less of a challenge to British policy than the previous six congresses had done.[52] In the period between the sixth and seventh congresses, the populist movement had grown strong enough to take part in changing the political language of citizenship and its associated social, political and civil rights. The continued changes to political language can be attributed to the political and social situation in Palestine in the aftermath of the August 1929 Wailing Wall riots.[53] The 1930 execution of three young Arab men charged for their role in the riots served as the particularly salient event for the national movement and the men immediately became martyrs.[54] The emerging populist movement characterised the three martyrs as patriotic citizens who defended the Arabs' political and civil rights.[55] As a result of the events from 1929 through early 1931, pan-Arab activists including 'Awni Abd al-Hadi appealed to the British to grant the 'religious and civil rights [that were] closely interrelated' with self-governing institutions. His views, and those of the more radical movement, articulated a post-1929 conceptualisation of distinct views on citizenship rights and duties.[56] In response, political, youth and social groups asked that the Arab Executive convene to discuss policies of non-cooperation with the Palestine Administration and a boycott. The fragmented political factions split over the tactics. As a consequence, the more radical nationalist groups assumed the task of carrying out measures of non-cooperation as an explicit duty of citizenship.[57]

From the beginning of the British administration of Palestine, the first writings by nationalist leaders and those in the press rarely included the term 'citizen' (*muwātin*) but rather used the Arabic term '*ahl Filastīn*' (Palestinian people) and 'natives of Palestine' (*abna' Filastīn*). Throughout the 1920s, the differences in the ever-evolving political language of nationality, nationalism and, later, citizenship were subtle. These early terms expressed a sense of secular communitarian belonging, similar to the way in which '*umma*' translated into 'community' in the era of nationalism. As noted previously, *muwātin* came into use in Arabic newspapers and documents printed by nationalist associations in Palestine alongside legislation that marked members of the Arab national community as having a legal status vis-à-vis the administration. However, the use of *jinsiyya* (nationality) continued to be dominant in reference to citizenship legislation. Yet the political language of citizenship changed in about 1930. As early as the 1931 strike and demonstrations in Nablus, the populist Arab leaders asserted their citizenship by informing officials that public demonstrations were active civil rights. Press editorials concluded that the inhabitants of Palestine knew their rights and their duties as citizens even if the government did not allow their exercise.[58] On the eve of riots in Jerusalem in October 1933, an article in the city's *al-Jamiyya al-'Arabiyya* stressed that the British did not consider the Palestinians as Arab nationals and urged the Arabs to assert their citizenship rights in Palestine through protest'.[59] The influence of the Istiqlal Party, ideologically linked to earlier pan-Arab national movements, can be seen in an analysis of the changing discussions of citizenship after 1930.

The Istiqlal Party, officially formed in 1931 as the first non-factional Palestinian political party, has been the subject of only two monographs.[60] The party was active for three years but its membership, principles and formation were crucial to the creation of a grassroots civic movement and to the evolution of a new meaning of pan-Arab citizenship. The party, based in Nablus, advocated Palestinian Arab citizenship as inseparable from an inclusive, wider notion of Arab nationality. Weldon Matthews refers to the party as a watershed: at once Palestinian, pan-Syrian and pan-Arab and the first of its kind to attempt to form a public, mass organisation whose adherents used different approaches to mobilise nationalist and civic sentiments.[61] Its founding members announced the party's charter at the same time as the sessions of the Islamic Congress convened in Jerusalem in December 1931. Drawn up in the home of Arab Executive member 'Awni Abd al-Hadi, the pact stated the anti-colonial demand for independence and called for a democratic government in Palestine as part of a pan-Arab federation. The idea of the federation necessitated that the Arabs of the former Ottoman provinces of Greater Syria be granted a federated citizenship based upon their Arab nationality.[62] The party included prominent members, young and veteran pan-Arab activists as well as writers, teachers, lawyers and other intellectuals from the upper and middle socio-economic classes such as Mohammad 'Izza Darwaza, Akram Zu'aytir, Hamdi al-Husayni, Ibrahim Shanti, 'Isa Bandak and Sheikh 'Izz al-Din al-Qassam.[63]

The Istiqlal Party, unlike the Executive, addressed its appeals to 'the citizens'. In 1933, the party's conference in Jaffa highlighted the vision of its executive committee for a full-scale boycott of the Palestine Administration. Istiqlalists characterised the boycott as a way through which citizens could demand rights, and the party encouraged the act of boycott as a duty of citizenship. By advocating actions such as boycotts, the party's populist leaders created a version of civil society in which all Arabs were represented as active citizens. To this end, members organised a range of political activities, public festivals and holidays, issued political statements through local leaders and connected with other groups that supported the peasants, workers and students.[64] Seven festivals, holidays and major conferences took place in the early 1930s under the party's auspices and included the celebration of Hittin Day in Haifa, memorial days for martyrs and commemorations of the British occupation of Palestine.[65]

One of the party's most prominent members, Sobhi al-Khudara, explained that national public opinion could be harnessed through the patronage of educated and non-educated Arab citizens using the language of rights and democracy.[66] In the early 1930s the party organised actions including strikes and boycotts of British goods, particularly in the city of Nablus. In late 1932 the party encouraged a general boycott of all British administrative functions and events. According to a statement issued by the party to High Commissioner Wauchope, these acts re-affirmed the civil rights of Arab citizens of Palestine. Similar to demands from other sectors of the citizenry, the Istiqlal Party argued that the citizens deserved equal employment opportunities as those of Jewish and British inhabitants, access to education and an independent parliament.[67] One of the most debated components of active citizenship was non-cooperation with the administration. During a 1933 conference of nationalist leaders, one speaker suggested that non-cooperation should start with the non-payment of direct taxes as a civic duty in order to force the British to abrogate the mandate. Although the meeting's members split over policy implementation, the tactic itself demonstrates the ways in which populist leaders attempted to put the language of citizenship into practice.[68] It is important to recognise that the Arab organisers of strikes and boycotts attempted to garner support from the rural and working classes in the early 1930s at conferences and public meetings, in part through accusations that British colonial policy caused the poor economic conditions faced by these classes.

After 1933, the activities of the Istiqlal Party ceased due to the lack of strong leadership. Members were periodically arrested, exiled, placed under house arrest and forced out of jobs as teachers and civil servants due to their campaigns for civil disobedience. At the same time, Palestine was in recovery after the urban riots of late 1933, which occurred in several cities after Arab demonstrations and marches against increased immigration figures and the mandate itself turned violent. The riots themselves, although not discussed here, and their interpretation in the press indicate that the language of active citizenship promoted by the Istiqlalists had made an impact on the citizenry: Arabs assembled in several cities to demand particular political rights from the government and did so through the practices advocated by the Istiqlal Party. However, with the loss of the Istiqlal Party's advocacy for a pan-Arab civic identity by 1934, other nationalist political groups of a younger generation stepped into the vacuum to represent – or fail to represent – Arab citizenship in Palestine on the eve of the Palestinian Arab revolt.

Even after its demise, the party's grassroots-styled activists saw themselves as a new generation inspired by anti-colonial leaders like Gandhi and by their links to the League to Combat Imperialism and to the Communist International.[69] During the early 1930s, these activists increasingly used public space for displays of nationalism, with the idealistic hope that the civic nature of their activities could bring the Arab population together on the basis of their common citizenship and the threats posed to that status by Zionism and the Mandate. Still, prior to 1936 these leaders largely failed to engage a large majority of peasants in active citizenship, as demonstrated by the lack of long-term involvement of the rural classes in the urban-based national movement and civil society. When peasants stressed their identities as citizens who were guaranteed certain rights by virtue of that identity, they did so mainly in response to economic pressures. This is evidenced in protest letters and testimonies of peasant associations to government officials that asked for, among other things, an agricultural bank, a reduction of tithes and taxes and agricultural and secondary schools in villages.[70]

By the mid-1930s a new type of 'civic' activism emerged in Palestine aimed at stemming the influx of Jewish immigrants and stopping the transfer of land from Arab to Jewish ownership. The new activists had a separate ideology from that promoted by the Istiqlalists and urban civil society, which had worked to change policy or to remove altogether the mandate administration from Palestine. Rather, a number of individual leaders from the peasant and working classes organised secret bands in the countryside and carried out guerilla-style tactics against the Jewish settlements in northern Palestine. Secret cells were also formed in urban shantytowns such as those in Haifa by Sheikh 'Izz al-Din al-Qassem, an itinerant preacher, teacher, marriage registrar and member of the YMMA and Istiqlal Party. These bands attempted to educate and mobilise citizens through the idea of a popular revolt against the government.[71] Guerrilla organisations and tactics later inspired these novice fighters to shape a new resistance movement and orchestrate the Palestine Revolt of 1936–9. Through the ideology of revolt as a means to achieve independence, the guerrilla groups played a role in shaping another meaning of Palestinian civic identity as they insisted that the revolt was a civic duty that Palestinian Arabs should support in order to 'gain back' their homeland from the British and, by extension, Zionist colonisers. Rebel leaders stressed to the population through memorandum, strongmen, publications and funds the importance of unwavering civic, social, economic and political support for their anti-mandate cause. They often did this through force or tactics of fear in the latter year of the revolt and publications couched these appeals in the language of citizenship duties and patriotism. Despite the tactics used by the populists to engage with a larger section of subaltern Palestinian society and to represent all Palestinians as citizens, the populist movement ultimately remained small and based in urban areas. For the rural population after 1933, citizenship rights and civic identity became less abstract once village leaders manipulated the populists' and the nationalists' vocabulary of rights and advocated a type of 'civic' behaviour meant to alleviate their poor economic situation – that of revolt against the British authorities and the Jewish settlers.

Conclusion

By 1935, the Istiqlal Party and the active youth movement had all but disappeared from Palestine. New political parties emerged through the efforts of leading personalities from either the Jerusalem-based Husayni or Nashashibi factions. Five parties of some importance and standing took the place of the Istiqlalists. Still, their platforms differed very little from each other and none initially advocated direct confrontation, demonstrations or non-cooperation against the administration.[72] The brief mobilisation and use of the language of citizenship rights and membership in Palestine through the exercise of those rights to dismantle the mandate had been snuffed out and replaced with a return to factional politics. The representations of citizenship, which had formerly been presented on the pages of Arabic periodicals, barely factored into the activities of the new political parties whose familial ties and sectarian politics dominated them.

Still, the half-decade prior to the Palestine Revolt was one in which the Istiqlalists and the more radicalised individuals associated with it shaped a particular representation of Palestinian citizenship as connected to what contemporary historians of citizenship call the bundle of rights granted to the nationals. This representation transformed the earlier proposals of an equal national identity between Arabs and Jews in Palestine into proposals for a future self-rule by the Arabs based on their majority status and 'Arab' nationality. By the middle of the 1930s, the terminology of citizenship used by the Arabs changed as demands for the rights of citizenship became more frequent and increasingly contested by the lower classes. The press published letters signed by 'citizens of' (*muwatinīn min*) rather than 'nationals of' (*qawmī* or *watanī min*), cultivating a broader sense of civic identity and the rights and duties that went along with this identity. As opposition to the mandate came to be advocated in stronger terms, citizenship was transformed from being a middle-class concept, transported to the Arab world from Western Europe, to becoming an active practice and expression of belonging for – and occasionally, by – the lower classes.

Numerous pieces of legislation and the growing emphasis by the Cabinet to manage tensions between the Arabs and Jews in Palestine contributed to the continued denial by the local administration to follow the League of Nations' prerogative to develop self-governing institutions in the mandate territories. The administration enshrined neither the rights nor the protections that both Arab and Jewish population demanded – be they political, social or civil aside from the provisions of the electoral and municipal council ordinances – in a constitution as both groups wished. The administration also never gave in to the demand to grant a representative council the power to draft a constitution or bill of rights, as in the other Arab mandates. Although the United Kingdom itself did not have a constitution, a fact that Arab leaders sometimes noted, their experience with the Tanzimat legislation, the 1908 constitution and similar documents in the wider region and bills of rights in Europe influenced this constant demand for rights to be enshrined in a written document. The mobilisation inherent in popular politics, such as that of the Istiqlalists, caused a shift in public opinion to focus on the failure of the mandate to provide for its citizens in the social, economic and political realms. Through this process, the historical agency of a more inclusive Arab citizenry allowed for new negotiations of identity and citizenship. As Partha Chatterjee has written, political institutions – in this case, citizenship in Palestine – must be linked into a network of norms in civil society that are independent from the state in order for the behaviours of such institutions to be put into wide and active practice.[73] The Palestinian Arabs succeeded in encouraging types of behaviours of active citizenship in civil society and associational life outside the realm of the state. Finally, the press must be considered as the medium through which the citizenry learned of, explained and challenged mandate legislation. As readership spread to rural areas, public displays of citizenship and civic identity such as protest marches, demonstrations, unionisation and strikes included the subaltern population who witnessed and became part of the national community of Arab citizens, often for the first time. When the Palestinian Arab general strike began in April 1936, it gathered massive support throughout the country, owing to the attention the press gave to it throughout its duration. The resurgence of an active citizenship was owed to the Arab community's experiences of the late 1920s and early 1930s and the mobilisation by nationalist leaders and groups against mandate legislation.

7

The Palestine Revolt and Stalled Citizenship

'There is no genuine enthusiasm to be observed in Palestine for Palestinian citizenship,' wrote the members of the Royal Commission in 1937 after their return from Palestine where they had been sent by the Government of Great Britain in order to investigate the causes of the general strike, adding that 'it is only the Arabs in South America who are really anxious for it. And under present conditions this does not surprise us . . . To the educated Palestinian Arab, who has always resented the separation of Palestine from Syria, the very idea of Palestinian citizenship is obnoxious as being associated with the Mandate and all it involves.'[1] The Palestine Royal Commission of 1937, known as the Peel Commission after its appointed chairman, is most often remembered as the first official British investigative body to suggest the partition of Palestine. The Commission recommended more than simply partition: Sir Earl Peel validated the long-standing demand of a number of Arab nationalist and local leaders and Arab Executive Committee members that Arab emigrants be given Palestinian citizenship in order to return to Palestine if they wished. Although the report is important in that it suggested that the tense situation in Palestine could be solved by partition, it can also be read as providing a broader understanding of the socio-political and legal institution of citizenship and its importance to the Arab and Jewish communities in Palestine in the mid-1930s. In particular, the report offers clear hints at contemporary notions and meanings of, and the vocabulary associated with, nationality and citizenship. It also offers suggestions for the future of an internationally recognised Palestinian citizenship. The Commission heard evidence between the end of 1936 and January 1937 as part of its attempt to uncover the reasons for the 'disturbances', or the early years of the Great Revolt (*al-thawra al-kubra*) in Palestine. As part of the investigation, a number of Arab witnesses testified on the issue of Palestinian citizenship and its inclusion in anti-Mandate protest demands – an opportunity that the authorities had never made available to the Arab population of Palestine.

The work of the Peel Commission and its final report demonstrate continuities and changes in both British and Arab perceptions of nationality, citizenship and rights by the end of 1937. Here, I attempt to shed light on the ways in which British and Arab actors continued to negotiate multiple definitions of 'the citizen' in the legal sphere and the socio-political meanings of citizenship during the six-month general strike in Palestine in 1936 and the first year and a half of the Palestine Revolt through 1937. In the latter half of the three-year revolt, alternating factions of rebel leaders, mostly lower-class Muslim villagers rather than the middle-class nationalist elites and intellectuals, attempted to assert their control over the revolt and garner support through various appeals to different groups in Palestinian Arab society. The tense situation between rebel leaders themselves in Palestine, between these leaders and the central command in Damascus and between the rebels and the British meant that the nationalists' pre-1936 language and vocabulary of nationality and citizenship transformed into a new language popularised by the rebels: this language prioritised expressions of patriotism, loyalty, anti-Zionism and action to support the continuation of the revolt until victory (that meant, for the rebels, an end to the mandate). The idea of citizenship as linked to a political status and bundle of rights had little currency among the rebel commanders although their aim of self-government and an end to Jewish immigration mirrored that of the middle-class Arab national leaders. While the previous chapter demonstrated the significance of the representation and the language of rights, duties and belonging to a broader understanding of citizenship and civic identity for the Arab population, this chapter offers insight into the changing language used by both the Arab population and the British administration during the general strike and revolt. This language evidences a shift in the understanding on the part of mandate officials about citizenship and the place of Palestine as linked to a broader British colonial model.

In a recent reflection on subaltern studies, Partha Chatterjee has suggested that the contemporary Indian peasant must be understood within a new framework of democratic citizenship – one that is definitely not subjecthood but that is perhaps fundamentally altered from the normative ideas of citizenship in Western liberal democracies. The suggestion is relevant to the history of the Palestine Revolt and the place of citizenship in it. I have argued thus far that the ideas and ideals of citizenship expressed by the Palestinian Arabs during the mandate were increasingly conceived of and understood within a conceptual framework of primordial or communitarian citizenship and nationality, alongside strong influences of democratic, liberal citizenship, while rooted in notions of *jus sanguinis* and *jus soli* nationality influenced by late Ottoman practice. The changes to Arab civic identity owing to the events of late 1935 through 1937 requires the historian to situate the Arab *fellahin* – whose livelihoods were greatly affected by the revolt – alongside the more middle-class nationalist and populist leadership as actors who contributed to and influenced new notions and expressions of Palestinian citizenship.

Following Chatterjee's argument, the rebels from rural Palestine (who became more and more numerous by the end of 1936) can be construed as political actors, rather than passive reactionaries, whose leaders presented themselves as members of 'the nation' mobilised against the British authorities.[2] However, the argument cannot be followed through at face value: the historian must be careful to take the nuances of peasant identities and actions into account. Rural insurgency from 1936 was stirred not only by the prior activities and propaganda of populist national leaders but also in reaction to increased economic problems in the countryside. Still the revolt cannot be characterised as one of an entirely reactionary nature on the part of the peasantry stirred to action by the notables. It must be stressed that the peasant leadership of agricultural and village associations did not use the actual term for 'citizen' with the same political, Western-influenced connotations that many middle-class or youth leaders had done from the early part of the decade. Rural Palestinians certainly knew the term for 'citizen' and the more radical nationalists frequently noted that the former had a number of 'citizenship rights': this language cropped up in the appeals for unity and support that they made to the *fellahin*, which linked the economic problems and the absence of sovereignty over land and resources in the countryside to the mandate's support of Zionism and its encouragement of land sales to Jews. The framework of the growth of mass political mobilisation that stemmed from land losses and economic-based grievances in Palestinian villages during the revolt allows historians to understand the expansion of civic notions and behaviours as well as the shelf-life of both in light of the nationwide revolt staged against the British.

Throughout the first phase of the revolt and as a result of the increase in violence by the Arab and British sides, authorities censored the press, vetoed the right of assembly and enacted emergency

regulations: all measures that primarily affected the Arab population and only rarely the Jewish immigrants and citizens.[3] Although
the six-month general strike itself under the direction of the Higher
Arab Committee (HAC) was mostly a peaceful show of civil disobedience influenced by the tactics adopted by the populist movement
since the early 1930s, at the same time insurgents in the countryside
(themselves loosely connected with the HAC and rebel leadership in
Damascus) embraced anti-British and anti-Zionist violence. After a
lull in violence once the strike came to a brokered end, insurgency
started again in September 1937 as a result of the publication of the
report by the Peel Commission that recommended partition of the
territory. The report emboldened the rebels towards greater violence
as it forced the British, particularly High Commissioner Arthur Wauchope, to pay attention to their actions. In some respects violence
halted the development of Arab civil society as tensions increased
between urban and rural Palestinians and as divisive sentiment
against Arab Christians spread.[4] Shortly before the mass outbreak
of revolt – and perhaps a contributing factor to the ability of rebels in the countryside to undertake attacks on British personnel and
Jewish settlements – Palestine's pan-Arab and populist Istiqlal Party
collapsed and the moderate political current again came to dominate
Arab politics.[5]

Meanwhile, the provisions of citizenship legislation that negatively impacted the Arab emigrants ceased to feature in the press in
the mid-1930s. The amendments to the citizenship order of 1925
had made little effort to solve the problem of statelessness for native
Arabs emigrants. As suggested by the Peel Commission's report
cited above, the grievances that remained over the citizenship legislation and the treatment of the Jewish immigrants as opposed to the
Arabs did not disappear but rather remained relevant at the advent
of revolt.

Palestinian Arab Civic Identity and the
General Strike of 1936

At the end of 1935, High Commissioner Arthur Wauchope wrote to
the Secretary of State for the Colonies of his growing concern over
what he reported as radical Arab groups in Palestinian villages. He
had cause for concern. That autumn, the death of Sheikh 'Izz al-Din
al-Qassam during a gun battle with British forces resulted in an out-
pouring of Arab nationalist and anti-colonial sentiment against the

British and it turned al-Qassam into a martyr for the liberation of Palestine. Al-Qassam came to Palestine from Syria in the early 1920s (avoiding a French-issued death sentence), worked as a preacher and social reformer in Haifa and gained a following with his anti-British appeals to the Muslim working class and students. He joined the Istiqlal Party and led the Haifa Young Muslim Men's Association (YMMA) for a time. He secretly organised cells of fighters known as the Black Hand Gang (*al-yad al-sawda'*), which included the unemployed, labourers and the peasantry, and planned to begin a revolt in the north of Palestine in late 1935.[6] Al-Qassam's death in November reinvigorated a specifically rural nationalist movement. The surge in nationalist activity came in spite of the atmosphere that was described by Bahjat Abu-Gharbiya, a friend of al-Qassam, as follows: 'in the 1920s and 1930s, an important popular national element formed for [the Palestinian Arabs] but Mandate authorities worked to reduce it from 1935 until . . . it was as if it did not exist'.[7]

The following section analyses the increasing normalisation of certain practices and expressions of citizenship in the months leading to the general strike of April through October 1936 and the subsequent spread of violent insurgency. The agrarian Arab population engaged to an extent with the urban middle-class nationalists' language of social, political and civil rights and duties of citizenship. The rhetoric that emphasised political rights to representation or civil rights to economic assistance, for example, became associated with expressions of discontent with the mandate such as strikes and protests that peasants and the urban labourers attended. Rural associations increasingly penned letters of protest to the Palestine Administration, expressing opposition to its policies and claiming to represent, in their own words, the 'citizens of the villages'. The general strike, which marked the start of the revolt and featured episodes of violence in the urban and rural areas, has been analysed in a number of studies, yet these works have not considered events from the perspective of the ways in which rights of citizenship were manipulated by rebel leaders and educated elites to feature at a wider discursive level within the tense Arab society-in-revolt.[8] This is hardly surprising since explicit slogans of citizenship by leaders and from civic associations were not a predominate feature of the strike. Yet the revolt's Arab commanders portrayed their rebellious actions as part of their civic and national duties and rights.

The strike marked a turning point: for the first time, it mobilised a language of rights alongside widespread physical violence, the latter of which was imagined by revolt leaders as a necessary and legal path towards the attainment of an independent and representative government in Palestine. It is important to note that the strike was part of a broader regional context of unrest and political struggles, such as in Syria and Egypt (although this is too large a discussion to include here), and it was also certainly influenced in part by Zionist labour organisation. Civic identity played a key role in the strike as Arab nationalist leaders heavily stressed that all Palestinian Arabs had the same rights associated with citizenship and they formed part of a wider civic and national community in Palestine. In a study on violence and civil society in Quebec and Ireland, Jeffrey Cormier and Phillipe Couton maintain that certain mobilising structures such as civil society organisations are necessary for the emergence of both non-violent and violent social movements.[9] The application of Cormier's and Couton's logic to the revolt years in Palestine helps to explain the historical connection between urban and rural networks that supported the strike and the violence – and significantly, the endurance of both despite superior British manpower and firepower.

Before al-Qassam's death in 1935, High Commissioner Wauchope began to advocate proportional representation in a new legislative council, one of the Arabs' most consistent, long-standing demands.[10] However, his attempt to reintroduce a plan for a legislative council after the failed attempt in 1922 (due to the Arab boycott of elections) did not come to fruition because Parliament refused to support the plan, exposing growing tensions between the local Palestine Administration and the Cabinet and Parliament in London. In response to frustration over the continued failure of the administration to introduce representative government into Palestine, 'independent groups' led by Arab young men such as secondary-school teacher and journalist Akram Zu'aytir in Nablus declared several general strikes in a number of urban centres. For example, the Arab Scouts in rural areas and the Youth Sports Club oversaw a November 1935 city-wide strike in Nablus to protest the 'Judaising' of Palestine and to ask for a representative council. Zu'aytir addressed letters of response to those who participated in the strike as 'thanks to you, the citizens!' (*shukrān lakum, al-muwātinīn!*) linking nationalist actions to a sense of civic duty. Similar language was used in other acts of civil protest. In Jerusalem, thousands attended a demonstration to mark the anniversary of the city's occupation by the British, and speakers such as the schoolteacher and newspaper editor Hamdi Husayni and the labour unionist Michel Mitri appealed to 'the citizens' to form a popular configuration of resistance.[11]

After the November 1935 strike, Wauchope noted – and began to fear – the links between the more radical civil society and youth groups in rural Palestine. Similarly, the demands for political representation at the village level alarmed officials. These groups and individuals advocated direct political action against the Palestine Administration by appealing for public and, at first, civil tactics. A meeting of local leaders in Nablus decided to support acts of non-cooperation including demonstrations, the resignation of Arab Government officials and a boycott of Jewish and British social and political events and declared their willingness to be imprisoned for the national cause. By that time, various urban nationalist leaders travelled to rural areas to speak in clubs and mosques. In the countryside, peasants expressed a greater interest in politics than they had previously.[12] Indeed, the Arab Scouts were particularly politically active in 1935 in villages. Young members explained their actions of spreading nationalist propaganda and encouraging non-payment of tithes in terms of national and civic duty.[13] Similarly, in Syria during the Great Revolt against the French, a romanticisation of Arab leaders took place within the context of the changing approaches to popular mobilisation in the national movement. To legitimise the leadership of the populist leaders, their figures had to be juxtaposed with 'unjust' leaders.[14] In Palestine, al-Qassam made these juxtapositions as he walked through the countryside to preach jihad (holy struggle) against the administration.

Public meetings became a standard way to chart the public opinion of the peasants and labourers and to encourage greater participation in political affairs. The gatherings of grassroots organisations influenced thousands of supporters to join demonstrations in towns and cities. By January 1936 a strong populist movement led by former Istiqlal leaders and Arab youth groups withdrew confidence from the Jerusalem-based political parties and gave their support to the young men's groups.[15] As a result of the changing political situation and the higher level of political activity in the countryside, active expressions of citizenship such as the use of the term itself in petitions, the establishment of rural clubs for Palestinian Arabs and letter-writing campaigns by which residents demanded a variety of 'rights', grew in number. Meetings, demonstrations and even non-payment of taxes and donations made to the National Land Fund allowed Palestinian Arab citizens to craft an ideology of citizenship duties during the revolt. In the months before the general strike began, the national committees in Nablus made the first appeal for citizens to stop the payment of taxes to the Mandate Government came in March 1936.

From the beginning, the Nablus leaders portrayed the refusal to pay taxes as a civic, national and wholly legal duty. However, in the countryside local groups took a more violent approach: small groups cut telephone wires, bombed bridges and blocked roads as a show of resistance to the government.[16] By early April 1936, after Parliament refused to support Wauchope's legislative council, villages and towns throughout Palestine bombarded the British administrators with petitions in support of the council, taking the lead from the national committees in Nablus.[17]

In April 1936, a number of Arab civil servants, urban tradesmen and transportation workers went on strike. In response, the administration issued the Emergency Regulations that criminalised calls for strikes and threatened those who encouraged the strike with legal action.[18] Regardless, nearly 140 Palestinian senior government officials in a letter to High Commissioner Wauchope explained their resignation in terms of civic duty. Their role, they explained in the petition, was to serve as a link between the government and all classes of Arab citizens.[19] The letter demonstrates the connection between the notion of 'duties' as supported by Arab civil society and the support for the call of non-cooperation with the government on the part of civil servants or the striking working and middle classes. The call for a comprehensive general strike, the first phase of the Palestine Revolt, came after murders in mid-April 1936: members of an Arab armed gang near Haifa killed two Jewish truck drivers.[20] The murders led to a cycle of Jewish reprisals followed by Arab counter-reprisals and within days the British imposed a curfew on Arab areas of the country.

Demonstrations turned violent as they spread to urban areas, with the Arabs expressing anger against increased Jewish immigration. Local leaders in Nablus urged the use of tactics of non-violence and took the lead in prompting other municipal authorities to form local committees that linked up to larger national bodies such as the Youth Congress and the Arab Patriotic Society (al-mujtam'a al-'arabī al-watanī) (formerly the Muslim–Christian Association). These leaders then announced a general strike in protest against immigration policy and the mandate, and prepared a statement that explained the purpose of national committees and asked for support from all Palestinian Arabs to recognise the Nablus leadership as representative of the population.[21] As the work by the urban Nablus strike committee began, slogans of non-cooperation appeared in letters supporting the committee. The committee soon received a letter from a Jerusalem club signed by 150 self-professed 'citizens' such as doctors, lawyers, union leaders, students, teachers and tradesmen. They announced their support for the practical implementation of 'no taxation without representation' (la dara'ib bilā tamthīl). In Nablus, Akram Zu'aytir and others agreed that the first serious political step was to embark on a campaign of civil disobedience by refusing to pay taxes. The letter from the Jerusalem club added that only through non-cooperation (alata'āwun) could the Arab population maintain its identity.[22]

By the end of April 1936, grassroots national committees swiftly formed in other Palestinian cities and towns and they unanimously agreed to adhere to the general strike. The committees, backed by press reports, called for all Palestinian Arab citizens to participate. On 25 April, the Mufti, Hajj Amin al-Husayni, met with the five largest political parties in Jerusalem and formed a coordinating body, the Higher Arab Committee (HAC), led by Hajj Amin. According to Swedenburg's study on the revolt, this committee represented an alliance between traditional notables and the newer middle-class urban radicals.[23] However, the national committees were often organised at a local level and their leaders did not want to follow the exclusive leadership of the elite.[24] Subhi Yassin's history of the revolt notes that local leaders and committees immediately demanded that the HAC support civil disobedience and the non-payment of taxes and yield to public opinion.[25]

By mid-May 1936, the HAC announced that the position of 'no taxation without representation' to be the hallmark of citizenship practice. The committee stated in a communiqué published in the press and addressed to the Palestinian Arabs that this would 'help preserve your identity and your nationality [qawmtik]'.[26] One observer, the Egyptian-Palestinian newspaper owner Mohamed 'Ali El-Tahir noted that the non-payment of taxes and the peaceful strike were the duties of 'citizens employed in the national cause' (al-qadiyya al-wataniyya).[27] The adherence by a large part of the Arab population to the HAC's request that the Arabs stop paying taxes as part of the general strike is a significant active expression of involvement in, and understanding of, civic and political behaviours of belonging. The communiqué took into account struggles elsewhere in history for independence, such as in the United States. The response by the Arab community proved to the mandate administration the power of both the individual and the collective. At first, the strike showed the diversity of Palestinian Arab civil society. Alongside the workers and the notables, the peasant leadership expressed its support and children refused to go to school.[28] National committees throughout

Palestine worked at the local level to ensure that the population received food supplies. Initially, certain groups were given strike funds in lieu of their salaries. The wealthy were asked to contribute money and women went door-to-door to fundraise and encourage *sumud* (steadfastness) and sacrifice.[29]

Meanwhile, although a number of village committees advocated civil disobedience such as the non-payment of tithes alongside their urban counterparts, other village leaders instead urged 'disobedience in all senses of the word', meaning armed revolt.[30] Violence was touted as a legitimate expression of citizenship and resistance to the mandate. Support for violence as a tactic to resist the government and the land policies that favoured immigrant settlers can be traced back to the organisation of countryside bands of rebels, even prior to the works of men like al-Qassam. Indeed, as noted above, civil society even in its nascent form in rural areas could be mobilised to support violent acts against government infrastructure and personnel using the language of colonial oppression to incite peasants. In Palestine by 1936, the rebels justified violent disobedience as the means to achieve fully the goal of forcing the British to surrender control of the country to the Arabs. The violence initially took place in the first weeks of the strike as Arab guerilla rebels, often from the countryside and who worked independently from the HAC, committed numerous murders and attacks on Jewish settlements and British police.[31] Soon after the strike began, a former Syrian Ottoman army officer who had fought against the French, Fawzi al-Din al-Qawuqji, assumed control of the rebel bands in Palestine and claimed his title to be commander-in-chief. One of the first communiqués issued by al-Qawuqji, addressed to the 'citizens', argued that the revolt was a humanitarian, religious and national duty of the Arabs in Palestine and of the entire Arab nation. Al-Qawuqji called on the citizens to take up arms as a matter of duty.[32]

Swedenburg's ethnographical study on the Palestine Revolt provides the insight that many peasants often depicted their identity as primordial and linked to the very land of Palestine – but they did not explicitly mention citizenship.[33] Rather, rural groups issued appeals in the name of Allah to the nation (*al-umma*), its native sons (*abna'*) or the noble people (*karīm al-sha'b*). The appeals contained localised narratives and arguments such as the need for the peasants to sacrifice themselves to protect their land (*ard*) and honour (*sharaf*) as Arabs. The link between land, economic stability and revolt is an important one as it seemed to be the driving force for many peasants to join guerilla bands of fighters under al-Qawuqji. Rural Arabs, unlike urban nationalists, thought of rights primarily as rights to land and fairer taxation. More recently, historian Michael Provence has demonstrated that since the revolt's commanders and many individual rebels had all been Ottoman subjects they had exposure to notions of nationalism and collective struggle through Ottoman education and conscription prior to 1918. These former Ottoman subjects communicated and mobilised through the language of popular patriotism and Arab nationality.[34] For some peasants and for urban labourers, the notion of civic rights and duties and their subsequent expression developed through a process that involved daily interactions with strike committees, strikers and the authorities. Throughout 1936, associations and press editorials encouraged active behaviours of political citizenship, suggesting that village and urban Palestinians alike begin legal proceedings and boycotts against the mandate government over the loss of civil and political rights.[35] For example, in Nazareth the Chamber of Commerce informed the high commissioner just as the general strike began that since the city's merchants would strike, the government should not send them any bills.[36] In a sense, both the rebels and the peaceful strikers crafted their own expressions of citizenship rights and duties even if they rarely articulated the term 'citizen'.

A number of Egyptians and Syrians worked in Palestine on railways and ports just as Palestinian Arabs lived and worked in Egypt and Syria. Emigrants in these two countries, and those in the Americas, were actively involved in supporting the events of 1936. These links served to emphasise further the notion of Arab nationality as an inclusive status tied to concepts of national and natural political rights throughout the Levant. Notably, El-Tahir, who became head of the Palestine Arab Committee in Cairo, wrote updates (republished from his newspaper and elsewhere in the press) on the strike for the emigrants in North and South America, and informed them of the intensification of violence and the tolls of dead, wounded and jailed. One of his letters stated that 'it becomes the duty of every Arab emigrant in the service of his country and his nation' to support the Palestinian Arabs' strike and revolt. El-Tahir and those who read his reports and newspaper editorials thus helped to export the discourse of civic duty as linked to the revolt into the Palestinian Arab diaspora.[37]

The general strike was called off after six months, in October 1936, as a result of negotiations between the HAC and other Arab leaders primarily in Iraq, Egypt, Transjordan and Arabia. Ultimately, the strike failed to paralyse the economy. Additionally, by that point the poorer segments of the Arab population expressed an often-dire discontent with the strike and the difficulties they incurred in their trade, particularly in the transportation of produce. Although the national committees and newspapers portrayed the strike as supported by all Palestinian Arabs, in reality their propaganda neglected to account for a large part of the population that simply could not afford to strike.[38]

Stalled Citizenship: From the Citizenry to the 'Population'

By early 1937, new British legislation put in place in order to quell the revolt in Palestine served to deny the few political and civil rights that the Palestinian Arabs had enjoyed before the outbreak of the revolt. The new Emergency Regulations impacted urban and rural Arabs as they were imposed from above by the military authorities sent to Palestine and by the British Government, and Matthew Hughes has termed these regulations de facto martial law.[39] This implementation was colonial in that the administration of Palestine adhered to imperial emergency and martial law provisions as models for the provisions specifically put into place in Palestine. Furthermore, the emergency situation made it increasingly difficult for the British to view the Arabs in any fashion as rights-bearing citizens, as it eroded civil and political rights. Here, it is useful to refer to the difference between 'the citizens' and 'the population' in light of the response to the Palestine Revolt by the authorities. In terms of policy and theory, 'the citizens' and 'the population' are often viewed as separate groups under colonial rule. Chatterjee has written that the concept of the citizen carries with it 'the ethical connotation of participation in the sovereignty of the state', while the concept of the population, by contrast, 'makes available to government . . . a set of rationally manipulable instruments for reaching large sections of the inhabitants of a country as the targets of their "policies." '[40] With the outbreak of collective violence in Palestine the British found it necessary to remove certain rights given to the Palestinian Arabs by treating them *not* as citizens of the mandate but rather as its colonised population. This is important: through the early 1930s the legislation around citizenship in Palestine continued to shape the legal status and the international recognition of 'the citizen' and small steps had been made through 1935 towards granting Arabs and Jews greater political rights to representation in a proposed legislative assembly. Additionally, the terms of the mandate and the League of Nations' Permanent Mandates Commission had made explicitly and repeatedly clear that Great Britain could not treat the inhabitants of the Palestine Mandate as colonial subjects. The sovereign imposition of emergency laws and martial law went against League policy (as did similar actions by Great Britain and France in other mandates previously) and caused friction between the international body and the government in London.

The legislation drawn up during the revolt in London, and the referral of British troops to Palestine served to classify the Palestinian Arabs in the minds of Cabinet officials in the metropole as simply the majority segment of Palestine's population. As such, they were subject to the terms of martial law without any need for further discussion and without the need for popular approval. During the Palestine Revolt, the examples of Chatterjee's 'manipulable instruments' included old and new British colonial legislation that was implemented by the administration: collective punishment, forced exile of certain individuals including most of the Arab leadership of the Palestine Communist Party,[41] the emergency and martial law regulations and military trials. While the Palestine Government could easily apply these public security measures on colonial populations it was more difficult to justify their application to a population of Palestinian citizens internationally recognised as British-protected persons and over whom Great Britain did not have full sovereignty. Not only were certain rights and privileges withdrawn from the Arab population, but the existence of Palestinian citizenship as separate from British colonial subjecthood became muddled. Mandate authorities increasingly placed the inhabitants of Palestine within a more broadly colonial category as a population to be made loyal to Great Britain. This was a direct result of the revolt and the British reaction to Arab violence as defensive to protect not only the mandate territory but Great Britain itself. During the revolt, the British in Palestine referred to the Arab citizenry collectively at best as 'the population' of the territory, and at worst as suspected guerrillas.

Under the regime's statutory martial law, a stage between full military control with martial law in Palestine and the continued exercise of civil powers under partial military control, officials could disregard the civil rights that offered certain protections for entire civilian populations of villages and towns.[42] Although Great Britain did not introduce a complete martial law ordinance in Palestine, related ordinances that sanctioned collective and punitive punishments primarily affected the Palestinian Arab inhabitants by turning them into colonial subjects. As historian Naomi Shepherd states, after the passage of the Mandate's Emergency Regulations by High Commissioner Wauchope in the early summer of 1936, 'the legal system of Palestine became harnessed to repression . . . [S]uccessive Emergency Regulations led to summary justice and the curtailment of civil rights.'[43] The regulations additionally allowed for all sorts of collective punishment measures, from imposing fines to demolishing Arab quarters of cities and Arab homes in villages. Despite the high commissioner's objections, Whitehall decided that the army and the Royal Air Force (RAF) be sent to Palestine as a show of force to contain insurgent Arab groups and to control areas once the violence intensified. The tactics meant to contain and stop the revolt were not new creations: a British volume on 'small wars' from the late 1890s supported collective punishment of 'uncivilised' natives and the book's recommendations had been used in Egypt and Iraq as well as in the Boer War, India and Ireland.[44]

By 1935, the imperial martial law ordinance had been amended so that it no longer required officials to prove a crime was committed before imposing collective punishment. After the outbreak of revolt in 1936, the British Government gave the High Commissioner's Office the power to apply collective punishment in municipal areas in response to crimes committed by rebels such as the cutting of telephone wires, the destruction of infrastructure and rifle fire.[45] Yet as Palestine was not a colony under full British sovereignty, theoretically the administration, the military and the Palestine Police were bound by international and British regulations that offered a standard for the proper treatment of civilian populations to maintain law and order during incidents of rebellion. The most well-known example of collective punishment actions during the general strike was the June 1936 demolition of the Arab quarters of the old city of Jaffa, which left up to 6,000 Palestinian Arabs homeless. More common were punitive acts committed by British soldiers in villages.[46] In 1936, collective fines started to be used as punitive measures under the Collective Punishment Ordinance and the Emergency Regulations. These types of punishments, done under a civil administration prior to the arrival of military authorities to Palestine, took away any sense of legal standing or presumed rights to protection of life, property or welfare. The Jewish Palestinians did not suffer collectively from either type of punishment. As a result, the civil and military authorities could continue to treat one set of recognised Palestinian citizens differently from the other set of citizens.

The Arab villagers recognised their lack of legal rights even during the strike. Residents of the village of Qula reported on the excesses of force, including home demolitions, by British soldiers. They referred to the actions of the soldiers as 'inconsistent with the principles of justice and humanity' and invoked the villagers' rights to an immediate legal inquiry. Despite their hopes for legal action, those citizens whose homes were demolished or partially destroyed by the British were not allowed to give evidence in court.[47] In fact, the citizens of Palestine could not take legal action against the government itself during the revolt but could only press civil charges against individual soldiers. The British justified their actions as defensive measures meant to protect the Government of Palestine. Simoni notes that during the years of revolt, any welfare offered by the British to the Arab population was halted as security became the overriding concern, thus widening the gap in the political relations between the Arab and Jewish communities.[48]

The emergency and collective punishment laws, particularly the 1937 Prevention of Crimes Ordinance, allowed for deportation and the detention of suspected criminals or politically active leaders. Throughout 1936, the authorities suspended Arab dailies thirty-four times.[49] In March 1937 the Palestine Defence Order-in-Council gave High Commissioner Wauchope the power to carry out a variety of defence measures in the interest of law, order and public safety. The order-in-council made the carrying of firearms punishable by death and the private possession of a firearm could result in a life sentence in prison; furthermore, it criminalised any meeting or procession including more than twelve people. Citizens risked imprisonment if they did not give the correct identification information and travel permit or passes to any official who requested such information.[50] Since the British Government classified the revolt as an internal insurrection, Arab suspects and rebels were denied treatment as civilians such as due process. After the murder of British District Commissioner Lewis Andrews by an Arab gang in September 1937, the Colonial Office authorised British soldiers to torture Arab suspects and non-combatant villagers in areas with heavy rebel activity in order to gather intelligence.[51] The HAC was declared illegal and its members forced to flee from Palestine or face arrest and deportation. In early 1937, civil society groups and Arabic newspapers sent numerous petitions to High Commissioner Wauchope to complain of the treatment of political and other prisoners.[52] According to the memoirs of Arab lawyer Hanna Nakkara, as a result of the Prevention of Crimes Ordinance arrests took place regularly and the British opened several detention camps for political detainees, a category that increasingly included intellectuals and workers.[53]

At the same time, as the revolt became more widespread, rebel leaders attempted to act as government figures. They implemented their own rebel courts and laws, and enforced certain civic duties. The Arab rebels also reduced Palestinian citizenship – in the form granted by the mandate – to a meaningless status by the end of 1937. The rebel leaders themselves did not directly address the issue of rights of citizenship but instead used rhetorical nationalist terminology and imposed their own vision of public order in line with their tactics in support of the rebellion. The rebels used a type of rhetoric that differed from that of the urban leadership and that of the British authorities. By 1937, in some important respects these rebels sought to offer certain rights and expressions of citizenship without being familiar with the term. They ordered the cancellation of rents and rural taxes and prescribed a certain style of dress in order to cement a sense of solidarity with the lower classes.[54] Rebel leaders did not recognise identity documents given to the Arabs by the government and went as far as to order the Palestinians to not show these documents to military or police officers.[55] The rebel leadership issued calls and demands to the population to resist the government using religious phrases and appeals to jihad. In doing so, these rebels represented a new version of civic public order and political and civil action. The defensive measures on the part of the British *and* the Arabs during the first half of the revolt shifted the understandings of the citizenry's rights, protections and objects of loyalty.

Palestinian Citizenship and the Royal Peel Commission

This penultimate section steps back from the 1936 general strike and the first year of the revolt. Through two case studies on citizenship requests and a closer inspection of the Peel Commission's recommendations on citizenship, it investigates the affects of legal changes to the acquisition and revocation of citizenship for Arabs and Jews. It also discusses the response by Arab nationalist leaders to the recommendations of the Peel Commission with regards to citizenship and partition. The Peel Commission arrived to Palestine in November 1936, just after the strike had been called off.[56] To put the actions of the commission and its interviewees into perspective, it must be emphasised that even during the first stage of the revolt the Colonial Office allowed for nearly 2,000 more entry permits to be given to Jewish immigrants. As a result, the Palestinian Arab leaders boycotted Peel and his colleagues until January 1937.[57]

In 1936, the Colonial Office defended its policy that gave Jewish immigrants an easier route to the acquisition of Palestinian citizenship by stating that officials in Palestine were obliged to keep citizenship legislation favourable for immigrants or risk litigation from the Jewish community negatively impacted by its provisions.[58] In the meantime, the Arab population had not seen any significant redress of their own grievances over the provisions. The following case studies serve to demonstrate that during the period of tumult and political and legal transformations caused by the revolt, citizenship continued to be a subject of contestation for individual Arabs. They testify to the unequal treatment in the grant and recognition of citizenship between Arabs and Jews.

The first case of a man born in Ottoman Palestine in the 1890s demonstrates how mandate politics played a role in influencing the treatment of natives who wished to return from abroad under extraordinary circumstances. Hussein Khalil Abu Ziyad left Palestine in the early 1920s and married an American woman in the United States, all while he retained his Ottoman nationality documents. Ziyad applied to the British consulate in California in 1934 to return to Palestine as a citizen and the consul requested the application be considered by the high commissioner. However, once the consul informed Palestine's Commissioner for Migration and Statistics that Ziyad was 'unsound and an inmate of a state hospital for the insane' as a result of a diagnosis with a form of dementia Ziyad's visa for Palestine was cancelled.[59]

By the end of 1936, the Colonial Office feared that the denial of Ziyad's return to Palestine could be given a 'political complexion [sic]' and that his exclusion from Palestine could not be justified under the mandate's 1933 Immigration Ordinance. The case had a legal element. Ziyad's lawyer stressed in early 1937 that his client appeared to be a 'Turkish citizen of Palestinian birth' who met all of the requirements of the Foreign Office consular instructions that permitted an individual's return to Palestine. The lawyer added that Ziyad's wife threatened to politicise the matter, which was most undesirable to the British Government in the climate of revolt in the mandate territory. In this connection, Ziyad's wife stated that she had recently discovered 'that, due to a British law passed at the time they [Britain] gave Palestine to the Jews as a National home, all Arabians then in foreign countries had to renew their citizenship or lose it'. Thus, Ziyad lost his citizenship and lacked both a passport and a visa to return. Still, the administration refused to admit Ziyad as a citizen of Palestine.[60]

In certain circumstances, Arabs born in Palestine posed problems in terms of classification dependent on their birth. In 1936 the question of the divestment of Ottoman nationality for certain Arabs confused Palestine and British authorities. The son of George Rock, an Ottoman subject naturalised as a British citizen in the 1890s, enquired as to whether his father's status made him a British subject or a Palestinian citizen. Although John George Rock was born in Palestine, his father had been a resident of Britain prior to 1914. When John George enquired as to his nationality in the 1930s, the British initially responded that he was Palestinian rather than British. In a series of interdepartmental correspondence on the case, the Home Office referred to the Ottoman Nationality Law of 1869 in its attempt to decide upon the status of John George Rock in late 1936. It found that according to the Ottoman law, since the elder Rock did not automatically lose his Ottoman nationality upon British naturalisation, John George could not be regarded as a British subject as he had hoped.[61] The issue of multiple loyalties came into the picture in the case of John George Rock. He stressed, as did his father, that the elder rock severed any ties with Turkey. At the time of John George's questioning as to whether he or his father were British subjects, his father proclaimed his readiness to give a statement that 'on [his] naturalisation he swore allegiance to the British Government and no one else'.[62] The case also demonstrates the uncertainty of the revolt years as to whether Palestinian Arabs such as John George, who assumed that he was in fact a British subject, would be loyal to Great Britain.

At the end of 1936 the Colonial Office and other departments were in discussion with the Palestine Administration over a proposal to draft another amended citizenship order-in-council. The outbreak of revolt and the activities of the Royal Commission in Palestine forced officials to pause their talks until the Commission published its report, which included recommendations on citizenship, naturalisation and immigration. As early as August 1936 the commission headed by Lord Peel received a memorandum from the Mandate Government that asked it to consider the division of Palestine under a cantonisation scheme. The cantonisation proposal meant that the mandate territory would become a federation of cantons, or self-governing units. The idea was an unpopular one with the British Government and with other members of the administration, but Peel and his colleagues studied it briefly.[63] To continue to analyse the multiple understandings of citizenship and nationality in Mandate Palestine, it is useful to question whether the cantonisation plan proposed a new structure for both statuses. A former administrator in Palestine, L. G. Archer Cust, submitted one of the cantonisation plans to the Commission. In essence, the scheme involved the formation of three cantons: Arab, Jewish and a mix of the two groups. The aim was to segregate Palestinian communities to avoid clashes of interests between Arabs and Jews. Cust's plan outlined the separation and autonomy of Jewish and Arab areas. For example, Jewish immigration and land sales could be permitted only in the Jewish canton. In the Arab canton, a central canton government and elected assembly would supervise the local bodies and Jewish immigration would be prohibited.[64] Palestine's Chief Secretary Sydney Moody was quick to ask other officials 'whether any of us know what cantonisation means?'[65] It was unclear whether Arabs and Jews would carry equal rights of citizenship, and the proposal neglected to mention the concept of Arab nationality. In theory and practice, the cantonisation plan went against Britain's mandatory obligations because the plan would effectively force the Arab citizens out of their traditional geographical areas through a population transfer if they decided not to live in the Jewish canton. Ultimately, the Peel Commission also rejected the scheme but its eventual recommendation of partition reflected persistent, deeper questions on nationality and citizenship in a partitioned Palestine.

In January 1937 the Commission heard evidence that explicitly criticised the mandate's citizenship legislation. With the Arabs' boycott of the Commission over, a number of outspoken leaders provided it with a different account from that of the mandate officials as to proposals for a future Palestinian government. A very small but vocal handful brought up the problems of Palestinian citizenship for Arab emigrants and contrasted the emigrants' situation with that of the Jewish immigrants. Importantly, their statements are examples of the ways in which discourses and definitions of nationality and citizenship had evolved from the early 1920s. These leaders stressed *jus sanguinis* and *jus soli* nationality provisions as equivalent to rights to citizenship in Palestine as well as to Arab nationality. Furthermore, the witnesses made clear attempts to connect their ideas of citizenship rights for the Arab emigrants with the provisions of nationality legislation in force in Great Britain.

The testimony of 'Awni Abd al-Hadi in early 1937 exemplifies some of the arguments and hopes of Arab middle-class and former Arab Executive body leadership for new citizenship regulations. His words to the Commission highlight the Arab nationalists' (often simplistic) understanding that the 1922 Legislative Election Order-in-Council was the first piece of legislation to allow any Jew to enter Palestine and receive citizenship with minimal restrictions.[66] The fears built up in the previous decade that Jewish citizens would become a majority in Palestine were evident. Abd al-Hadi's testimony also suggests that immigration statistics were actively compiled by Palestinian activists. He stated that at least 4,000 Jews entered Palestine on tourist visas yearly and then were subsequently 'lost'. As these individuals were not claimed as immigrants or as citizens they were excluded from the numbers of Jews who settled and contributed to the economic capacity of the territory.[67] However, Arab witnesses presented a great deal of nationalist-oriented rhetoric and demands to the Peel Commission, which seemed to weaken the potential impact of the testimony on citizenship, naturalisation and immigration statistics.

Akram Zu'aytir and Abd al-Hadi's colleague, schoolteacher Muhammed 'Izza Darwazah, gave similar statements to the Peel Commission. Both argued that the Arabs' claims in Palestine were based on their centuries-long residence as Arab nationals. They argued, based on the development of notions of citizenship from the early 1920s, that citizenship status in Palestine was a natural right based on birth and descent in the territory.[68] Furthermore, 'Isa Bandak, the leader and activist touted as an expert on Palestinian nationality and citizenship due to his lobbyist efforts in support of all Palestinian Arabs to receive citizenship, testified before Lord Peel. Bandak urged the Commission to implement the Arabs' own suggestions in its future report on the issue of citizenship.[69] Still these Arabs who spoke to the Commission, all upper- and middle-class individuals and self-professed nationalist leaders, couched their grievances in nationalist language and rarely explained in specific terms which rights citizenship entailed. The rebel leaders and the rural population as a whole were not directly represented to the Commission.

Finally, the testimony of the popular leader Abd al-Latif al-Saleh, who both rural and urban Palestinian Arabs regarded with respect, is unique in that it traced the concept of Arab nationality from Ottoman times through to the creation of citizenship in Palestine. Al-Saleh commented directly on specific cases in which the administration denied citizenship to native-born Palestinian Arabs. Al-Saleh also linked citizenship in Palestine to British colonial policies, thereby placing Palestine into a larger narrative of British imperialism as he referenced colonial settlement and the nature of colonial economies as tied to Great Britain. In addition, he stressed that the prejudice against the emigrants, rendered without nationality, was 'quite apparent' and indeed the latter was 'forbidden by international law'. Al-Saleh spoke of the discourse of citizenship rights in stating that the mandate text did not distinguish 'civil rights' from 'religious rights'.[70] The civil rights to citizenship were instead under the umbrella of religious rights and, as a result, citizenship came to be governed by religious communities.

The Arab nationalists in Palestine were not the only ones asked to offer testimony to the Commission on the issues of citizenship and immigration legislation. Mandate officials (and Jewish leaders) did as well but it was the testimony of Palestine's Commissioner for Migration and Statistics, Major E. Mills, which matched up with the arguments given on citizenship figures by the Arab interviewees. Mills's statements supported the Arabs' argument that the administration categorised Jewish citizens separately from Arab citizens in matters of immigration, emigration and naturalisation. His testimony also suggests the importance placed by administrators upon information-gathering on Jewish immigrants in order for the government to prove the success of the mandate's Jewish national home policy. Mills admitted to the Peel Commission in 1937 that 'the natural increase of the population has not been tabulated by citizenship', and instead explained that at the end of 1936, 43 per cent of the estimated 384,000 Jewish inhabitants were Palestinian citizens. In fact, he added that the number of Jews resident 'unofficially' in Palestine was much higher. It could then be surmised that less than 43 per cent of immigrants actually took Palestinian citizenship.[71] Mills's figures are reminiscent of debates from the late 1920s and early 1930s in which the administration revealed that many of the Jewish voters in the municipal elections were not actually citizens of Palestine. The figures given to Peel show that less than half of the Jewish population could legitimately claim the rights to Palestinian citizenship in 1937.

For Great Britain, these figures compiled on citizenship, naturalisation and immigration called into question the success of the mandate's extension of Palestinian citizenship to the Jewish immigrants, and thus the success of the Jewish national home policy itself. The low numbers of Jewish citizens, out of the total population of Jews in Palestine, highlighted questions regarding the loyalties of this population to the Palestine Government. In sum, the Commission did not look favourably upon provisions of citizenship and the dual system that separated Arab and Jewish residents. In its final report issued in July 1937 the Royal Commission recommended the alleviation of the Arabs' grievances in large part through the partition of Palestine. The report had sections devoted to citizenship

and naturalisation of both Arabs and Jews. It provided information on the means by which the government attempted to facilitate
the Jewish national home policy. For example, the report stated
that so-called naturalisation field officers visited the outlying Jewish villages and settlements specifically to ensure that immigrants
naturalised.[72] Out of just over 6,000 applications for naturalisation made in 1935, more than 1,500 were accepted by a field officer from Jewish settlements. The Commission also noted that in
1936, out of the 384,000 Jewish residents of Palestine, 92,000 were
recent immigrants unable to qualify for naturalisation. Peel and his
men affirmed what Great Britain feared, that the high percentage
of non-citizen Jews was due to the fact that the chief allegiance of
many immigrants was to the Jewish community rather than to the
Palestine Government.[73]

Two months before the Royal Commission report recommended
partition, Lord Peel asked the Palestine Administration and Whitehall whether either objected to the inclusion of certain recommendations on the issue of citizenship in the final report. The Commission
made clear that first and foremost it planned to recommend revisions to the citizenship order-in-council in the direction desired by
the Arabs, specifically to enable all natives to obtain citizenship.
The Commission was extremely favourable to the Arab argument
that the hardship for those Arab emigrants who did not sever their
connections with Palestine loomed large as a grievance for all of
the Arabs.[74]

The British Colonial and Foreign Offices objected to the recommendations. The British Government re-stated its long-standing
objection:

> It is undesirable to grant Palestinian citizenship to persons who
> have been absent from Palestine for several years and who have no
> intention of returning to Palestine within a reasonable period and of
> residing there permanently . . . [I]n many cases, the principle object
> of applications . . . is to obtain British protection for the purpose of
> pressing claims against the Governments of the countries in which
> they reside. Further, it is undesirable on general grounds to create a
> class of persons permanently resident abroad who would be entitled
> to British protection.[75]

As explained in Chapters 4 and 5, this argument was used for more
than fifteen years against stateless Palestinian Arabs. The Commission

further noted that mandate officials failed to take the initiative to consult or survey the emigrants themselves through British consuls.

The Commission's official report included the testimony by the Arab witnesses. It noted the figure of approximately 40,000 emigrants who had lost their chance to acquire Palestinian citizenship due to the 1925 citizenship order requirements. In particular, those interviewed noted that emigrants found one particular question on the mandate's form for Arabs who intended to 'opt' for ipso facto citizenship: that of 'where do you intend to reside?' Thus, answers usually listed the applicant's current country of residence rather than Palestine. The Commission stated that, as a result, out of more than 9,000 applications, only 100 were accepted by the mandate administration.[76] The Peel Commission considered that the Arabs had a genuine grievance as to the denial of citizenship for emigrants and that the British should utilise every effort to restore to these Arabs 'a right ordinarily enjoyed by the nationals of civilized peoples'. The Commission's report addressed the Palestinian Arab emigrants who did not take up any other nationality after they left Palestine as 'people who do not wish to be regarded as Turkish citizens' and who owed no allegiance to Turkey; further, Turkey did not want their allegiance. Instead, the emigrants had long 'regard[ed] Palestine as their country where their relatives still live' and that 'on the whole they maintain a substantial connexion [sic] with their families and their hope is to return to Palestine . . . to retire'. As for the mandatory, the Commission wrote that the administration knew the position of the emigrants and supposedly took all measures to facilitate their return and travel but large numbers of Palestinian Arabs in Latin America were unable to opt for citizenship and return to Palestine.[77] From the report, it is evident that Peel and his colleagues supported the argument of the Arabs against the mandate's citizenship provisions.

The Peel Commission concluded that it was 'reasonable and proper' that protection should be extended to the Arab emigrants by the mandatory. Indeed, it seems that the Commission felt that the emigrants' situation was important enough to be discussed despite objections by the British to the report. The Commission understood the attitudes of the middle-class nationalists towards Palestine's citizenship legislation:

> There is no genuine enthusiasm to be observed in Palestine for Palestinian citizenship. It is only the Arabs in South America who are really anxious for it. And under present conditions this does not surprise

us. Jewish immigrants may well hesitate to abandon the citizenship of some old established state in favour of citizenship in a country of which the future seems so uncertain. To the educated Palestinian Arab, who has always resented the separation of Palestine from Syria, the very idea of Palestinian citizenship is obnoxious as being associated with the Mandate and all it involves.[78]

Ten years after the first stirrings of discontent over the citizenship order, the voices of the emigrants and their supporters finally found public resonance and official expression in the report of the investigative commission. For the Arabs, however, the recommendation of partition overshadowed the report's favourable attitude toward citizenship legislation.

As is well known, the Arab leadership rejected the Peel report's suggestion of partition of Palestine. Although the report recommended that Palestine be split into an Arab and Jewish state with the designated holy areas (that is, sacred places such as Jerusalem and Nazareth) under an international mandate, it recognised the problems that that partition would cause for nationality and citizenship. The Commission referred to the initial and complicated problem of the status of Arabs in the Jewish state and vice versa, and expressed their hope that another body could 'avail itself of the service of experts on Nationality and Minority problems'.[79] It did recognise that those experts would need to design nationality and citizenship regulations broadly in order to accommodate the demands of the Arabs and the Jews in the territory. The Commission listed three possibilities for the implementation of the national and civic status of the inhabitants of the partitioned territories. First, it suggested that complete and full citizenship be given to every adult Arab who resided in the Jewish state if he wished. Of interest, the report also noted that nationality and citizenship were not the same and the differences could cause problems as states increasingly defined themselves in ethno-national terms. It was also noted that Arabs in the Jewish state may be given the option of citizenship in the co-national 'Mother State' on the other side of the border, meaning the Arab state.[80] The first option, to be sure, was quite new for the British Government since such flexible nationality and citizenship legislation had not been implemented in any of Great Britain's colonies or possessions.

In a partitioned Palestine, the Commission stated the second option to be the need for an inclusion of a minority statute as part of the constitution of the Jewish state in order to recognise the Arabs who resided within that state as a 'National Minority'. Presumably the same would be done in the Arab state, although the report envisaged that the number of Jewish residents was likely to be low given that the administration would be able to stop Jewish immigration and land purchases. Yet the rights to be given to national minorities were unclear. The third suggested option was that a 'Nationality Statute' recognise the Arab Palestinians as 'an Equal Nationality on par with the Jews, as a "*staatsvolk*," ' meaning that the Jewish state would be composed of and administered by the two constituent, equal nationalities.[81] The third option supported an egalitarian notion of citizenship for both groups.

British officials in London and in Palestine interpreted the recommendations in different ways. The report suggested that the third was the most feasible option as the one most likely to ensure cooperation from the Arabs in the administration of the Jewish state and to prepare the territory for a future union in a federation. The principle of bi-nationalism would be part of both the Arab and Jewish states. Some colonial officials argued that a minority nationality would not be adequate for either partitioned state because nationality would not be held equally and the minority group would not exercise the full political rights of citizenship.[82] In response to the report, the Higher Arab Committee commenting on the plans for minority and majority citizenships in a new Palestinian state argued the inadequacy of minority nationality. The HAC felt partition was simply neither possible nor acceptable.[83]

Each of the three options, if implemented, represented an attempt to create an efficient system of documentary identity, which had increased in global and colonial importance since the signing of the Treaty of Lausanne. These options were the expression of classifications of national identity and citizenship status as 'from above'. The Commission did not consider that the Arab and Jewish leaders themselves may be directly involved in the implementation of new nationality and citizenship regulations. Moreover, although the partition of Palestine meant that the Arab and the Jewish states would administer their respective territories autonomously, the legislative framework of the new status, including provisions of citizenship, would be devised by Great Britain. Despite the space given by the Peel Commission to Palestinian voices, the Commission did not address the Arabs' hope to design their own citizenship laws through an elected, representative parliament.

Proposed Amendments and Changes to Citizenship Legislation

Strong opposition to the plan for partition from within sections of the British Government, the Arab leadership and the Zionist Organisation prohibited its implementation. The Foreign Office objected to the Peel Commission's recommendation of partition and of unity between the Arab Palestinian state and Transjordan, while the Colonial Office endorsed it as the only acceptable solution to the situation in Palestine. The Foreign Office felt, as the Arab nationalist leaders had believed and voiced for nearly two decades, that the British could not possibly fulfil the mandate's obligations.[84] Since the partition scheme and options for new national statuses were not actually implemented in accordance with the Peel Report, the British Government in London and the Palestine Administration could begin the draft of an amended citizenship order in line with the report's other recommendations regarding Palestinian citizenship. The draft amendment of the citizenship order did not see official publication for two years after the Peel Report.

The events of 1936 and 1937, including the general strike, outright violent revolt and the work of the Peel Commission in Palestine highlight the multiple meanings for different segments of the Arab population on nationality, citizenship, civic duties and civic loyalties to the ambiguous 'nation'. The new atmosphere in Palestine after 1935 changed the Arab and the British understandings of the rights, duties and expressions of Palestinian citizenship as a result of the violent measures taken by the British administration to stop the Arab population from participating in the revolt. For a number of reasons, Palestinian citizenship lost some meaning during the revolt. On the one hand, the British military and civil authorities recommended emergency regulations and martial law measures such as collective punishment and the treatment of all civilians as rebels be applied only towards the Arab population. On the other, the Arab rebel leaders did not fully support liberal notions of citizenship such as due process and democratic representation as shown by their actions during the revolt. Hallmarks of citizenship practices such as non-payment of taxes and the general strike rested uneasily with those Palestinian Arabs who called for civic duties to be undertaken through violent resistance to the government.

Throughout the revolt, the vocabulary of citizenship and nationality did not change substantially. Rather it was partially appropriated by the Arab rebels in order to fit the concepts of citizenship and nationality into their view of a future Palestine independent from British control and Zionist influence. Still, the assumed legal parameters of citizenship were expressed actively through Arab support for the revolt. For example, protests, the non-payment of taxes and even the new, albeit non-democratic, measure of due process implemented by rebel courts transformed citizenship into a more tangible status of belonging to the Arab nation of Palestine. Yet the parallel legislative and judicial system put into practice by the peasant rebels during the revolt fell short of providing rights to the Arab population. Instead, it allowed for Arab civilians to be tried in rebel courts as 'traitors' and 'collaborators' without recourse to protections typically offered by civil constitutions. At the same time, the Peel Commission referred to problems caused by the citizenship legislation highlighting British favouritism for Jewish immigrants. The civil administration was not bound to implement the report's recommendations since the British Government did not require it to do so. The testimony of Arab national leaders on the issue of citizenship and their statistics on Jewish citizens are also telling. While heavily influenced by nationalist rhetoric and propaganda against mandate policy, it is difficult to construct a nuanced historical narrative based on the words of a few educated political leaders and writers. One can assume that these Arabs represented the feelings and beliefs of the majority of the population but it is difficult to gauge the extent to which mass notions of civic identity changed during the revolt. Similarly, the peasant rebel leaders did not have the full support of the wider population. What is clear, as shown by the actions of the rebels and the words and conclusion of the Peel report, is that by 1937 Arab nationality and Palestinian citizenship were imagined as distinct statuses as each entailed a different type of political, civic and social belonging to Palestine. The rights, protections and duties associated with this belonging also varied according to urban and rural leadership. These distinctions are crucial to the understanding of the process of citizenship and national identity affiliation in Palestine after the end of the revolt.

8

Conclusion – The End of the Experiment: Discourses on Citizenship at the Close of the Mandate

In 1938, the last full year of the Palestine Revolt, most of Palestine's more radical Arab leaders including former Istiqlalists and members of the Higher Arab Committee (HAC) had been deported to the Seychelles following their involvement in the general strike and revolt. Most remained interned as political prisoners through 1939. For these men, Palestinian citizenship seemed to be a meaningless status. As he began a hunger strike to protest his imprisonment, former Jerusalem mayor Husayn Khalidi wrote to High Commissioner Harold MacMichael (Arthur Wauchope's replacement) of his shame in 'remember[ing] I carry a British passport'. That passport issued by the Palestine Administration, wrote Khalidi, 'cannot accord its bearer the element once famed [of] British justice which accorded every citizen a right to stand his trial and defend himself'. Here, Khalidi referred to the lack of citizenship rights despite holding Palestinian citizenship – a legal status created by Great Britain – that he and many other Arabs had long envisioned would eventually confer such rights. Deported without a trial and held as a political prisoner on an island in the possession of Great Britain, Khalidi lamented to no effect in a petition to the high commissioner that '[w]e are either subjects of Your Majesty's Government and Empire or we are not'. If the former were true, Khalidi begged MacMichael to 'submit that we are entitled to some sort of protection, and such treatment consistent with the fact that we are human beings', such as rights of due process and return to Palestine.[1] The following year, the Foreign Office reaffirmed that Palestinian nationality did not reflect nationality in an ordinary sense, nor did it confer rights. Since the start of the mandate, the Palestinian Arabs had not given up demanding that the British grant them the bundle of rights that the former assumed were natural based on their Arab membership in the historical community and nation of Palestine. Instead, because the mandate territory was not an independent nation and since the mandatory had done very little to advance self-governing institutions, Palestine's inhabitants held a specialised and apolitical form of British-protected person or protégé status.[2]

The Palestine Revolt ultimately ended in 1939 as a failure for the Arab citizens of the mandate and their supporters outside of Palestine who desired self-government entirely free from British trusteeship. The revolt, like the general strike in 1936, ended due to Britain's overwhelming military and legislative power harnessed to arrest, deport and execute suspected rebels. For their part, Palestine's Arab leadership rejected the 1937 Peel Commission plan to partition the country between its Arab and Jewish inhabitants, but their calls for renewed strikes in opposition to the mandate had little effect. In addition to the deportations of urban Arab national leaders the mandate authorities executed more than 100 rebels and destroyed hundreds of houses. Arab deaths totalled 5,000 and the number of Arabs detained totalled more than 5,500.[3] The Palestinian Arab nationalist movement effectively split into a number of factions and a stark division emerged between the rural and the urban Arab leaders. In addition, a less stark but significant division started to grow between Christian and Muslim communities. Any inkling of a populist movement that could encompass all classes of Palestinian Arabs had little chance of succeeding and even the Mufti, Hajj Amin al-Husayni, had fled to Beirut during the revolt and did not return.

In the final months of the revolt in 1939, the British Government issued a new White Paper that for the first time described future limits to Jewish immigration and land purchases in Palestine, greater Arab involvement in the mandate government and the promise of independence within ten years. The 1939 White Paper ultimately meant very little, since both the Palestinian Arab leadership, which adhered to the opinion of the exiled Mufti, and the Zionist Organisation rejected its proposals.[4] At that time, Great Britain was increasingly pulled into European political events and could not devote significant resources to the post-revolt problems in Palestine. Despite their rejection of it, the Arabs affirmed the significance of the White Paper: they believed that the past two decades of appeals to Great Britain made a number of inroads. For the study of citizenship and political identity, the policy paper seemed to promise that Arab political control over Palestine could be tantalisingly close at hand. Once Jewish immigration and land purchases were curtailed, many nationalist leaders surmised, mandate institutions and legislation could be challenged and dismantled. Of course, the White Paper also seemed to signify that at the centre, Great Britain's Conservative Government warily realised the danger of continued support for rising immigration and the aims of Zionism in Palestine.[5]

The international situation in the late 1930s, particularly with regard to Germany's Jewish policy, affected Palestinian citizens in more ways than the related increase in both Jewish immigration and naturalisation. The Palestine Administration and, by extension, Whitehall, attempted to balance the mandate policy of support for Jewish immigration at a time when Germany began to clamp down on its Jewish citizens, with giving sufficient attention to the Arab demands for self-government. Great Britain also calculated its response to the Peel Commission report and although Whitehall ultimately refused to consider partition of Palestine, the government also knew that certain conditions proposed in the report to benefit the Arab inhabitants needed to be met. This final chapter explores the immediate reactions by Great Britain and the Mandate Government to the increase in Jewish immigration to Palestine and the changes made to the mandate's citizenship legislation in the wake of the revolt and the Peel report's recommendations. Significantly, on the eve of the Second World War citizenship in Palestine continued to be a crucial issue for Arab inhabitants and emigrants, as both groups increasingly feared the impact upon their communities as a result of the benefits and rights that accompanied citizenship status for Jewish immigrants and new Jewish refugees. The Arab community and its understanding of nationality, citizenship and political membership in the envisioned nation-state had changed greatly by 1939: this understanding was shaped by the immediate post-war disintegration of the Ottoman Empire and the accompanying transformations to political, social and civic interactions, and political institutions introduced (often inadvertently) by the existence of the mandate administration and the inclusion of Palestine in the British imperial system between the two world wars. The shifting demographics also changed the Arabs' perception of space, territory, civic behaviour and identity as it strengthened their sense of responsibilities, rights and duties within Palestine. Ultimately, high immigration and naturalisation figures in the years following the end of the Palestine Revolt in 1939 pushed up the percentage of Jewish citizens in Palestine vis-à-vis the Arab citizens. The outbreak of war in Europe and the subsequent impact on British administration in the mandate territory meant that Palestinian citizenship never fully evolved into a meaningful status that provided Palestinians with equal rights and duties as members of a nation-state.

Immigration, Nationality and Documentary Identity on the Eve of War

Significant changes to the perception of Jewish identity and immigration began to take place within Europe just as the attention of Great Britain was drawn away from the political situation in Palestine at the end of the 1930s. These changes affected the Arab citizens of the mandate as well. The treatment of Jews in Germany beginning in the early 1930s forced the Palestine Administration to differentiate between Arab and Jewish Palestinians when each left Palestine for international travel. It fell upon Great Britain to provide Germany with assurances that certain Palestinian citizens who requested residence in Germany for professional or academic reasons were in fact Arab, rather than Jewish, citizens. This is evidenced by an internal Colonial Office discussion on Germany's requirement that Great Britain forward a note of identification for a Palestinian Arab doctor, Mafid Abd al-Hadi. The office noted that it was evident that Abd al-Hadi was suspect due to his *Palestinian* nationality.[6] However, the suspicion of immigrants went both ways: the Palestine Administration received a number of warnings from the British Government to ensure that all persons who entered the mandate territory were genuine immigrants who did not attempt to evade immigration controls or seek political refuge.

In 1938, the Foreign Office warned the Crown's consular officers to be aware of individuals who impersonated Palestinian citizens in order to request Palestine passports. The problem had been widespread since the early 1930s, but with the increased number of Jews who sought Palestinian citizenship for political reasons, the Foreign Office hoped to stem any attempts by immigrants to use their nationality only for diplomatic protection. In particular, the office aimed the warning at a growing number of European Jews who requested Palestine passports for identification and travel purposes but who could not produce proof of their actual Palestinian citizenship.[7] The same problems that the administration encountered in the early 1930s persisted into the latter years of the decade. For example, a significant number of Jewish women tried to evade immigration regulations by entering false marriages with Palestinian citizens. In the first five months of 1938, Palestine's Commissioner of Migration and Statistics withheld Palestine passports from seventy-three Jewish women in Poland who falsely claimed to be legitimately married to Palestinians. E. Mills, the commissioner, noted that although his department withheld hundreds of passports altogether, incidents of so-called marriages of convenience decreased as immigration authorities carried out strict identity checks. Even so, out of almost 4,500 Palestinian Jewish marriages in 1936, half ended in divorce only two years later.[8] As the high commissioner and the Colonial Office simultaneously worked on draft citizenship amendment orders, both struggled with questions of how to prevent such abuses of Palestinian citizenship status and naturalisation in an internationally turbulent time period.

The 1938 Annual Report of the administration to the League of Nations included the year's summary of nationality issues and special cases. The report noted that in most special cases, the high commissioner granted naturalisation for Jewish immigrants regardless of whether those immigrants met the qualification of three years' residence in Palestine prior to their application to naturalise. In total, the administration issued more than 9,000 nationality certificates in 1938, which brought the total of certificates issued since 1925 to nearly 54,000 out of almost 61,000 applications. In 1938, more than 18,000 individuals acquired Palestinian citizenship, including wives and children of male immigrants, and possessed nationality certificates. Despite the high figures, the administration noted that compared to previous years, the number of naturalised citizens for the year actually dropped. Officials blamed the decrease on the disturbances and violence of the previous two years of revolt. Out of those naturalised in 1938, the majority were Polish and German Jews. In addition, ninety-two 'Turkish' individuals, forty Syrians and seventeen Egyptians became Palestinian citizens.[9]

The Palestine Administration issued a large number of Palestine passports in 1938 – nearly 15,600 – in spite of the disturbances. Officials noted that many Palestinian Arabs sought passports once they found themselves unable to cross freely into Syrian, Lebanese and Transjordanian territory. Palestinian Arabs who voluntarily left Palestine due to the revolt also needed passports.[10] Although officials tried to keep tabs on whether Jews who sought Palestine passports were actually entitled to them, a number of Jews who lived outside of Palestine and claimed to be too ill or poor to return were able to have their passports renewed by the administration. In most of these cases, the Palestine Administration consulted with the

Colonial Secretary and granted extensions of individual passport validity until the passport's holder claimed that he or she could return. Despite long absences and repeated failures of such Jewish Palestinian citizens to return to Palestine, most did not have their passports or certificates of naturalisation revoked.[11]

The Palestine passports themselves became symbolic of the seemingly unending internal administrative disagreements over Palestinian nationality and the role of Great Britain in providing documentary identity to Arab and Jewish citizens. Husayn Khalidi's letter to the high commissioner in 1938 is just one example of the complexities caused by the disagreements. In early 1939, the Foreign Office – then officially charged with Palestine policy – proposed that Palestine passports no longer have their covers labelled as a British passport but rather as 'Passport – British Mandated Territory of Palestine'. The change came as a response to two factors: the first, a larger move by the Dominions Office to have 'British Passport' printed on any passport issued by a British protectorate. Dominions officials felt Palestinians were as similar to British-protected persons as possible and the Foreign Office agreed that British passports did not mislead other nations as to the status of Palestinian citizens as not under the full sovereignty of Great Britain. However, other officials noted that since Palestinians were aliens under British immigration legislation, their claim to British passports was indeed misleading, and criticised the label 'British passport' because it gave an impression that holders were entitled to certain privileges. One Foreign Office member suggested the change because the then-current form of the passport 'was ambiguous to the ordinary man, particularly the ordinary Palestinian and he (unfortunately) cannot by any means be relied on to have an exact and correction notion of what a passport is or what the rather complicated international situation of Palestine is'.[12] Foreign officials suggested the change to the wording of the passport for a second reason. A court case at the end of 1938 that involved a Jewish Palestinian, *Rex vs. Ketter*, resulted in a legal report by the Court of Criminal Appeal titled 'Citizen in Palestine not a British subject'.[13] Palestinian citizens who also claimed British nationality often faced different treatment as to their status both within Great Britain and abroad. The court case affirmed that Palestinian citizenship did not translate to ipso facto British nationality.

Within Palestine, the administration also instituted a wider use of documentary identification cards. Through the final year of the Palestine Revolt, High Commissioner MacMichael discussed proposals for identity cards with Colonial Secretary Malcolm MacDonald.

The men concluded that compulsory cards would stem illegal immigration but they both realised the difficulties in obtaining cooperation from the Jewish community. In the final months of 1938, the Palestine Government instituted a voluntary system of identification cards with the hope that the population would become accustomed to showing their cards. By the end of 1938, more than 170,000 citizens had identity cards and, of that number, in the region of 90,000 were Arabs. However, the administration feared that Palestinian Arabs could be easily induced to destroy their identity documents for political reasons.[14] By the end of the first two decades of the civil administration, identity cards continued to be issued on a strictly voluntary basis. It is interesting to note that although some officials within Great Britain pressed for a more inclusive Palestinian citizenship for Jews, the Jewish community in Palestine did not wholeheartedly support compulsory identification cards or other measures to ensure they were documented as citizens.

Jewish Identity and Changes to Palestinian Citizenship

Shira Robinson argues that in post-Ottoman Palestine, the turn-of-the-century concept of 'racial unmixing' through the creation of states for one specific people (as popularised by British colonial official Lord Curzon) took on a decidedly more racialised cast in the mandate era. The Yishuv leadership posited Jewish immigrants and Jewish citizens as a racial, rather than religious, community. By the second decade of the mandate, the British also placed the Jewish immigrants into the 'white race' category. The British and, later, the 1947 United Nations Special Committee on Palestine (UNSCOP) visualised Palestine's Jews as composing their own racial – albeit white – group that was thus entitled to self-rule in part of Palestine.[15] The proposed exclusiveness of a Jewish Palestinian citizenship was not new – Chaim Weizmann had proposed a separate nationality for the Palestine's Jews even before the ratification of the mandate – and at the time of the growing Jewish refugee situation in the late 1930s members of Parliament began to discuss a greater racial segregation in the application of Palestinian citizenship as well.

After the release of the Peel Commission report in the summer of 1937, High Commissioner Wauchope and the Colonial Office separately drafted their own amended citizenship order-in-council in response to the report's recommendations for changes to the existing legislation. Up until that time, the process of drafting a new amended order had been deferred until the publication of the report. As in previous attempts to amend the 1925 Palestine Citizenship Order-in-Council, the administration questioned whether amendments would contravene the Treaty of Lausanne's nationality provisions. It remained recognised protocol that the other signatories of the treaty were required to approve proposed amendments to the mandates' citizenship laws.[16] Yet, unlike the previous years of debate over citizenship, the new issue of security played a major role both in terms of the need for the British to prevent further violence by the Arabs and to manage the ever-growing German and Polish Jewish immigrants.

In the first half of 1938, the Colonial Office expressed alarm after *The Times* published details of a bill introduced by a Member of Parliament that proposed a universal Palestinian citizenship for *all* Jews. Officials in the Colonial and Foreign Offices immediately feared the Arab reaction once news of the bill became known in Palestine. They quickly expressed the hope that the bill would not progress further. The under-secretary for the Colonial Office met with the bill's sponsor, Commander Locker-Lampson, and the latter explained that he meant the bill to only be 'a "gesture" . . . a matter more of "emotion" and he had not expected a division' as a result of its provisions. The sponsor affirmed his hopes that Great Britain would offer protection in the form of extra-territorial Palestinian citizenship for about 200,000 Jews in central European states.[17] Although after the secretary's discussions with the sponsor himelf, Locker-Lampson, the latter withdrew the proposed bill to extend Palestinian citizenship to all Jews. The Colonial Office stated that if such a freer grant of citizenship was contemplated for Jews outside of Palestine, 'it would be imperative not to overlook the claims of Arabs born in Palestine who are living abroad and have no opportunity in the present law to become Palestinian citizens'.[18] However, the mandate's citizenship legislation could not have been changed by the bill since an act of Parliament could not change the existing legislation in Palestine. Rather, only the king could do so through an order-in-council. In addition, United Kingdom legislation required that citizenship be based on domicile.

The Colonial Office also expressed the belief that if Palestine were partitioned in the future, the Jewish state would enact its own nationality law and definition of a Jew.[19] That definition complicated matters for the administration as it and the Colonial Office drafted changes to citizenship legislation. The discussions that arose out of attempts to resolve the complicated definition of 'Jewish' harked back to similar discussions that took place on the nationality of Jewish individuals in the early 1920s between the Palestine Arab Executive, including Musa Kazim al-Husayni, and the British Colonial Office. The settlement upon a proper definition of 'Jewish' had long been avoided by British and mandate officials despite numerous Arab requests for the definition of nationality in relation to the Jewish national home.

By 1938 the government in Great Britain increasingly gave attention both to the Jewish refugee problem in central Europe and to a fear that Palestine was far too small a territory to play any significant role in its solution. Other political leaders agreed with the idea behind the bill noted above, and the possible solution it posed. Colonial officials continued to stress to Cabinet that if all Jews were granted Palestinian citizenship, Great Britain would be obliged to undertake special duties 'to the Jewish race as a whole'. Such a view had been resisted by successive British governments since the time of the Balfour Declaration in 1917; instead, the Colonial Office stated that governmental obligations were 'strictly limited to facilitating the Zionist ideal of the establishment of a national home for Jews in Palestine (an ideal to which large numbers of Jews are indifferent, or even hostile)'. A number of specific changes suggested to Palestinian citizenship were 'fundamentally inconsistent with accepted British principles of nationality laws', according to the Colonial Office, which began to make this stance publically clearer. Despite the problems with the proposal to extend Palestinian citizenship to Jews throughout the world, the House of Commons split the vote perfectly on Locker-Lampson's bill before its withdrawal, with 144 votes in support and 144 votes in opposition.[20]

The late 1930s ushered in a flurry of Jewish lobby efforts to influence the proposed amended citizenship order. The Jewish Agency requested that Jewish refugees from Germany be given the 'full rights of citizenship' upon their arrival into Palestine, which would entail that the administration overlook the two-year residency period required before these immigrants could naturalise. The Home Office declined to consider the suggestion while High Commissioner MacMichael expressed his disagreement with it, noting that the provision would 'differentiate between Jews in Palestine on the grounds of nationality'. Indeed, no longer would the distinction in citizenship be between Jews and Arabs but between Jews of different origins and political backgrounds. The status of German Jews in British territories as 'enemy subjects' would actually become a privilege if the administration enacted the suggestion. The Jewish

Agency's plan could have allowed one group of Jews to receive natu-ralisation under exceptional circumstances. In a climate of increas-ing anxiety over a new war, MacMichael did, however, note that it could be beneficial to grant Jews in Palestine who joined His Maj-esty's Armed Forces immediate citizenship upon enlistment.[21]

The problematic situation of Palestinian Arab natives abroad received attention once again in light of the proposed bill and the Peel Commission recommendations as the Palestine Administration and the Colonial Office drafted versions of a citizenship order-in-council amendment. In fact, the Middle East Division of the Colonial Office wrote to Palestine's Chief Secretary Sydney Moody in mid-1938 that the department had not forgotten the question on grants of citizen-ship to persons born in Palestine and resident abroad. The Colonial Office and other officials in London analysed Peel's recommenda-tions for these Arabs who could not receive citizenship. The office's draft amendment met the points made by the Royal Commission but expressed hope to further quantify the meaning of 'unbroken personal connection' with respect to the need to offer citizenship to those emigrants who demonstrated such a connection.[22] By 1938, the draft amendment had been seen and re-drafted by the Colonial, For-eign and Home Offices of the British Government.[23] Although draft amended orders were started by both the Palestine Administration and the Colonial Office in 1937, they floated between departments and individual officials until 1939. Only then was the amended citi-zenship order-in-council published.

The drafts of the new amendment focused on the status of Jew-ish immigrants, married Jewish women and children, all of which had remained unsolved by the 1931 amendment. The usual debate over changes ensued, particularly as to whether a married woman's nationality depended entirely on her husband and whether women could be naturalised as Palestinians separately from their husbands. The League of Nations had debated the same issue earlier in the 1930s but the Government of Great Britain and its Dominions Office did not agree with demands by women's organisations to implement such a change. After much discussion, in May 1939 High Commis-sioner MacMichael accepted the final draft for the amended order-in-council, minus one final change that involved questions over how the administration could deprive minors of citizenship. The admin-istration initially intended for the amended order to end the nearly decade-long debate over the naturalisation of women separately from their husbands. The 1939 amendment's Article 6 clearly stated that the citizenship status of women was governed by their husbands.

This came despite the insistence from various governmental officials in Great Britain that separate naturalisation facilities would bar the entrance of 'undesirables' into Palestine.

Two months later, on 25 July 1939, His Majesty's Government ratified the new Palestine Citizenship (Amendment) Order-in-Council of 1939. The primary change in the new amendment, which revoked the 1931 order's Article 12, allowed that an alien woman married to a Palestinian citizen did not become a Palestinian by reason of marriage but, rather, she would receive a certificate of naturalisation on separate terms from her husband.[24] The problem of undesirables in Palestine who evaded immigration controls remained only tenuously solved. For the Palestinian Arabs, the changes made to Article 2 of the principle (1925) order had a significant impact. The changes affected the status of Palestinian-born Arabs who resided abroad: those who possessed Ottoman nationality on the date of the 1925 Palestine Citizenship Order-in-Council, or continued to hold Turkish citizenship, and who had 'since maintained an unbroken personal connection with Palestine and intend to resume permanent residence in Palestine' were given the opportunity for the first time to acquire Palestinian citizenship by stating their option for it. The option was, as it had always been, subject to the consent of the Government of Palestine and those who chose to opt could not hold any other nationality but Turkish. The article allowed for two years from the date of the amendment for natives to exercise their option for citizenship, and allowed natives to send their applications to do so to any British consul to be forwarded to the Director of Immigration in Jerusalem.[25] The amended Article 2 exclusively benefited the Palestinian Arabs by offering natives abroad the chance to take on citizenship that had been denied for nearly fifteen years. The victory was significant for the Arab Palestinians in that the government finally met the demands of the emigrants and their nationalist lobby group. The change had also come less than two years after the publication of the Royal Peel Commission recommendations, which included a proposal to extend Palestinian citizenship to all Arab natives abroad. Indeed, the change came after significant discussion between the Colonial, Foreign and Home Offices. The Home Office in particular felt that the Treaty of Lausanne allowed states to offer certain options in cases of nationality not provided for in the treaty itself thus allowing 'default' Turkish nationals to choose Palestinian citizenship.[26]

The final amendment to the Palestine citizenship legislation came in 1942. A new amendment granted an extension of the initial two-year timeframe for option for citizenship (as included in the 1939 Amendment Order) to six years.[27] Despite the changes to legislation to allow for native Palestinians to return to their homeland and choose its citizenship, only a small number of individuals did so. From 1925 to 1946, fewer than 500 native Palestinian Arabs who lived outside of Palestine actually returned and acquired citizenship. The reasons for the small numbers of returnees are not entirely clear. As Mutaz Qafisheh rightly argues, a number of factors played a role as to how and why emigrants returned as Palestinian citizens. He suggests that the discretion exercised by the high commissioners had a negative impact on Palestinian Arabs who applied to opt for citizenship but could not prove a definitive, unbroken personal connection with their homeland. Perhaps just as important was the international context after 1939 – the outbreak of war in Europe meant that immigration to Palestine became more restrictive not only for Jews but also for Arabs born in the territory.[28] Furthermore, many Arabs had since established businesses, social networks and familial roots outside of Greater Syria, territory that some of them left prior to 1914.

The Palestine Citizenship Order-in-Council of 1925, and the subsequent amended articles and amended orders that replaced it, transformed the Palestinian Arab and the Jewish immigrant populations into the citizenry of a quasi-colonial state. For the Arab inhabitants, the orders did something more: the provisions differentiated the formerly Ottoman nationals born in Palestine from Arabs (and other ethnic groups) born elsewhere in Greater Syria. The institutions and the new political, civic and social interactions created and maintained due to the British-administered government shaped new public spaces and new systems of meaning and power that Palestinian Arab leaders linked directly to their notions of citizenship and nationality. Although the Palestinian Arab leadership conceived of themselves as Palestinians long before the citizenship order – and for some time before the beginning of the civil administration – these national and local leaders also saw themselves as Arab nationals alongside Syrian, Lebanese and Iraqi Arabs. The citizenship legislation changed that perception both ideologically and in practical, on-the-ground ways. In the middle of 1939, less than ten years before the mandate ended and Palestine's Jewish citizens declared the establishment of Israel, the British Government asked Palestine's High Commissioner MacMichael to give an assurance that the mandatory would invest the same amount of energy into preventing illegal Arab immigration into the territory as it did in preventing illegal Jewish immigration. In response to MacMichael's assurance, government officials asked

whether the answer proved that the Arabs of Palestine were 'a separate and distinct people from Arabs of other countries'.[29] The answer
to the latter question, even without MacMichael's assurances, can
most certainly be demonstrated by the preceding twenty years of
legislation, discourses, representations and behaviours that shaped
Palestinian nationality and citizenship.

Conclusions: Citizenship at the End of the Palestine Mandate and upon the Creation of Israel

The Palestine Administration and the British Government acted in
nearly all cases related to citizenship, nationality and passports from
1918 to the year that saw the final changes to citizenship legislation,
1942, to maintain the status quo support for the mandate's terms
that supported Jewish immigration and naturalisation as the primary
means through which the Jewish national homeland could be established under the auspices of the mandate itself. For at least the first
decade of the civil administration, the first consideration for all of the
proposed legislation and regulations, whether by the local administration officials or the officials and policy-makers in Whitehall, was
towards the facilitation of this aim in as much as it did not contradict
or call into question wider British imperial policy and norms. Citizenship legislation received the same preliminary caution and treatment,
although this legislation never progressed beyond its original aim to
regulate the legal and international status and documentary identity
of Palestine's population. Thus, citizenship legislation was crucial to
the success of the mandate policy, and the Palestine Administration
and Great Britain ultimately surrendered to the need to maintain a
successful policy and hold ultimate imperial authority in Palestine by
regulating citizenship in the ways that it did – ways that did favour
continued Jewish immigration. Even so, the 1925 Palestine Citizenship Order-in-Council left various questions as to the status of the
Arab and Jewish natives and inhabitants of the territory unsolved: it
created more debate – within Palestine, Whitehall and the Arab (and
Jewish) diaspora than it resolved in the long and short term. Neither Great Britain nor Palestine's attorney-general clearly differentiated in vocabulary between nationality and citizenship despite the
practical differences emphasised by the mandate administration and
the persistent appeals by the Arab community to design citizenship
acquisition as based upon a primordial notion of Arab and Ottoman
nationality. This lack of differentiation in terminology plagued the

Palestine Administration for some time, in large part because the Arabs conflated the two terms and applied this conflation to their understanding of Jewish nationality in Palestine.

The new, mainly middle-class political public in Palestine, as elsewhere in the interwar and post-colonial period, was an essential part of the creation, vocabulary, behaviours, and development of types of representations of citizenship. Alongside new civil society organisations and the practices that they encouraged, the political public firmly separated itself from the administration and thus negotiated citizenship and nationality within a particular discursive space. The groundwork for the discussions of citizenship came out of the steady rise of mass politics bolstered by the Arabic press and as a reaction to British legislation in Palestine, including the reactionary hopes that this administration would grant self-governing institutions managed by the Arabs. The vocabulary of citizenship and nationality and the discussions on both that had been known since the mid-nineteenth century were the resources used by the Palestinian Arab educated leaders to explain, define, strengthen and challenge the construction of citizenship by the government. In their own civic and political associations, the emigrant community reflected upon the differences in meaning between nationality and citizenship, and the practical differences between the national and the citizen of a state. Particularly through use of the term '*jinsiyya*' (nationality) rather than '*muwatana*' (citizenship), the emigrants and their supporters and the press within Palestine, reinforced a conflation of the two terms.

The British presence in Palestine and the institutions that the mandate established ultimately supported the conditions necessary to foster the Arabs' claims to rights *to* Palestine. These conditions thus promoted the growing and general sense of participatory rights and duties and by the early 1930s, rural and lower-class Palestinian Arabs actively demanded greater rights and protections from the administration. Yet before Palestinian citizenship and the Palestinian citizen vanished upon the proclamation of Israel as a Jewish state, the practical expressions of citizenship and the rights and duties associated with it, had stalled or regressed as spaces and tentative institutions for those expressions closed. The revolt, and the subsequent Peel Commission report, confirmed the unequal distribution of rights, benefits and protections of mandate citizenship between Arabs and Jews in Palestine and the discontent felt by the former group over such a situation. At the same time, the Arab rebels refused to consider a future Palestine in which Arabs and Jews could hold an equal citizenship status.

Despite the attempts of Palestine's high commissioners to effect any favourable changes to citizenship legislation for the Arab emigrants, none actually succeeded in changing the *structure* of that legislation. Tensions within the administration and between Palestine and London contributed to the application and approval of various legislative measures for Palestine. As needs no explanation here, at the end of November 1947 the new United Nations General Assembly voted to partition Palestine (Resolution 181) and thus absolve Great Britain from further responsibility over the territory. The 1947 UN Resolution 181 referred to Palestinian citizens in relation to elections for the proposed partitioned Arab and Jewish states: according to the UN, those given the right of the franchise, the most basic political right of citizenship, were to be those over the age of eighteen who were Palestinian citizens resident in Palestine, as well as Jews and Arabs resident in Palestine who were not yet Palestinian citizens but would sign a note of intention to become citizens. 'Citizens' continued to be mentioned, albeit ambiguously, in terms of rights and freedoms given to all residents of the future Arab and Jewish states. Chapter 3 of Resolution 181 specifically focused on citizenship. Palestinian citizens, according to legislation, in Palestine outside of Jerusalem and those Arabs and Jews without citizenship who lived in Palestine would become citizens of the state of their residence upon independence, and have all the civil and political rights of citizenship. The residents of Jerusalem were to become automatically citizens of the City of Jerusalem unless they gave intent to opt for citizenship of the Arab or Jewish state. Jerusalem citizens were to have the appropriate civil and political rights regardless of nationality.[30]

The declaration of a Jewish state on 15 May 1948 and the intensified fighting between the Jewish militias and the Arab and Palestinian armies and irregulars before and after this date led to an exodus of from 250,000 to 350,000 Palestinian Arab citizens from the territory. From 1948 until 1952, when Israel passed its Nationality Law, Palestinian Arabs were effectively stateless because Israel's Supreme Court held that Palestinian citizenship terminated on 14 May 1948. The Israeli Nationality Law was not a *citizenship* law. In fact, the law affirmed the denaturalisation of the Arabs as retroactive from the date of Israel's declaration of statehood. Article 3 of the law stated that children born to stateless Palestinian Arab parents were also stateless.[31] A nationality committee convened under the command of Ben-Gurion in 1949 but until 1952 the legal status of Israeli citizenship for Jews and Arabs both did not exist. Robinson has recently shown that for both Palestinian Arab citizens of Israel (post-1951) and Palestinian Arabs who remained outside of Israel after 1948, the Israeli state's citizenship law was framed to stop Palestinians from returning to their original homes from exile or from remaining in their homes.[32] She argues that David Ben-Gurion, Israel's first prime minister, charged Israel's first policy-makers as early as 1947 to draft a future constitution that would reconcile Jewish statehood with popular democracy. This proved impossible: the Arabs in Israel were instead 'invited' to become a part of the new state as its citizens but such a status was not enshrined as a democratic principle.[33]

In an odd twist, Israel's immigrant Jewish population came to be called 'native nationals' of the land after 1948 despite the fact that they were not nationals of the land prior to May 1948, nor were they a native-born population. Israeli policy-makers categorised the Arabs, on the other hand, as foreigners or aliens (*zarim*).[34] However, the discourse of democratic and rights-based citizenship claims continued to permeate petitions and demands submitted to the new government by its recently created Arab Israeli citizens. Instead of a democratic, rights-based citizenship, these Arabs received their Israeli citizenship by virtue of their residence in the territory upon the date of the passage of the 1952 Israeli Nationality Law. This method of offering citizenship mirrored the Lausanne Treaty's provisions for the ways in which the same status was automatically conferred in the Arab mandate territories. Additionally, as Lena Dallasheh has recently shown, negotiations over citizenship continued immediately after May 1948 in Arab-majority areas of Israel such as Nazareth, taking the form of negotiations over rights to water resources and land.[35]

The Palestinian Arabs who came under Jordanian administration in the West Bank did not receive Jordanian nationality until the West and East banks were united under one administration in 1950. All Arabs with Palestinian citizenship prior to 15 May 1948 (except for Jews) and permanently resident in the Hashemite Kingdom received Jordanian nationality after 1950. Meanwhile in Gaza under Egyptian Administration, the Basic Law of 1955 stipulated a constitution for the Gaza Strip and kept all laws in force from the 1922 Order-in-Council as long as they did not contradict the Basic Law. Gaza's 1962 Constitutional Order emphasised Palestinian identity and affirmed Gaza to be an integral part of Palestinian territory – its inhabitants did not receive Egyptian nationality. Instead, the 1962 order stated that all Palestinians, in Gaza and elsewhere, were one national entity with one Palestinian nationality.[36] Four years after the formation of the Palestine Liberation Organisation (Harakat al-Tahrir al-Filastini) (the PLO), the Palestinian National Charter of 1968 included Article 4 that stated that Palestinian identity passed by blood, *jus sanguinis*, and the aftermath of the Arab expulsion in 1948 from the mandate territory did not negate that identity nor cause a loss of membership as Palestinians in the Palestinian community. Article 5 then defined the Palestinians, for the first time officially under a Palestinian quasi-government, as 'those Arab nationals who, until 1947, normally resided in Palestine regardless of whether they were evicted from it or have stayed there. *Anyone born after that date, of a Palestinian father – whether inside Palestine or outside it – is also a Palestinian.*' The following article stated that Jews who normally resided in Palestine before the opening of the country to Zionist settlement were also Palestinian. At the same time, the Charter declared the mandate over Palestine and everything based upon it as null and void, noting that Judaism was not an independent nationality and that Jews were citizens of the states to which they belonged originally.[37]

In 1995, the interim government created by the Oslo Accords, the Palestinian Authority (PA), drafted a citizenship law but did not publicise or pass it. Citizenship could not have been regulated by the PA anyway, since the authority operated under Israeli occupation.[38] Next, the third Draft Palestine Constitution gave citizenship to any Palestinian resident of Palestine before 1948. It envisioned that citizenship pass by descent through mothers and fathers and, importantly, that it would pass indefinitely without time limits. Further, all those former citizens with the right of return were to have Palestinian nationality.[39] The most recent official mention of Palestinians in the context of nationality is from the Basic Law of the PA in 2003 but the law fails to define Palestinians and is unclear as to whether Palestinians resident outside of the West Bank and Gaza can claim the rights of citizenship, including the franchise. Article 7 of the Basic Law states that 'Palestinian citizenship shall be regulated by law' and Articles 21 through 33 list the political, civil and social rights of citizenship.[40] According to the Draft Constitution of 2003, Palestinian nationals who are not citizens will indeed have representation in a future Advisory Council.[41] Within Israel, new government policies and certain political ideologies since the second intifada have created a consciousness that Arab citizens' citizenship is not real citizenship in the sense of civil and political rights. The Israelis see citizenship as a 'conditional privilege' for their Arab residents rather than a right.[42]

At the core of citizenship inclusion in the modern state is the way that the status allows for the regulation of power. Citizenship determines the criteria for membership into the decision-making processes of a state, and it determines who receives the state's assistance and benefits. In the case of an independent Palestinian state, the criteria for citizenship must be more than superficially stated in order to give Palestinian nationals – whether refugees or not – clear terms for membership in that state and hence access to its decisions and benefits. The laws of state succession that governed the transfer of nationality after the end of the First World War no longer apply. Other legal norms and arguments have taken their place such as the argument by Victor Kattan that all Palestinians have been denationalised following the end of 1948, and remain without nationality until the time when a Palestinian state will be able to provide such nationality.[43]

British colonial officials in Palestine and London debated for two years in the early 1920s on the subject of whether to pass a citizenship law. They debated whether to first define the citizenry in order to give them the right to vote without a constitution, or whether to give citizenship first to allow for a constitution to be formed by elected representatives. Ultimately, the Palestine Administration did not enact either option as such. The legacy continues even today: the same issue applies to the current situation in the West Bank, Gaza Strip and wherever Palestinian nationals have been scattered: should citizenship and the electorate in a Palestinian state be defined first without a constitution or basic law in order for the citizens to draft a constitution, or must citizenship be imposed first without representative decisions made upon its provisions? If nationality is decided upon as the criteria for citizenship, it is essential to recognise the Palestinian national and the Palestinian citizen as two different statuses; thus, nationality does not necessarily translate into citizenship. If the right of return is the criteria for determining citizenship, due to international law all Palestinian nationals (as all have the right to return) will be deemed citizens.

Indeed, historically, the Palestinian Arabs – and likewise the Palestinian Jews – never became 'national citizens' during the mandate in the sense that scholars today define the phrase. In the absence of an autonomous nation-state, national citizenship remained out of reach. Part of the blame for this absence is to be laid indirectly on the actions of the British Administration, led largely by imperial concerns as well as initial disinterest in how legal citizenship impacted political understandings of rights, and the ways through which the administration in Palestine and the government in Great Britain bureaucratised citizenship and categorised the citizens by their respective religious communities. This, in turn, can be partly framed by Britain's perception of Palestine within the imperial and international contexts and the need felt by Great Britain that Palestine to conform to both contexts despite its international position. Without a doubt colonial, or mandate, citizenship was imposed upon, and experienced by, Arabs and Jews in Palestine unequally. The institutionalisation of citizenship, and the nature of that insitutionalisation, ensured that the mandated citizens themselves had no share in their status – it was not a citizenship that they envisioned nor was it *for* them.

Notes

Notes to Chapter 1

1. 'A change of the present government', 25 September 1929, *Sawt al-Sha'b*.
2. Some exceptions exist for studies on the French in Algeria, and the reverse, Algerian Muslim immigrants to France. One example is Ian Coller's *Arab France: Islam and the Making of Modern Europe, 1798–1831* (Berkeley: University of California Press, 2010). However, these studies do not offer regional comparisons or place the context of the changing international system of the interwar period at their centre.
3. Minutes of the 24th session of the Council, Geneva, April 1923, *League of Nations Offical Journal*, 4th Yr. No. 6 (June 1923): 567–8.
4. Rogers Brubaker, *Nationalism Reframed: Nationhood and the National Question in the New Europe* (Cambridge: Cambridge University Press, 1996), p. 3.
5. For a fuller analysis, see Rieko Karatani, *Defining British Citizenship: Empire, Commonwealth, and Modern Britain* (London: Frank Cass, 2003).
6. Engin F. Isin, 'Theorizing acts of citizenship', in *Acts of Citizenship*, eds Engin F. Isin and Greg M. Nielson (London: Zed Books, 2008), pp. 17–18.
7. Helen Haste, 'Constructing the citizen', *Political Psychology* 25 (June 2004): 428.
8. William Hanley, 'When did Egyptians stop being Ottomans? An imperial citizenship case study', in *Multilevel Citizenship*, ed. Willem Mass (Philadelphia: University of Pennsylvania Press, 2013), p. 108.
9. Hanley, 'When did Egyptians stop being Ottomans?', p. 95.
10. Benjamin Thomas White, *The Emergence of Minorities in the Middle East: The Politics of Community in French Mandate Syria* (Edinburgh: Edinburgh University Press, 2011), p. 34.
11. This perception of the Palestinian Arabs immediately after 1918 is somewhat akin to what William Hanley describes for Egyptian subjects under multi-layered Ottoman imperial and British protection after 1882. See Hanley, pp. 90–3.

12. Alan Lester, 'Imperial circuits and global networks: Geographies of the British Empire', *History Compass* 4 (2006): 129.
13. Kathleen Wilson, *The Island Race* (London: Routledge, 2003), pp. 11–16.
14. Ann Laura Stoler, *Carnal Knowledge and Imperial Power: Race and the Intimate in Colonial Rule* (Berkeley: University of California Press, 2002), p. 98.
15. Regionally, nowhere is this truer than the case of the French in Algeria and their decision in the nineteenth century to treat Algerian Jews (and Christians) as French nationals.
16. M. Page Baldwin, 'Subject to Empire: Married women and the British nationality and status of Aliens Act', *Journal of British Studies* 40 (October 2001): 525–7.
17. Wilson, *The Island Race*, p. 40.
18. Niraja Gopal Jayal, *Citizenship and its Discontents: An Indian History* (Cambridge, MA: Harvard University Press, 2013), p. 30. Also see the work of Stoler (above) and Frederick Cooper, *Colonialism in Question: Theory, Knowledge, History* (Berkeley: University of California Press, 2005).
19. Frederick Cooper, *Citizenship between Empire and Nation: Remaking France and French Africa, 1945–1960* (Princeton: Princeton University Press, 2014), p. 33.
20. Cooper, *Citizenship*, p. 4.
21. Ann Dummett and Andrew Nicol, *Subjects, Citizens, Aliens and Others: Nationality and Immigration Law* (London: Weidenfeld and Nicolson), pp. 2–3.
22. Ilana Feldman, *Governing Gaza: Bureaucracy, Authority, and the Work of Rule, 1917–1967* (Durham, NC: Duke University Press, 2008), pp. 194–6.
23. Jurgen Habermas, 'Citizenship and national identity', in *Theorizing Citizenship*, ed. Ronald Beiner (Albany: State University of New York Press, 1995), pp. 258–73; Angus Stewart, 'Two conceptions of citizenship', *The British Journal of Sociology* 6 (March 1995): 66.
24. Rogers Brubaker, *Citizenship and Nationhood in France and Germany* (Cambridge, MA: Harvard University Press, 1992), pp. 123–4.
25. Rogers Brubaker, *Nationalism Reframed: Nationhood and the National Question in the New Europe* (Cambridge: Cambridge University Press, 1996), p. 33. Similar meanings for these concepts specific to the Arab world can be found in Gianluca P. Parolin, *Citizenship in the Arab World: Kin, Religion and Nation-State* (Amsterdam: Amsterdam University Press, 2009), p. 13.

26. According to the narrative of citizenship as linked with the nation-state, the city was the space in which groups defined their identity, rights and duties as citizens; ibid., pp. 34–41. For more, see Thomas Janoski and Brian Gran, 'Political citizenship: Foundations of rights', in *Handbook of Citizenship Studies*, eds Engin F. Isin and Bryan Turner (London: Sage, 2002), p. 13.

27. John Torpey, *The Invention of the Passport: Surveillance, Citizenship and the State* (Cambridge: Cambridge University Press, 2000), pp. 4, 58–71, 116–23.

28. David Miller, *Citizenship and National Identity* (Cambridge: Polity Press, 2000), p. 83.

29. Bryan S. Turner, 'Contemporary problems in the theory of citizenship', in *Citizenship and Social Theory*, ed. Bryan S. Turner (London: Sage, 1993), p. 4. Citizenship allows for three classes of rights: civil, political and social, which Marshall identified as part of the stages of citizenship formation. The first stage of this formation is the development of civil rights, such as the definition and institutionalisation of individual freedoms and securities in the state. The next step was the formation of political citizenship, inaugurated when individuals participate in politics. Political rights include the franchise, due process and rights to fair trials. Social citizenship, the third stage, advances once rights of social entitlement, such as welfare, are introduced by the state for its citizens.

30. However, one must be especially careful when defining Ottoman nationality in terms of instances or absences of certain rights and duties associated with membership in a nation-state. See Engin F. Isin, 'Citizenship after Orientalism: Ottoman citizenship', in *Challenges to Citizenship in a Globalizing World: European Questions and Turkish Experiences*, eds F. Keyman and A. Icduygu (London: Routledge, 2005), p. 33.

31. Michelle U. Campos, *Ottoman Brothers: Muslims, Christians, and Jews in Early Twentieth Century Palestine* (Stanford: Stanford University Press, 2011), p. 61.

32. See the application of this in the centre and in the Empire's provinces in Erol Ülker, 'Contextualising 'Turkification': Nation-building in the late Ottoman Empire, 1908–18', *Nations and Nationalism* 11 (2005): 613–36.

33. For a more general discussion on the late nineteenth-century British perceptions of the Near East see Michelle Tusan, *Smyrna's Ashes: Humanitarianism, Genocide, and the Birth of the Middle East* (Berkeley: University of California Press, 2012), pp. 3–8, as well as Toby Dodge, *Inventing Iraq: The Failure of Nation Building and a History Denied* (London: Hurst and Co., 2003).

34. The mindset of colonial officials on the issue of citizenship did not radically change after the end of the First World War. The influence of Indian identity legislation was significant for the Middle East, and especially Palestine. The colonial government in India divided the Indian population into different communities and argued that the population was not politically mature enough to hold citizenship. See the first chapter of Gopal Jayal, *Citizenship and its Discontents*, pp. 6–21; also see Jennifer Pritts, *A Turn to Empire: The Rise of Liberalism in Britain and France* (Princeton: Princeton University Press, 2005), pp. 97–8, 139–43.

35. To be sure, research into such terminology in the post-Ottoman Arab Levant would be very much welcomed. Jonathan Marc Gribetz has recently written a study on race in Jewish/Zionist and Arab encounters in the late Ottoman period. He argues that the category of the 'nation' did not dominate discourse in these encounters but race and religion certainly did. See Gribetz, *Defining Neighbors: Religion, Race, and the Early Zionist–Arab Encounter* (Princeton: Princeton University Press, 2014).

36. Helen Haste, 'Constructing the citizen', *Political Psychology* 25 (June 2004): 420.

37. Newer works on late Ottoman Palestine and identity include Michelle U. Campos, *Ottoman Brothers*; Yuval Ben-Bassat, *Late Ottoman Palestine: The Period of Young Turk Rule* (London: I. B. Tauris, 2011); Abigail Jacobson, *From Empire to Empire: Jerusalem between Ottoman and British Rule* (Syracuse: Syracuse University Press, 2011); A.W. Said Kayyali, *Palestine: A Modern History* (London: I. B. Tauris, 1978); Kushner, David, ed. *Palestine in the Late Ottoman Period* (Leiden: Brill, 1986); Alexander Scholch, *Palestine in Transformation, 1856–1882* (Washington, DC: Institute for Palestine Studies, 1993); Beshara Doumani, *Rediscovering Palestine: Merchants and Peasants in Jabal Nablus, 1700–1900* (Berkeley: University of California Press, 1995); Hasan Kayali, *Arabs and Young Turks: Ottomanism, Arabism, and Islamism in the Ottoman Empire, 1908–1918* (Berkeley: University of California Press, 1997).

38. See the article of Awad Halabi, 'Liminal loyalties: Ottomanism and Palestinian responses to the Turkish War of Independence, 1919–1922', *Journal of Palestine Studies* 41 (spring 2012): 19–37.

39. Torpey, *The Invention of the Passport: Surveillance, Citizenship and the State*, 5.

40. Will Hanley, 'Papers for going, papers for staying: Identification and subject formation in the Eastern Mediterranean', in *A Global Middle East: Mobility, Materiality and Culture in the Modern Age, 1880–1940*, eds Liat Kozma, Cyrus Schayegh and Avner Wishnitzer (London: I. B. Tauris, 2015), p. 178.

41. The Syrian and Lebanese *mahjar* have been the focus of a number of more recent histories of Arab emigration in the late nineteenth and early twentieth centuries but those emigrants from Palestine have been largely left out of these studies. See newer works such as: Jacob Norris, 'Exporting the Holy Land: Artisans and merchant migrants in Ottoman era Bethlehem', *Mashriq & Mahjar: Journal of Middle East Migration Studies* 1 (fall/winter 2013): 14–40; Stacy Fahrenthold, 'Transnational modes and media: The Syrian press in the *Mahjar* and emigrant activism during World War I', *Mashriq & Mahjar: Journal of Middle East Migration Studies* 1 (spring 2013): 32–57; Camila Pastor de Maria Campos, 'The Mashriq unbound: Arab modernism, *Criollo* nationalism, and the discovery of America by the Turks', *Mashriq & Mahjar: Journal of Middle East Migration Studies* 2 (fall/winter 2014): 28–54; Andrew Arsan, *Interlopers of Empire: The Lebanese Diaspora in Colonial French West Africa* (Oxford: Oxford University Press, 2014). Less recent works include Nancie L. Gonzalez, *Dollar, Dove, and Eagle: One Hundred Years of Palestinian Migration to Honduras* (Ann Arbor: University of Michigan Press, 1992); Roberto Marin-Guzman, *A Century of Palestinian Immigration into Central America* (University of Costa Rica, 2000); Manzar Foroohar, 'Palestinians in Central America: From temporary emigrants to a permanent diaspora', *Journal of Palestine Studies* 40 (spring 2011): 6–22; Kenny Saade and Kathy Saade, 'The power of place: Katrina in five worlds', *Jerusalem Quarterly* 35 (autumn 2008): 5–30; Christina Civantos, *Between Argentines and Arabs: Argentine Orientalism, Arab Immigrants and the Writing of Identity* (Albany: State University of New York Press, 2005); Kemal Karpat, 'The Ottoman emigration to the America, 1860–1914', *International Journal of Middle East Studies* 17 (May 1985): 175–209; Albert Hourani and Nadim Shehadi, eds, *The Lebanese in the World: A Century of Emigration* (London: I. B. Tauris, 1992); Akram Fouad Khater, *Inventing Home: Emigration, Gender, and the Middle Class in Lebanon, 1870–1920* (Berkeley: University of California Press, 2001); Sarah Gualtieri, *Between Arab and White: Race and Ethnicity in the Early Syrian American Diaspora* (Berkeley: University of California Press, 2009); Adnan Musallam on Bethlehem's emigrants in *Folded Pages from Local Palestinian History in the 20*th *Century: Developments in Politics, Society, Press and Thought in Bethlehem in the British Era, 1917–1948* (Bethlehem: WIAM Conflict Resolution Center, 2002) (Arabic and English); Jeffery Lesser, '(Re)creating ethnicity: Middle Eastern immigration to Brazil', *The Americas* 53 (July 1996): 45–65.

42. Of note, see Bernard Wasserstein, *The British in Palestine: The Mandatory Government and the Arab–Jewish Conflict, 1917–1929*, second edition (Oxford: Basil Blackwell, 1991); Barbara J. Smith, *The Roots of Separation in Palestine: British Economic Policy, 1920–1929* (Syracuse: Syracuse University Press, 1993); Mark LeVine, 'The discourses of development in Mandate Palestine', *Arab Studies Quarterly* 17 (winter and spring 1995): 95–124; Aida Asim Essaid, *Zionism and Land Tenure in Mandate Palestine* (London: Routledge, 2014).

Notes to Chapter 2

1. This characterisation is rather unfair in its sweeping nature but it is true that numerous officials posted to Palestine had little training, and did not speak Arabic or for that matter, Hebrew. Michael J. Cohen, 'Direction of policy in Palestine, 1936–1945', *Middle Eastern Studies* 11 (October 1975), 247.
2. Memo on meeting with High Commissioner, 30 October 1922, M/4/16.
3. Cohen, 'Direction of policy', 240–1.
4. David Lambert and Alan Lester, 'Introduction', in *Colonial Lives across the British Empire: Imperial Careering in the Long Nineteenth Century*, David Lambert and Alan Lester, eds (Cambridge: Cambridge University Press, 2006), pp. 2, 25.
5. Bernard Wasserstein, *The British in Palestine*, p. 109. See also Naomi Shepherd, *Ploughing Sand: British Rule in Palestine, 1917–1948* (New Brunswick, NJ: Rutgers University Press, 2000) and Zachary Lockman, 'Railway workers and relational history: Arabs and Jews in British-ruled Palestine', *Comparative Studies in Society and History* 35 (July 1993): 601–27.
6. Until that point, Great Britain continued to implement colonial structures of control in places far from the metropole regardless of increased resistance by colonised populations. Histories on India in the early twentieth century present one example, but see also Jonathan Saha, *Law, Disorder and the Colonial State: Corruption in Burma c. 1900* (Basingstoke: Palgrave Macmillan, 2013).
7. Susan Pedersen, 'The meaning of the mandates system: An argument', *Geschichte und Gesellschaft* 32 (October to December 2006): 560–82.
8. Susan Pedersen, 'Introduction: Claims to belong', *Journal of British Studies* 40 (October 2001): 447.
9. Wm. Roger Louis, 'The United Kingdom and the beginning of the Mandates System, 1919–1922', *International Organization* 23 (winter 1969): 74–5.

10. Aaron Klieman, 'The divisiveness of Palestine: Foreign Office versus Colonial Office on the issue of partition, 1937', *The Historical Journal* 22 (June 1979): 423–4.
11. Roger Louis, 'The United Kingdom and the beginning of the Mandates System', p. 91.
12. Klieman, 'The divisiveness of Palestine', pp. 425–6.
13. Cohen, 238–40.
14. For instance, see the more general history by A. J. Sherman, *Mandate Days: British Lives in Palestine, 1918–1948* (London: Thames and Hudson, 1997); Norman and Helen Bentwich, *Mandate Memories, 1918–1948* (London: Hogarth Press, 1965); Ronald Storrs, *Orientations* (London: Nicholson and Watson, 1943); and Edward Keith-Roach, *Pasha of Jerusalem: Memoirs of a District Commissioner under the British Mandate* (London: Radcliffe Press, 1994).
15. Roger Louis, p. 93. Class B and C mandates were for 'lesser civilized' former German colonies in Africa and the Pacific. The Arab mandates were A mandates, categorised as such due to their near-readiness for self-government.
16. Lugard had been a former governor-general in colonial Nigeria and devised a widely accepted treatise on indirect colonial rule.
17. Michael Callahan, *Mandates and Empire: The League of Nations and Africa, 1914–1931* (Portland: Sussex Academic Press, 1999), pp. 34–5. The Allies drafted policies that gave the League stronger powers such as complete supervision over the mandates, the right of their inhabitants to appeal to the League and the establishment of a mandate commission that was to receive annual reports on each mandate.
18. Ibid., pp. 70, 72–5.
19. Charles R. Crane and Henry C King. *King–Crane Report on the Near East*, 28 August 1919 (New York: Editor and Publisher, Co., 1922). The commission consisted of two Americans sent to greater Syria to survey the inhabitants of the former Ottoman provinces as to their opinions on the mandate system and their preferences for a mandatory power. The two men visited both urban and rural areas and received numerous petitions and delegations by Arab leaders. At the same time, the Arab leaders voiced their opposition to Article 22 of the League Covenant because it did not clarify how each mandate could be abrogated. See Callahan, *Mandates and Empire*, pp. 193–4. The official preamble of the Palestine Mandate charter had twenty-eight articles and included the provisions of the Balfour Declaration. In contradiction with the League Covenant that stated that advice and assistance to the mandate administration could come from the mandatory, the mandate charter gave the Zionist Organisation privilege to assist the

mandate administration. The mandate charter itself allowed for the mandatory to have full powers of legislation and administration, in contradiction with Article 22 of the Covenant.

20. Matthias B. Lehmann, 'Rethinking Sephardi identity: Jews and other Jews in Ottoman Palestine', *Jewish Social Studies* 15 (fall 2008): 93.

21. Sarah Abrevaya Stein, 'Protected persons? The Baghdadi Jewish diaspora, the British State, and the Persistence of Empire', *The American Historical Review* 116 (February 2011): 85.

22. Future Constitution of Palestine Zionist Proposals with Secretary of State's Amendments, 27 Feb. 1919, FO 608/98/8. This proposal was essentially a constitution for Palestine, or a draft mandate, written by the Zionist Organisation in late 1918 in anticipation of the Versailles Conference. The proposal was not discussed at the conference since the Allies did not make a decision on the Ottoman Empire's territories. This draft was reviewed then by the Foreign Office and commented upon in April 1919.

23. An ordinance to regulate the acquisition of the status of Palestinian subjects, Feb. 1921, *Norman Bentwich papers*, GB 165-0025/2/69–71.

24. Zionist Proposal for the future of Palestine with Secretary of State amendments, 20 March 1919, FO 371/2/10.

25. Roger Louis, pp. 74–5.

26. Norman Bentwich, 'Palestine nationality and the mandate', *Journal of Comparative Legislation and International Law* 21, Third Series (1939): 231.

27. Sukanya Banerjee, *Becoming Imperial Citizens: Indians in the Late Victorian Empire* (Durham, NC: Duke University Press, 2010), p. 3.

28. Cooper, *Citizenship*, pp. 16–20.

29. Sarah Abrevaya Stein, 'Citizens of a fictional nation: Ottoman-born Jews in France during the First World War', *Past and Present* (February 2015): 229–30. See also the forthcoming monograph by Sarah Abrevaya Stein, *Extraterritorial Dreams: European Citizenship, Sephardi Jews and the Ottoman Twentieth Century* (Chicago: University of Chicago Press, 2016).

30. Aviva Ben-Ur, 'Identity imperative: Ottoman Jews in wartime and interwar Britain', *Immigrants and Minorities* (2014): 175.

31. Stein, 'Protected persons?', pp. 87–90. British-protected persons and British subjects were accorded the same treatment until the 1934 British Protected Persons Order, a uniform regulation that marked the difference between the two statuses. The order defined a protected person as an individual without any other nationality but who belonged to British protectorates, trust or mandated territories with the exception of Palestine and Transjordan.

32. Foreign Office minute, 16 March 1921, GB 165-0025/2/85–6.
33. For more on the debates over nationality for parts of the imperial realms and especially for both British and immigrant married women, see Baldwin, 'Subject to Empire'.
34. Samuel to Curzon, High Commission of Egypt correspondence paper no. 337, 7 October 1920, FO 141/495/1.
35. Favourable treatment included appeals to the Mixed Courts, which heard commercial and civil cases of non-Ottoman subjects, using French law codes. This can be seen as a type of capitulation granted to Europeans in the Ottoman Empire. The Native Courts tried civil cases on the basis of Ottoman law.
36. Samuel to Curzon, High Commission of Egypt correspondence paper no. 337, 1 Nov. 1920, FO 141/495/1.
37. Ibid.
38. For more on Ottoman travel regulations, see Christoph Herzog, 'Migration and the state: On Ottoman regulations concerning migration since the age of Mahmud II', in *The City in the Ottoman Empire: Migration and the Making or Urban Modernity*, Ulrike Freitag, Malte Fuhrmann, Nora Lafi and Florian Riedler, eds (Oxford: Routledge, 2011), pp. 117–34.
39. Passports for Jews and Arabs of Palestinian or Syrian Origin memo, 5 July 1920, CO 323/831/19.
40. As discussed prior, the Ottoman Nationality Law of 1869 granted nationality by both provisions of *jus sanguinis* and *jus soli*.
41. Foreign Office Circular, 31 December 1920, CO 323/831/81.
42. Passports for Arabs of Palestinians or Syrian Origin memo, 7 July 1920, CO 323/831/338.
43. Some examples of studies depicting the impact of British laws and regulations include Martin Bunton, 'Inventing the status quo: Ottoman Land-Law during the Palestine Mandate, 1917–1936', *The International History Review* 21 (March 1999): 28–56; Assaf Likhovski, *Law and Identity in Mandate Palestine* (Chapel Hill: University of North Carolina Press, 2006); Ronen Shamir, *The Colonies of Law: Colonialism, Zionism, and Law in Early Mandate Palestine* (Cambridge: Cambridge University Press, 2000); Ylana Miller, *Government and Society in Rural Palestine, 1920–1948* (Austin: University of Texas Press, 1985).
44. Ten years after the Palestine constitution passed international law scholar S. D. Myres argued that Great Britain and the League were meant to act jointly as guardians of their 'ward' (the inhabitants), but none of the laws and regulations implemented in the early 1920s provided for such a set-up. S. D. Myres, Jr, 'Constitutional aspects of the

Mandate for Palestine', *Annals of the American Academy of Political Science and Social Science* 164 (November 1932): 3–8.

45. Palestinian Nationality memo, August 1921, CO 733/14/117.

46. The Palestine Order-in-Council, 10 August 1922 and Palestine Legislative Election Order, 10 August 1922.

47. Status of applicants for Palestinian citizenship under the Electoral Order-in-Council, Home Office paper, 25 September 1922, CO 733/32/32.

48. Municipal Government memo from Edward Keith-Roach to Herbert Samuel, 14 February 1921, CO 733/1/7.

49. Fruma Zachs and Basilius Bawardi, 'Ottomanism and Syrian patriotism in Salim al-Bustani's thought', in *Ottoman Reform and Muslim Regeneration: Studies in Honour of Butrus Abu-Manneh*, Itzchak Weismann and Fruma Zachs, eds (London: I. B. Tauris, 2005), p. 111.

50. Municipal Government memo from Edward Keith-Roach to Herbert Samuel, 14 February 1921, CO 733/1/7.

51. C. Luella Gettys, 'The effect of changes of sovereignty on nationality', *The American Journal of International Law* 21 (April 1927): 269.

52. Memo, Herbert Samuel to Secretary of State for the Colonies, 17 July 1921, GB 165-0025/2/54–5.

53. Memo, Lucien Wolf to Colonial Office, 13 May 1921, GB 165-0025/2/91.

54. Colonial Office annex, 16 March 1921, GB 165-0025/2/88–9.

55. Memo, Launcelot Oliphant to Foreign Office, 21 May 1921, GB 165-0025/2/96.

56. Memo, Herbert Samuel to Secretary of State for the Colonies, 17 July 1921, GB 165-0025/2/54–5.

57. The mandate authorities and the Zionist Organisation paid greater attention to non-European Jews only in the 1930s. Prior to the creation of Israel, Yemeni Jewish immigration to Palestine began to occur in significant numbers but Arabic-speaking Jews elsewhere did not follow the trend of the Yemeni or European Jews. For more see Aviva Halamish, 'A new look at immigration of Jews from Yemen to Mandatory Palestine', *Israel Studies* 11 (spring 2006): 59–78.

58. Memo, R.H. Campbell to Foreign Office memo, 27 May 1921, GB 165-0025/2/97.

59. Palestinian Nationality Order draft, 7 June 1921, CO 733/12/13–14. See also, *Report by HMG to the Council of the League of Nations on the Administration of Palestine and Transjordan*, 1925 (London: HMSO, 1926).

60. Memo, John Pedder to Home Office, 7 June 1921, GB 165-0025/2/60.

61. Palestinian Nationality Draft Ordinance, Samuel to Curzon, 9 February 1921, CO 733/9/391.

62. Memo, John Pedder to Home Office, 7 June 1921, GB 165-0025/2/62.

63. Zionist attitude on the draft Palestinian Nationality Order, 7 June 1921, CO 733/12/12.

64. Foreign Office Minute on Draft Ordinance, 9 February 1921, CO 733/9/406.

65. Examples of this can be found in letters from 1922 contained in the file CO 733/27.

66. Minutes of the 24th session of the Council, Geneva, April 1923, *League of Nations Offical Journal*, 4th Yr. No. 6 (June 1923): 567–8.

67. Ibid., pp. 568–70.

68. Endorsement of Provisional Certificates memo, 8 May 1923, CO 733/55/487–91.

69. Palestinian nationality draft, 19 November 1923, CO 733/56/490–7. The Home Office cited two other 'curious' cases of Tonga and Zanzibar.

70. Palestine Constitution draft, August 1921, CO 733/14/170.

71. British naturalisation for persons employed under the Palestine Government, Home Office memo, November 1923, CO 733/56/490–7.

72. Extension of Imperial Preference to Palestine memo, January 1924, CO 733/63/31–2. See also Palestinian Nationality Letter from the Institute of Civil Engineers to the Palestine Government, 20 November 1924, CO 733/84/331.

73. Memo from Herbert Samuel on Provisions in the Palestine Legislative Council Election Order-in-Council, 26 December 1923, CO 733/52/451–3.

74. Fees for certificates of Palestinian nationality and laissez-passers memo, 24 August 1923, FO 371/38.

75. Observations on the Order-in-Council revisions, 12 May 1924, CO 733/68/313–20. The Zionist protests against the revisions are included in this file.

76. Nationality Order-in-Council draft, October 1924, CO 733/271–3.

77. Cohen, p. 241.

78. '*Al-ra'iyyā al-uthmāniyyun āsbahu filastīniyyīn*' [Ottoman subjects become Palestinians], *Al-Huquq Scientific and Education Journal* II (August 1925). By virtue of the treaty the former Ottoman nationals, the largest national group in Palestine, would be able to opt for Turkish nationality.

79. For contemporary arguments see H. S. Q. Henriques and Ernest J. Schuster, ' "Jus Soli" or "Jus Sanguinis"?', *Problems of the War* 3 (1917): 119–31; James Brown Scott, 'Nationality: Jus Soli or Jus Sanguinis', *The American Journal of International Law* 24 (January 1930): 58–64, and Peter A. Speek, 'The meaning of nationality and Americanization', *American Journal of Sociology* 32 (September 1926): 237–49.

80. Nationality Order-in-Council, 1924, CO 733/75/271.

81. Mutaz Qafisheh, *The International Law Foundations of Palestinian Nationality: A Legal Examination of Nationality in Palestine under Britain's Rule* (Leiden: Martinus Nijhoff Publishers, 2008), p. 75.
82. Ibid., 95.
83. Palestine Citizenship Order-in-Council, 30 January 1925, CO 733/88/383–98.
84. Qafisheh, p. 97.
85. On the Lebanese mandate (and, by extension, Syrian) nationality order, see Rania Maktabi, 'The Lebanese census of 1932 revisited: Who are the Lebanese?', *British Journal of Middle Eastern Studies* 26 (November 1999): 219–41.
86. Palestine Citizenship Order-in-Council, 30 January 1925, CO 733/88/383–98.
87. Qafisheh, p. 96.
88. As mentioned above, Palestinians abroad encountered these difficulties long before the order was passed and their record can be found in numerous memos in the British Colonial Office records and Palestine press. More instances can be found in Qafisheh's *The International Law Foundations of Palestinian Nationality*.
89. Endorsement of Provisional Certificates memo, June 1923, CO 733/55/545.
90. Palestinian Nationality Order-in-Council draft, 8 July 1924, CO 733/80/599.
91. E. F. W. Gey van Pittius, ' "Dominion" nationality', *Journal of Comparative Legislation and International Law* 13 (1931): 199–202 for an interwar account of the complexities of Dominion status; see also the comparative case of Ireland: Mary E. Daly, 'Irish nationality and citizenship since 1922', *Irish Historical Studies* 32 (May 2001): 377–407.
92. Constitutional Position of Palestine memo, 20 February 1925, CO 733/105/45.
93. Local Government Interim Report, 11 July 1924, CO 733/71/230–86.
94. Memo on the situation in Palestine, October 1925, CO 733/107/511.

Notes to Chapter 3

1. '*Al-asad wa al-fa'r*' [The lion and the mouse], 25 March 1925, *Mir'at al-Sharq*.
2. '*Ila qurā'nā fī kul makān*' [To our readers everywhere], 25 March 1925, *Sawt al-Sha'b*.
3. Raymond A. Rocco, *Transforming Citizenship: Democracy, Membership, and Belonging in Latino Communities* (East Lansing: Michigan State University Press, 2014), p. 94.

4. For more on this in the context of European nation-state building, see Stuart Hall and Bram Gieben, eds, *Formations of Modernity* (Cambridge: Open University, 1992), 96–7.

5. Awad Halabi has recently depicted these Palestinian Arabs as at an intermediate stage in terms of their political community, as they maintained strong links with an Ottoman identity in the early 1920s. See Halabi, 'Liminal loyalties'.

6. Here again, I reference an argument followed throughout the chapter by Raymond Rocco on the links between associative life and the strengthening of communal and communitarian identity and political practices that enabled claims to citizenship and to the rights associated with that status. Rocco, *Transforming Citizenship*, p. 104.

7. The factionalism of politics in Ottoman Jerusalem and Mandate Palestine is linked to what Albert Hourani has defined as 'the politics of notables'. These 'politics' referred to the competition for jobs and favours by notable, elite and well-connected Arabs in the provinces of the Ottoman Empire, and the notables were far removed from popular politics or mass mobilisation when it occurred against the Mandate. See Albert Hourani, 'Ottoman reform and the politics of notables', in *Beginnings of Modernization in the Middle East: The Nineteenth Century*, eds William R. Polk and Richard L. Chambers (Chicago: University of Chicago Press, 1968), pp. 41–68.

8. Recent works that move away from a rigid nationalist history include Campos, *Ottoman Brothers;* Selim Deringil, ' "They live in a state of nomadism and savagery": The Late Ottoman Empire and the post-colonial debate',*Comparative Studies in Society and History* 45 (April 2003): 311–42; Ussama Makdisi, 'Ottoman Orientalism', *The American Historical Review* (June 2002): 768–96; Karen M. Kern, *Imperial Citizen: Marriage and Citizenship in the Ottoman Frontier Provinces of Iraq* (Syracuse: Syracuse University Press, 2011); Karen M. Kern, 'Rethinking Ottoman frontier policies', *The Arab Studies Journal* 15 (spring 2007): 8–29; Thompson, *Colonial Citizens.*

9. Nawaf A. Salam, 'The emergence of citizenship in Islamdom', *Arab Law Quarterly* 12 (1997): 140.

10. Kern, 'Rethinking Ottoman Frontier Policies', p. 8.

11. Kemal H. Karpat, *Studies on Ottoman Social and Political History: Selected Articles and Essays* (Boston: Brill, 2002), p. 640.

12. William Hanley, 'When did Egyptians stop being Ottomans?', p. 96.

13. Ibid., p. 93.

14. A comparison and developed analysis of changing national categorisations at the bureaucratic level in the Empire's Eastern provinces, as represented in the Ottoman censuses, can be found in Ipek K. Yosmaoglu,

'Counting bodies, shaping souls: The 1903 Census and national identity in Ottoman Macedonia', *International Journal of Middle Eastern Studies* 38 (February 2006): 65–6.

15. Some insightful work on these two terms has been done by Uri Davis. See Davis, '*Jinsiyya* versus *Muwatana*: The question of citizenship and state in the Middle East', *Arab Studies Quarterly* 17 (winter/spring 1995): 19–50; and Davis, 'Democratization, citizenship, Arab unity, and Palestinian autonomy: A critical reading of the New Middle East', in *Citizenship and State in the Middle East: Approaches and Applications*, eds Nils A. Butenschon, Uri Davis and Manuel Hassassian (Syracuse: University Press, 2000), pp. 225–45 .

16. Hanley, p. 93.

17. Scholch, *Palestine in Transformation*, p. 12.

18. Ibid., pp. 12–14. See also a similar argument: Butrus Abu-Manneh, 'The Christians between Ottomanism and Syrian nationalism: The ideas of Butrus Al-Bustani', *International Journal of Middle East Studies* 11 (May 1980): 287–304.

19. Al-Tahtawi was influenced in part by French intellectuals and ideas during his time in Paris in the 1830s. Although he held *sharia* as the highest authority, his writings frequently use the terms for 'patriotism' and 'homeland', '*hubb al-watan*' and '*watan*'. He wrote of duties of citizens toward their homeland and of rights of freedom for citizens. See Albert Hourani, *Arabic Thought in the Liberal Age 1798–1939* (Cambridge: Cambridge University Press, 1983), pp. 78–83.

20. Salam, 'The emergence of citizenship', pp. 141–2.

21. Ussama Makdisi, 'After 1860: Debating religion, reform, and nationalism in the Ottoman Empire', *International Journal of Middle East Studies* 34 (November 2002): 601–17.

22. Ibid., pp. 605–8.

23. *Nafir Suriya* 4, 25 October 1860, in *Al-Mu'allam Boutros al-Bustani: Dirāsa wa thā'iq* [The Teacher Boutros al-Bustani: A Study and Documents] (Beirut: Publications de la Revue Fikr, 1981), pp. 121–2.

24. For the full text of the constitution see 'The Ottoman Constitution, promulgated 23 December 1876', *The American Journal of International Law* 2, No. 4, Supplement: Official Documents (October 1908): 367–87.

25. Salam, p. 144.

26. Ülker, 'Contextualising "Turkification"', pp. 615–16.

27. Keith David Watenpaugh, *Being Modern in the Middle East: Revolution, Nationalism, Colonialism, and the Arab Middle Class* (Princeton: Princeton University Press, 2006), p. 64.

28. For some further background to this, see Andrew Arsan, "This is the age of associations': Committees, petitions, and the roots of interwar Middle Eastern internationalism', *Journal of Global History* 7 (July 2012): 166–88.
29. Rocco, p. 87.
30. Ibid., p. 104.
31. James Gelvin, 'Demonstrating communities in post-Ottoman Syria', *Journal of Interdisciplinary History* 25 (summer 1994): 29.
32. Mustafa Kabha, *The Palestinian Press as Shaper of Public Opinion, 1929–1939: Writing up a Storm* (London: Valentine Mitchell, 2007), p. xv.
33. Ayalon, *Reading Palestine*, p. 107.
34. C.A. Bayly, *Empire and Information: Intelligence Gathering and Social Communication in India, 1780–1870* (Cambridge: Cambridge University Press, 1996), p. 39.
35. For example, the Literary Society of Bethlehem undertook the task to sponsor a large demonstration in late February 1920 in response to the King–Crane Commission report release in Paris and in support of complete independence and unity of Syria and Palestine. Without propaganda on the report and explanations of its aims on the part of the press and literary societies, this demonstration would likely not have drawn a diverse crowd or a crowd aware of the matters at hand. It was noted that 'citizens' from towns and rural areas of Jerusalem subdistrict attended. See Adnan Musallam, 'From wars to *Nakbeh*: Developments in Bethlehem, Palestine, 1917–1948', *Al-Liqa'* (Bethlehem) 30 (July 2008): 7–36.
36. For more of ideology as a part of communities of discourse and their discursive features, see Robert Wuthnow, *Communities of Discourse: Ideology and Social Structure in the Reformation, the Enlightenment, and European Socialism* (Cambridge, MA: Harvard University Press, 1989), pp. 12–18.
37. Sessions of the Fifth Palestinian Arab Congress, Nablus (August 1922), Arab Executive Committee files, ISA/M/4/3.
38. Gelvin, *Divided Loyalties*, p. 183.
39. 'Abd al-Wahhab al-Kayyali, *Wathā'iq al-Muqāwama al-Filastīniyya al-'Arabiyya did al-Ihtilāl al-Britānī wa al-Zioniyya, 1918–1939* [Documents of the Palestinian Arab Resistance against the British and Zionist Occupation] (Beirut: Institute for Palestinian Studies, 1967), p. 3.
40. Two of the best studies of the early national movement in Palestine from secondary literature are Muslih, *The Origins of Palestinian Nationalism* and Yeshoshua Porath, *The Emergence of the Palestinian-Arab National Movement 1918–1929* (London: Frank Cass, 1974).

41. A. W. Said Kayyali, *Palestine: A Modern History* (London: I. B. Tauris, 1978), p. 61.
42. Campos, *Ottoman Brothers*, pp. 100–7.
43. Gelvin, 'The social origins of popular nationalism in Syria', p. 648.
44. Gelvin, *Divided Loyalties*, p. 145; emphasis in the original.
45. *Wathā'iq al-Haraka al-Wataniyya al-Filastīniyya min Awrāq Akram Zu'aytir, 1918–1939* [Documents of the Palestinian National Movement from the Papers of Akram Zu'aytir] (Beirut: Institute of Palestine Studies, 1979), pp. 7–8.
46. Ibid., pp. 7–8. The letter cited here referred to the majority Arab population as 'guests' in their own country.
47. Civil rights had, however, been part of the terminology in government from the period of Young Turk rule from 1908. It was used seemingly without explanation in relation to electoral rights and the law of association. Eligibility for the franchise and to stand for election to the Ottoman Parliament, as well as to join a public association, was granted only to men who had not been deprived of their 'civil rights'.
48. Parolin, *Citizenship in the Arab World*, pp. 24–5.
49. *Min Awrāq Akram Zu'aytir*, p. 11; Al-Kayyali, *Wathā'iq*, p. 3.
50. Dora Glidewell Nadolski, 'Ottoman and secular civil law', *International Journal of Middle East Studies* 8 (October 1977): 531. Foreign individuals, however, had been permitted to purchase Ottoman land since the 1860s. For more, see Anis F. Kassim, ed., *The Palestine Yearbook of International Law*, Vol. 1 (Cyprus: Al-Shaybani Society of International Law, 1984), p. 22.
51. Hanna Nakkara, *Lawyer of the Land and the People* (Haifa: Al-Asawar Publishers, 1980), p. 67.
52. *Min Awrāq Akram Zu'aytir*, May–July 1922, pp. 243–51. For a detailed study, see Martin Bunton, *Colonial Land Policies in Palestine 1917–1936* (Oxford: Oxford University Press, 2007).
53. *'Jam'iyya al-qara'* [Village Associations], 11 Augusr 1920, *Mir'at al-Sharq*. For example, the Nablus Village Association in 1920 took on the task of helping the farmer understand that he had the same rights as any other Palestinian through the use of pamphlets and village meetings.
54. Khariya Qasmiya, ed., *Min mudhakkirat 'Awnī Abd al-Hadī* [From the Memoirs of 'Awni Abd al-Hadi] (Beirut: Institute for Palestine Studies, 2002), p. 139.
55. *'Ila al-sha'b al-'arabī al-filastīnī al-karīm'* [To the noble Palestinian Arab people], 31 December 1920, *Mir'at al-Sharq*.
56. *Min Awrāq Akram Zu'aytir*, pp. 65–71.
57. Ibid. These civil rights freedoms included those of speech and the press.

58. Ibid., 18.
59. *'Al-'adl!'* [Justice!], 25 February 1920, *Mir'at al-Sharq.*
60. *Min Awrāq Akram Zu'aytir,* 26 November 1920, p. 41. Also see Anita Shapiro, 'The ideology and practice of the joint Jewish–Arab Labour Union in Palestine, 1920–1939', *Journal of Contemporary History* 12 (October 1977): 672.
61. *'Surīyun nahnu um 'arab?'* [Are we Syrians or Arab?], 1 June 1920, Bayt Laham, from Adnan A. Musallam, *Folded Pages from Local Palestinian History in the 20th Century: Developments in Politics, Society, Press and Thought in Bethlehem in the British Era, 1917–1948* (Bethlehem: WIAM, 2002), pp. 99–102.
62. *Min Awrāq Akram Zu'aytir,* 125.
63. Ibid.
64. Ibid., 10 September 1921, p. 146.
65. Advisory Council meeting minutes, 4 November 1921, CO 733/6/184–5.
66. *Min Awrāq Akram Zu'aytir,* 212.
67. 'A Unity of Citizenship', 27 August 1921, *Mir'at al-Sharq.*
68. Thompson, *Colonial Citizens,* pp. 76–77.
69. Marcella Simoni, 'A dangerous legacy: Welfare in British Palestine, 1930–1939', *Jewish History* 13 (fall 1999): 81–3.
70. Agnes Shuk-mei Ku, 'Contradictions in the development of citizenship in Hong Kong: Governance without democracy', *Asian Survey* 49 (May/June 2009): 511.
71. A. L. Tibawi, 'Educational policy in Mandatory Palestine', *Die Welt des Islams* 4 (1955): 15–18, and *Min Awrāq Akram Zu'aytir,* p. 101.
72. *'Al-tamthīl fī filastin'* [Representation in Palestine], 29 November 1920, *Mir'at al-Sharq.*
73. *Min Awrāq Akram Zu'aytir,* p. 87.
74. Kayyali, *Palestine,* p. 89.
75. *Min Awrāq Akram Zu'aytir,* p. 65.
76. Interim Report of the Haycraft Commission, 16 August 1921, CO 733/5.
77. Wasserstein, p. 115.
78. Al-Kayyali, *Wathā'iq,* p. 63.
79. Wasserstein, pp. 121–4.
80. *'Al-ruh al-wataniyya'* [Spirit of Nationalism], 3 March 1920, *Mir'at al-Sharq.*
81. *Min Awrāq Akram Zu'aytir,* p. 299.
82. Al-Kayyali, *Wathā'iq,* p. 73. The congress also resolved to oppose a major concession proposed by the government to Zionist leader Pinhas Rutenberg and his electric company as well as any future concessions

and monopolies. For more see Smith, *The Roots of Separation*, p. 118. The Rutenberg Plan gave the mineral rights of the Jordan River to the aforementioned entrepreneur to provide hydroelectricity to the district of Jaffa.

83. Various scholars of the national movement list the mid-1920s in Palestine as a period of relative calm – for example, the work of A. W. Said Kayyali (*Palestine: A Modern History*) and Y. Porath (*The Emergence of the Palestinian-Arab National Movement 1918–1929*) take this view. However, the press from the period shows continued interest in the national movement's demands. Further, during this time, new political parties formed as members of the Husayni and Nashashibi factions broke rank. None of these recognised parties took a particularly radical or original stance and infighting among them continued.

84. '*Risāla muftuha ila Lord Plumer*' [Open Letter to His Excellency Lord Plumer], 26 August 1925, *Sawt al-Sha'b*.

85. '*Al-shaq al-thānī min wa'd Balfour: huquq al-watanīn al-midaniyya wa al-sīyāsiyya*' [The second part of the Balfour Declaration: The national civil and political rights], 21 December 1924, *Mir'at al-Sharq*.

86. '*Taqrīr al-mandub al-sāmī 'ain filastin*' [Decisions of the High Commissioner on Palestine], 19 July 1925, *Mir'at al-Sharq* and '*Al-watan al-qawmīal-sha'b al-yahudī*' [National home of the Jewish people], 26 July 1925, *Mir'at al-Sharq*.

87. '*Taqrīr al-mandub al-sāmī 'ain filastin*' [Decisions of the High Commissioner on Palestine], 19 July 1925, *Mir'at al-Sharq*. This conversation came as a response to Colonial Office discussions on whether a Jewish national home entitled all Jews to be nationals of that home even if they possessed citizenship of another country; see 'Discussion of citizenship/nationality', 1925, CO 733/102/159–60.

88. Ibid.

89. '*Al-watan al-qawmī al-sha'b al-yahudī*' [The national home of the Jewish people], 26 July 1925, *Mir'at al-Sharq*.

90. In fact, the official translation of the order into Arabic also used 'nationality law' (*qānun al-jinsiyya al-filastīniyya*) rather than translating 'citizenship order'. The Arabic-language scientific and legal journal *al-Huquq* also used 'nationality' (*jinsiyya*) rather than 'citizenship' (*muwātana*). More citations of the terminology used in the press are included throughout this chapter and the next. Mutaz Qafisheh's work (*The International Law Foundations of Palestinian Nationality*) also notes the translation of nationality rather than citizenship.

91. Adnan A. Musallam, 'Palestinian Arab press developments under British rule with a case study of Bethlehem's *Sawt al-Sha'b* 1922–1939',

Bethlehem University Journal 5 (August 1986), www.bethlehem-holy-land.net/Adnan/bethlehem/Sawt_Al-Shab.htm (accessed 15 September 2015).

92. '*Qānun al-jinsiyya tahīzāt huquq al-'arab*' [The law prejudices the rights of the Arabs], 21 October 1925, *Mir'at al-Sharq*.

93. Ibid.

94. '*Bālgh rasmī*' [Official communication], 19 December 1925, *al-Ittihad al-'Arabī*.

95. '*Sīyāsa al-hukuma al-hādara*' [Current government policy], 8 July 1922, *Mir'at al-Sharq*.

Notes to Chapter 4

1. British Legation, La Paz memo, 8 April 1927, CO 733/142/45–6.

2. For a general discussion on the linkages between the diaspora and the homeland, and the creation of discourses of nationalist sentiment, the homeland and nation-building within the diaspora, see Helena Lindholm Schulz and Juliane Hammer, *The Palestinian Diaspora: Formation of Identities and Politics of Homeland* (London: Routledge, 2003), pp. 10–20.

3. Citizenship Order-in-Council memo, June 1925, CO 733/104/201.

4. Khater, *InventingHome*, 88–9.

5. Isin, 'Theorizing acts of citizenship', pp. 17–18.

6. Specialised studies include Gonzalez's *Dollar, Dove, and Eagle*; Marin-Guzman, *A Century of Palestinian Immigration into Central America*; Foroohar, 'Palestinians in Central America'; and work by Adnan Musallam on Bethlehem's emigrants. Jacob Norris has written about Ottoman-era migration of Christian Palestinians to Latin America, the US and Russia in the sale of holy land artifacts such as olive wood and mother-of-pearl carvings. See Jacob Norris, *Land of Progress: Palestine in the Age of Colonial Development* (Oxford: Oxford University Press, 2013).

7. See Civantos, *Between Argentines and Arabs*, p. 7. Civantos notes the problem of accurate records of immigrants due to illegal entries and departures, and non-standardised terms to record the immigrants' origins; Karpat, 'The Ottoman emigration to the America'. Karpat's study is one of the most widely cited, but it must be noted that Arabs immigrated to places other than the Americas during the Ottoman and post-war period, including Russia, the Philippines and throughout West Africa. It must be remembered that emigration took place between the

'global south' or 'third world', and not exclusively from the third world to the 'first world'.

8. Gonzalez, *Dollar, Dove, and Eagle*, pp. 25–8. The Americas were certainly not the only destination for Palestinian emigrants during this time period but it was the destination that drew the highest numbers of migrants. The current work of William Clarence-Smith shows that Syrians and Palestinians in the Philippines at the same time faced similar problems with returning home due to the expiry of Ottoman passports and the loss of consular protection.

9. For more on the situation of Arabs in Haiti in the pre-war years, see Brenda Gayle Plummer, 'Race, nationality, and trade in the Caribbean: The Syrians in Haiti, 1903–1934', *The International History Review* 3 (October 1981): 520–1.

10. Adel Beshara, 'A rebel Syrian: Gibran Khalil Gibran', in *The Origins of Syrian Nationhood: Histories, Pioneers and Identity*, ed. Adel Beshara (London: Routledge, 2011), p. 144.

11. Maria del Mar Logrono Narbona, 'A transnational intellectual sphere: Brazil and its Middle Eastern populations', in *The Middle East and Brazil: Perspective on the New Global South*, ed. Paul Amar (Bloomington: Indiana University Press, 2014), 200.

12. San Salvador Palestine Colony to Lloyd George, 7 March 1919, *Min Awrāq Akram Zu'aytir*, p. 10.

13. The phenomenon of mutual aid to political associations in the mahjar started during the First World War as well, particularly in North and South America. For more on this, see Stacy Fahrenthold, 'Transnational modes and media: The Syrian press in the Mahjar and emigrant activism during World War I', *Mashriq & Mahjar: Journal of Middle East Migration Studies* 1 (spring 2013): 30–54, and as a comparison with the situation between Syria and the Syrian diaspora in the mid-1920s, Reem Bailony, 'Transnationalism and the Syrian migrant community: The case of the 1925 Syrian revolt', *Mashriq & Mahjar: Journal of Middle East Migration Studies* 1 (2013): 8–29.

14. '*Āmjama'iyyāt al-wataniyya fī al-mahjar*' [Nationalist societies in the diaspora], 12 February 1927, *Sawt al-Sha'b*.

15. Al-Kayyali, *Wathā'iq*, p. 83.

16. '*Al-mahājra*' [The migrant], 30 June 1920, *Mir'at al-Sharq*.

17. '*Ādārah juāzāt al-safar*' [The department of passports], 29 September 1920, *Mir'at al-Sharq*. A temporary type of passport for Palestinians was used since 1920 under the Mandate but these were not proper passports – Palestinian passports (as separate from British passports) were issued beginning in 1926. For more, see Qafisheh, 147–9 and Palestinian passports, 11 June 1926, CO 733/114/514–30.

18. Travel facilities for Palestinian Arabs in South America memo, August–December 1922, CO 733/27/518–21.

19. ''Arīd' [General news], 14 April 1924, *Sawt al-Sha'b*.

20. Ibid.

21. 'Thuwra Honduras' [Honduras Revolution], 31 May 1924, *Sawt al-Sha'b*.

22. 'Kitāb wajuāb' [Response letter], 14 August 1924, *Sawt al-Sha'b*.

23. 'Filastīniyyun fī al-mahjar: kīf ya'udun ila bāladhum bashula' [Palestinians in the diaspora: How they can return with ease], 14 December 1924, *Mir'at al-Sharq*.

24. 'Al-shaq al-thānī min wa'd Balfour: huquq al-watanīn al-midaniyya wa al-sīyāsiyya' [The second part of the Balfour Declaration: The national civil and political rights], 24 December 1924, *Mir'at al-Sharq*.

25. Protection of Palestinians in Honduras memo, 15 June 1925, CO 733/104/35–8.

26. Travel facilities for Palestinians in Hayti, 16 April 1925, CO 733/103/353–6.

27. Foreign Office circular on the acquisition of Palestinian citizenship, 21 December 1925, ISA/M/223/38.

28. Ibid.

29. 'Al-muhajarīn wa al-jinsiyya' [The emigrants and nationality], 15 May 1926, *Sawt al-Sha'b*.

30. Ibid.

31. Ibid.

32. 'Al-muhajarīn wa al-jinsiyya al-filastin' [The emigrants and Palestinian nationality], 23 May 1926, *Sawt al-Sha'b*.

33. 'Sawt al-mahjar' [Voice of the diaspora], 4 September 1926, *Sawt al-Sha'b*.

34. 'Ikuwān al-muhajarīn' [Immigrant brothers], 26 May 1926, *Sawt al-Sha'b*.

35. 'Al-yahud wa al-jinsiyya filastīniyya' [The Jews and Palestinian nationality], 11 August 1926, *Sawt al-Sha'b*.

36. 'Al-muhājarun wa jinsīthum' [The emigrants and their nationality], 24 November 1926, *Sawt al-Sha'b*.

37. 'Ila al-mandub al-sāmī: līs min yadāfa' ain al-'arab fī al-mahjar' [To the high commissioner: Arabs in the diaspora are not defended], 21 July 1926, *Sawt al-Sha'b*.

38. 'Bishā'n al-muhājarīn fī Honduras' [Regarding the emigrants in Honduras], 28 July 1926, *Sawt al-Sha'b*. For more on anti-Arab sentiment, see also Civantos, *Between Argentines and Arabs*, pp. 7–12.

39. 'Tamdīd qānun al-jinsiyya' [Extension of the law], 1 September 1926, *Sawt al-Sha'b*.

40. 'Sawt al-mahjar' [Voice of the diaspora], 4 September 1926, *Sawt al-Sha'b*.

41. 'Al-intidāb hadhā ām āsta'bād?' [Is this the mandate or slavery?], 18 March 1927, *al-Jamiyya al-'Arabiyya*.

42. *'Jinsiyya al-muhājarīn'* [The nationality of the emigrants], 2 February 1927, *Sawt al-Sha'b*.
43. *'Al-ghabin al-āhaqq bal-muhājarin al-'arab'* [Continued injustice for the Arab emigrants], 12 March 1927, *Sawt al-Sha'b*.
44. *'Huwl mu'tamar al-jinsiyya'* [Concerning the Nationality Conference], 30 May 1927, *al-Jamiyya al-'Arabiyya*.
45. *'Al-mujtam'a min al-waheda al-filastīniyya'* [Society for Palestinian Unity], 5 July 1927, *Filastin*. The other groups included Tampico's Sons of Palestine Society and the Society for the Unity of Palestine and East Jordan.
46. Ibid.
47. Ibid.
48. Ibid.
49. *'Sawt min Mexico'* [Voice from Mexico], 11 August 1927, *al-Jamiyya al-'Arabiyya*.
50. Petition by Palestinian Arabs in Honduras, 4 June 1927, ISA/M/223/38. These individuals also asked what right any British officer had to change their nationality for them since they were 'Palestinians, born, bred and reared, and no power of earth can sever our claims and rights as Palestinians'.
51. *'Risāla muftuha ila mandub sāma'* [Open letter to the High Commissioner], 6 February 1928, *al-Jamiyya al-'Arabiyya*.
52. *'Ila al-ma'āmlāt: al-jinsiyya al-filastīniyya'* [To workers: Palestinian nationality], 29 October 1928, *Sawt al-Haqq*.
53. *'Nadā' lilsha'b al-'arabīal-filastīnī mukhalis: qānun al-jinsiyya tahīzāt huquq al-muhājarīn'* [Appeal to the loyal Palestinian People: The Nationality Law prejudices the rights of the emigrants], 26 May 1927, *Mir'at al-Sharq*.
54. Appeal to the noble British people from the Committee for the Defense of Arab Emigrant Rights to Palestinian Nationality (Jerusalem: Al-Quds Printing House, February 1928), reprinted in Musallam, *Folded Pages*, 201–10.
55. Memorandum submitted to the High Commissioner for Palestine by the Committee for the Defense of Arab Emigrants Rights to Palestinian Nationality, September 1927, CO 733/142/47–8.
56. Memo, S. S. for the Colonies to Ormsby Gore, 29 July 1927 and Memo, Symes to Amery, 21 June 1927, CO 733/142/53–63.
57. Ibid.
58. Appeal to the noble British people from the Committee for the Defense of Arab Emigrant Rights to Palestinian Nationality, in Musallam, *Folded Pages*, 201–10.

59. Memo, S. S. for the Colonies to Ormsby Gore, 29 July 1927 and Memo, Symes to Amery, 21 June 1927, CO 733/142/53–63.

60. '*Al-difāʿ ʿain al-jinsiyya al-muhājarīn*' [The defense of the emigrants' nationality], 9 February 1928, *al-Jamiyya al-ʿArabiyya*.

61. Appeal to the noble British people, in *Folded Pages*. The appeal elaborated that many emigrants who extended their stay outside of Palestine in the years just after the outbreak of World War I did not receive official notice of the fall of the Ottoman Government. It noted that upon the outbreak of the war, the German consulates took charge to defend all individuals who held Ottoman nationality. Despite German protection, many Arabs of Greater Syria resorted to dependence on Britain and France, the allies of the Arabs in the war. That allied sentiment posed a problem: only those Ottoman merchants and traders abroad who recorded their names with the German consuls during the war were identified as Ottoman nationals after the end of the war, as the British and French consuls did not record the names of Arabs who identified with the Ottoman Empire.

62. Ibid. The article stated that the children born to natives from all countries separated from the Ottoman Empire were to be recognised as nationals of their parents' country of origin.

63. Memo, Colonial Office to HM Consul, San Salvador, 28 October 1927, CO 733/142/12–19.

64. Memo, the British Legation, Mexico to Austen Chamberlain, 10 August 1927, CO 733/142/22.

65. Central Palestine Society to Secretary of State for the Colonies, 17 June 1927, ISA/M/223/38.

66. The Turkish Republic introduced its own, and rather complex, citizenship legislation in the years following the War of Independence. The government passed a law relating to Ottoman subjects in 1927: those outside of Turkey during the War of Independence and who did not return lost their Turkish citizenship (this, however, applied to former Ottoman subjects resident within the borders of the Republic). In large part, Turkish citizenship regulations were restrictive. See Soner Çağaptay, 'Citizenship policies in interwar Turkey', *Nations and Nationalism* 9 (2003): 601–19.

67. Citizenship applications, 1927, CO 733/142/2–4.

68. Ibid.

69. Ibid.

70. Memo, Foreign Office to Colonial Office, 20 October 1927, CO 733/142/19–24.

71. Memo, Colonial Secretary Ormsby Gore to High Commissioner, 9 December 1927, CO 733/142/10.

72. '*Rad 'ala wazīr alā-sta'māriyya*' [Reply to the Colonial Minister], 29 March 1929, *Sawt al-Sha'b*.
73. '*Al-da'ua 'ala mudīr al-muhājra*' [The lawsuit on the Director of Immigration], 10 April 1929, *Sawt al-Sha'b*.
74. '*Risāla min El Salvador*' [Letter from El Salvador], 15 May 1929; '*Muhājarun El Salvador*' [El Salvador emigrants], 5 June 1929, *Sawt al-Sha'b*.
75. Memo, Foreign Office to Colonial Office, 28 July 1927, CO 733/142/34–7.
76. '*Rad 'ala wazīr alā-sta'māriyya*' [Reply to the Colonial Minister], 29 March 1929, *Sawt al-Sha'b*.
77. '*Al-filastīniyyun al-'āi'dun ila al-watan*' [The return of the Palestinians to the homeland], 15 February 1930, *Sawt al-Sha'b*.
78. '*Lajna al-difā' taqābil al-mandub al-sāma*' [Committee for the Defense meeting with the High Commissioner], 18 February 1933, *Sawt al-Sha'b*.
79. Palestine Royal Commission Report: Nationality Law and Acquisition of Palestinian Citizenship, May–June 1937, CO 733/347/4.

Notes to Chapter 5

1. Revocation of Naturalisation certificates and Palestinian citizenship memo, 5 December 1930, CO 733/179/2/4.
2. The cases of Jewish citizens abroad are numerous but scattered through the mandate archives over about two decades. Some examples can be found in the correspondence contained in the files CO 733/142 and CO 733/357/2.
3. See, for instance, correspondence memos entitled Travel Facilities for persons whose applications for Palestinian citizenship have been rejected, CO 733/142/8.
4. The links between progress, entrepreneurialism and colonial policies towards European Jewish merchants and businessmen within British imperial possessions is explained further in Norris, *Land of Progress*, pp. 75–85.
5. Emma Hunter, 'Dutiful subjects, patriotic citizens, and the concept of "good citizenship" in twentieth-century Tanzania', *The Historical Journal* 56 (2013): 260. Also see Emma Hunter, *Political Thought and the Public Sphere in Tanzania: Freedom, Democracy and Citizenship in the Era of Decolonization* (New York: Cambridge University Press, 2015), p. 43; Christopher Joon-Hai Lee, 'The 'native' undefined: Colonial categories, Anglo-African status and the politics of kinship in British Central Africa, 1929–38', *Journal of African History* 46 (2005): 455–78.

6. Norris, 84 –5.
7. Stoler, 27; 43. The same can be applied to the judicial system in Palestine, as shown in Assaf Likhovski, 'In our image: Colonial discourse and the Anglicization of the law in Mandatory Palestine', *Israel Law Review* 29 (summer 1995): 297–301.
8. Shira Robinson has demonstrated that throughout the Mandate, British policies caused a gradual change in the classification of the population in terms of race, but so, too, did the policies of the *Yishuv* itself in promoting notion of the Jews as a 'racial' group in Palestine distinct from the Arabs. By the 1930s, the Yishuv posited the Jews as 'European white men'. See Shira Robinson, *Citizen Strangers: Palestinians and the Birth of Israel's Liberal Settler State* (Stanford: Stanford University Press, 2013): pp. 9–17.
9. Joon-Hai Lee, 'The "native" undefined', 461–2. For a similar analysis on these statuses and citizenship for the case of French colonies, see Emmanuelle Saada, *Empire's Children: Race, Filiation, and Citizenship in the French Colonies*, translated by Arthur Goldhammer (Chicago: University of Chicago Press, 2012), pp. 69–80.
10. Stoler, p. 24.
11. Harald Fischer-Tine and Susanne Gehrmann, 'Introduction', in Fischer-Tine and Gehrmann, eds, *Empires and Boundaries: Rethinking Race, Class, and Gender in Colonial Settings* (London: Routledge, 2008), p. 5.
12. Patrick Ettinger, *Imaginary Lines: Border Enforcement and the Origins of Undocumented Immigration, 1882–1930* (Austin: University of Texas Press, 2009), p. 7.
13. Stoler, p. 27.
14. Frederick Cooper, 'Citizenship and the politics of difference in French Africa', in *Empires and Boundaries*, p. 108.
15. Palestine Citizenship Order-in-Council, 30 January 1925, CO 733/88/383–98.
16. For more, see Pinhas Ofer, 'The Commission on the Palestine Disturbances of August 1929: Appointment, terms of reference, procedure and report', *Middle Eastern Studies* 19 (January 1983): 104–18 and Martin Kolinsky, *Law, Order and Riots in Mandatory Palestine, 1928–1935* (Basingstoke: Macmillan, 1993).
17. Future Constitution of Palestine, Zionist Proposals with Secretary of State's Amendments, 27 February 1919, FO 608/98/8.
18. Citizenship – Proposed Nationality of Jews memo, 1933, CO 733/247/8/3.
19. Ibid., 28 July 1933, CO 733/247/8/8–10.
20. Norris, p. 37.

21. Confidential Report by Josiah Westwood, 26 July 1928, the papers of Leopold Amery, AMEL 1/5/46.
22. Torpey, *The Invention of the Passport*, p. 116. For a study on the North American historical equivalent see Ettinger, pp. 15–16.
23. Qafisheh, p. 146.
24. Memo on Palestine passports, 11 June 1926, CO 733/114/514–15. Inside, a note requested that the holder pass freely and be given protection in the name of His Majesty's Government.
25. Ettinger, p. 6.
26. Torpey, pp. 4–12.
27. Ibid., 122–7. Governments were, however, not obliged to admit bearers of Nansen Passports into their territories.
28. For a fascinating study on this phenomenon of Ottoman Jewish aliens in Britain, see Aviva Ben-Ur, 'Identity imperative: Ottoman Jews in wartime and interwar Britain', *Immigrants and Minorities* (2014): 1–33.
29. Reconsideration of applications from persons resident abroad, 1927, CO 733/142/18/3–4.
30. Ibid.
31. Memo, Government Office in Jerusalem to Colonial Office, 18 September 1927, CO 733/142/8/16–17.
32. Palestine Passports memo, 11 June 1926, CO 733/114/517.
33. Period of validity of Palestine Passports memo, 16 November 1926, CO 733/118/142.
34. Home Office memo on Palestine Passports, October 1926, CO 733/121/482–7.
35. Draft instructions to consuls, June 1926, CO 733/114/530.
36. Art. 4 of the 1925 Citizenship Order-in-Council referred to individuals more than eighteen years of age who made a declaration to become a Palestinian citizen within two years of the order if he was born in Palestine as an Ottoman, was resident for at least six months prior to the date of declaration and had not acquired a foreign nationality; Art. 5 referred to individuals who made a declaration of intent to opt for citizenship in accordance with Art. 2 of the 1922 Legislative Council Election Order and had a provisional certificate of Palestinian nationality, had been resident of Palestine and declared his desire to become a citizen according to Art. 4; Art. 7 referred to individuals naturalised as Palestinian citizens and thus who met the qualifications for naturalisation.
37. Period of validity of Palestine passports, 16 November 1926, CO 733/118/142.
38. Mae M. Ngal, *Impossible Subjects: Illegal Aliens and the Making of Modern America* (Princeton: University Press, 2005), p. 4.

39. Palestine Citizenship Order-in-Council memo, 30 January 1925, CO 733/88/383–98.
40. Colonial Office memo on Administration Policy, 27 February 1926, CO 733/112/86–7.
41. For a discussion of these confusing and often overlapping statuses of inhabitants of a variety of British possessions in the nineteenth century and early twentieth, see Dummett and Nicol, *Subjects, Citizens, Aliens and Others*, 114–16.
42. Stoler, p. 39.
43. Colonial Office memo on Administration Policy, 27 February 1926, CO 733/112/86–7.
44. British naturalisation of persons resident in Palestine, April 1928, CO 733/167/5/1.
45. One reason included the identification by many of Palestine's Jews with the Yishuv as their 'state' and the guarantor of rights, duties and welfare.
46. Government offices memo on the rise in fees for naturalisation, 28 November 1929, CO 733/171/14/12.
47. Memo on the issue of birth of Palestinian children abroad, 17 December 1925, CO 733/121/716.
48. Irene Bloemraad, 'Who claims dual citizenship? The limits of postnationalism, the possibilities of transnationalism, and the persistence of traditional citizenship', *International Migration Review* 38 (summer 2004): 390–2.
49. Palestinian naturalisation, 25 August 1926, CO 733/116.
50. Ibid. It should be recalled that for native Arab emigrants, the Foreign Office instructed consuls to treat them as Turkish nationals. By the mid-1920s, many faced deportation from Latin America since they were without nationality papers – colonial officials did not step in to help as a matter of practice, as was done with stateless Jews.
51. Reconsideration of applications from persons resident abroad circular, 1927, CO 733/142/18.
52. Ibid.
53. Citizenship Order-in-Council memo, 1925, 16 May 1929, CO 733/171/14/1–5
54. Bunton, 'Inventing the status quo', pp. 49–51. Bentwich was also depicted in contemporary sources as 'the blind leading the blind' in reference to his role in drafting pieces of legislation.
55. Reconsideration of applications from persons resident abroad, 9 December 1927, CO 733/142/18.
56. Citizenship Order-in-Council memo, 1925, 16 May 1929, CO 733/171/14.

57. Ibid.
58. Memo from High Commissioner to Colonial Office, 26 April 1929, CO 733/171/14.
59. Ibid.
60. Ibid.
61. Foreign Office memo, 18 July 1929, CO 733/171/14/30.
62. Memo, Foreign Office to Colonial Office, undated [1929] CO 733/171/14/34.
63. Memo, Home Office to Colonial Office, 12 August 1930, CO 733/185/7/26.
64. Memo, High Commissioner Chancellor to Colonial Office, [undated] 1930, CO 733/185/7/32. Such a power to give or take away citizenship should, according to High Commissioner John Chancellor, be 'reasonably restricted'. Colonial Secretary Lord Passfield, who replaced Amery in 1930, agreed. See Passfield to High Commissioner, 18 January 1930, CO 733/185/7/34.
65. Memo, Foreign Office to Colonial Office, 5 April 1930, CO 733/185/7/29.
66. Citizenship (Amendment) Order 1931, Home Office, 23 July 1931, CO 733/203/13/23.
67. Citizenship Order-in-Council, 1930, CO 733/185/7/10.
68. Bentwich's subsequent appointment was that of lecturer in international law at the Hebrew University in Jerusalem. See Norman and Helen Bentwich, *Mandate Memories, 1918–1948* (London: Hogarth Press, 1965).
69. The connections were feared with some reason: anarchism in the Levant was not a new ideology and claimed a number of supporters in the late nineteenth century and early twentieth in places such as Syria and Egypt, as well as in Greece, and links with European anarchists were common. For more on the post-1914 situation, see Ilham Khuri-Makdisi, *The Eastern Mediterranean and the Making of Global Radicalism, 1860–1914* (Berkeley: University of California Press, 2010).
70. A broader study on the topic of subversion and intelligence gathering in the Middle East is that of Martin Thomas, *Empires of Intelligence: Security Services and Colonial Disorder after 1914* (Berkeley: University of California Press, 2008).
71. Again, the US presented similar cases and terminology at the time. See Ettinger, pp. 16–17. The term 'undesirable', used in reference to aliens, came out of Great Britain's 1905 Aliens Act. It was used more frequently after the First World War within the United Kingdom; see Dummett and Nicol, p. 112.

72. Dummett and Nicol, pp. 93–94. The British were also informed by experiences with Indian nationalists and India's more radical, and often violent, diaspora in the United States and Canada in the early twentieth century. Britain's reactions to the Ghadar Movement showcase an example of fears of radically subversive diasporas. See Maia Ramnath, 'Two revolutions: The Ghadar movement and India's radical diaspora, 1913–1918', *Radical History Review* 92 (spring 2005): 7–30.

73. Norris, pp. 38–9.

74. Citizenship Order-in-Council, June 1934, CO 733/257/9/4–6; emphasis in the original.

75. Memo, Colonial Office to Chief Secretary, June 1934, CO 733/257/9/60.

76. Ibid.

77. Citizenship Order-in-Council, 25 September 1934, CO 733/257/7.

78. Nationality: Revocation of Certificates of Naturalisation, 20 August 1934, ISA/M/710/14.

79. A file of correspondence on this topic can be found in Naturalization Certificates, CO 733/357/2.

80. '*Mudhakara 'ala huwl qānun al-hijra*' [Note on immigration law], 9 January 1928, *al-Jamiyya al-'Arabiyya*.

81. The letter from Marcos, along with similar letters from Musa Kazim al-Husayni and other Arab leaders in Nablus and Bethlehem, addressed to the high commissioner and colonial secretary, and responses can be found in CO 733/142/8, Citizenship Applications.

82. Citizenship Order-in-Council Amendment Order, 30 May 1932, CO 733/220/12/2–3.

83. Ibid.

84. Ibid.

85. Memo, High Commissioner to Secretary of State for the Colonies, 18 June 1932, CO 733/220/12.

86. Ibid., 9 May 1932.

87. Citizenship Order in Palestine, 1933, CO 733/238/14/3–4. Wauchope even noted that the Palestine Government would receive increased revenue from the naturalisation fees for Jewish women: Memo, High Commissioner to Foreign Office, June 1933, CO 733/238/14/39; emphasis in original.

88. Ibid., 31 August 1933.

89. Memo, Dominions Office to Colonial Office, 31 August 1933, CO 733/238/14/5–6; emphasis added.

90. Memo, Colonial Office to Dominions Office, December 1933, CO 733/238/14/11–13.

91. National Status of female British subjects who marry Palestinian citizens memo, August 1934, CO 733/268/18/3.

92. On the United States' Immigration Quota Act, 1925–1965, see Eric J. Hooglund, 'Introduction', in Eric J. Hooglund, ed., *Crossing the Waters: Arabic-Speaking Immigrants to the United States before 1940* (Washington, DC: Smithsonian Institute Press, 1987), p. 2.
93. *Palestine Statement of Policy by His Majesty's Government, presented by the Secretary of State of the Colonies to Parliament.* Cmd. Paper 3692. London: HM Stationery Office, October 1931 [Passfield White Paper].
94. Extract from the Official Report of the Arabs in Palestine, 27 June 1934, CO 733/251/4/33.
95. Robinson, *Citizen Strangers*, p. 117.

Notes to Chapter 6

1. *'Idrāb ghadān!'* [Strike Tomorrow!], 22 August 1931, *Mir'at al-Sharq*.
2. For more on this argument and modern examples, see William Safran, 'Citizenship and nationality in democratic systems: Approaches to defining and acquiring membership in the political community', *International Political Science Review* 18 (July 1997): 313–14.
3. *'Al-tamthīl fī filastin'* [Representation in Palestine], 29 November 1920, *Mir'at al-Sharq*. The Ottoman Education Law required that an elementary school be opened in every community and that a secondary school be opened in every large town of the Empire.
4. Laura Robson, *Colonialism and Christianity in Mandate Palestine* (Austin: University of Texas Press, 2011), p. 54.
5. Engin F. Isin and Patricia K. Wood, *Citizenship and Identity* (London: Sage, 1999), p. 4.
6. The field of Subaltern Studies has been immensely influential in studies of post-colonialism, but the members of the Subaltern Studies School mostly focused on the colonial, post-colonial and national histories of India. The concept of the subaltern citizen during the late nineteenth century and early twentieth in the Levant has yet to be truly explored. For more on subaltern citizens, see Gyanendra Pandey, 'The subaltern as subaltern citizen', *Economic and Political Weekly* 41 (November 2006): 4,735–41. Additionally, very few studies specifically focusing on the 'subaltern' citizen in the Middle East have been written, and most deal with the era after the mandate system ended. For example, see John Chalcraft, *The Invisible Cage: Syrian Migrant Workers in Lebanon* (Stanford: Stanford University Press, 2009) and Stephanie Cronin, ed., *Subalterns and Social Protest: A History from below in the Middle East and North Africa* (London: Routledge, 2008). Studies on civil society Tsarist

Russia offer different, and interesting, comparisons with the Palestine Mandate. Similar to Russia in the nineteenth century, the print
culture in the Arab provinces of the Ottoman Empire became one
of the most important elements to facilitate the emergence of civil
society. By the turn of the twentieth century, other elements at work
in Russia formed the structure of civil society such as universities,
city councils, urbanisation and thousands of voluntary associations
whose many projects formed networks, diffused public knowledge
and created a sense of participation. See Joseph Bradley, 'Subjects
into citizens: Societies, civil society, and autocracy in Tsarist Russia',
The American Historical Review 107 (October 2002): 1,106–19.

7. Margaret R. Somers, 'Rights, relationality, and membership: Rethinking the making and meaning of citizenship', *Law and Social Inquiry*
19 (winter 1994): 65, 78–9.

8. Hunter, ' "Our common humanity" ', p. 296.

9. Rachel Sieder, ' "Paz, progreso, justicia y honrade": law and citizenship
in Alta Verapaz during the regime of Jorge Ubico', *Bulletin of Latin
American Research* 19 (July 2000): 284–5.

10. Ibid., p. 292.

11. Memo, High Commissioner Plumer to Amery on the Legislative Council,
19 February 1926, CO 733/112/491.

12. Miller, *Government and Society in Rural Palestine*, p. 44.

13. Tamir Goren, ' "Cooperation is the guiding principle": Jews and Arabs
in the Haifa Municipality during the British Mandate', *Israel Studies*
11 (fall 2006): 111.

14. Municipal Franchise Ordinance 1926, CO 733/113/371–7.

15. '*Qānun al-baladiyyāt al-jadīd*' [The new municipal law], 10 November
1926, *Al-Ittihad al-'Arabī*.

16. '*Intakhābāt al-baladiyya*' [Municipal elections], 13 February 1927,
Al-Ittihad al-'Arabī; '*Ihtajājā nādīal-'amāl min yāffā*' [Protest of the
Jaffa Worker's Club], 7 February 1927, *Al-Jamiyya al-'Arabiyya*.

17. Municipal elections: Verification of Palestinian citizenship of voters
memo, 1933, ISA/M/205/37.

18. Municipal elections: Verification of Palestinian citizenship of voters,
1933, ISA/M/205/37.

19. Jacob Norris, 'Toxic waters: Ibrahim Hazboun and the struggle for
a Dead Sea concession, 1913–1948', *Jerusalem Quarterly* 45 (spring
2011): 31.

20. '*Dā'ra al-ashghāl*' [Department of Works], 12 November 1928, *Sawt
al-Haqq*.

21. '*Darbāt la darā'ib: wājab al-lajna al-tanfīdhiyya*' [Strike from taxes:
duty of the Executive Committee], 13 October 1926, *Sawt al-Sha'b*.

22. *'Harakat al-'amāl fī filastin'* [Workers' Movement in Palestine], 23 August 1928, *Mir'at al-Sharq*.
23. Grievances of the Educated Moslem Young Men Congress, 1932–1933, ISA/M/294/22.
24. *'Mādhā tākhdh al-hakuma min al-fellāh'* [What the government takes from the *fellah*], 14 November 1926, *Al-Ittihad al-'Arabī*. For more on tithes, see Matthews, *Confronting an Empire*, p. 204.
25. Migdal, *Palestinian Society*, pp. 12, 217.
26. From the unpublished manuscript of memoirs by Hanna Nakkarah on the history of the expropriation of Arab land in Palestine, to be cited as 'Hanna Nakkarah Book', 87–88. I am extremely grateful to the family of Mr Nakkarah: his daughter Naila and her husband Butrus Abu-Manneh, who allowed me to access and to cite this manuscript.
27. *'Ihtajājā 'ala sha'b gaza'* [Protest of the people of Gaza], 10 December 1928, *Al-Ittihad al-'Arabi*.
28. *'Nadā' bishā'n qānun al-muqtarah: teswiyya al-arādī'* [Appeal regarding the planned law: Land Settlement], 1 January 1929, *Al-Ittihad al-'Arabī*.
29. *Min Awrāq Akram Zu'aytir*, 334–44.
30. Matthews, *Confronting an Empire*, p. 2.
31. Eugene Weber, *Peasants into Frenchmen: The Modernization of Rural France 1870–1914* (London: Chatto and Windus, 1977), pp. 303, 336.
32. *'Lilmu'alamin fi al-mudāris'* [To the teachers in the schools], 22 July 1931, *Mir'at al-Sharq*.
33. Dipesh Chakrabarty, *Habitations of Modernity: Essays in the Wake of Subaltern Studies* (Chicago: Chicago University Press, 2002), p. 19.
34. Matthews, *Confronting an Empire*, pp. 56–9.
35. *'Muqarat mu'tamar jama'iāt al-shabān al-filastin'* [Decisions of the Palestine Youth Congress], 26 November 1928, *Sawt al-Haqq*.
36. *'Ila al-shabāb: iqtaham al-mīdān wa tanzīm sufufakum'* [To the young people: storm the field and organise your ranks], 7 January 1930, *Mir'at al-Sharq*. Furthermore, the British authorities kept a file on Akram Zu'aytir and his political activities even after his tenure as a teacher in Acre and the Galilee ended. The Department of Education felt that he 'indulge[d] in matters not considered satisfactory' with his pupils. See ISA/M/1012/15, July 1929. Gandhi's march across India early that year further inspired Zu'aytir: he encouraged the youth to walk across Palestine to spread patriotism, discourage land sales and encourage a boycott of foreign goods.
37. Foundation law of the Youth Club of Bethlehem, 1928, in Adnan Musallam, *Folded Pages*, p. 211.
38. *'Tafāsīl mu'tamar al-shabāb al-'arabī al-filastīniyya al-āwal fī yāffā'* [Details of the First Palestinian Arab Youth Conference in Jaffa], 6 January 1932, *Al-Jamiyya al-'Arabiyya*.

39. Joel Beinin, *Workers and Peasants in the Modern Middle East* (Cambridge: Cambridge University Press, 2001), p. 77.

40. Joseph Migdal, *Palestinian Society and Politics* (New York: Macmillan, 1980), pp. 237, 249.

41. '*Min sh'inhā tahasīn al-wada' al-iqtasādī fī filastin?*' [Will the economic situation improve in Palestine?], 23 May 1928, *Mir'at al-Sharq*.

42. Village Cooperative Society, Acre, 1928, ISA/M/5000/15.

43. Lockman, 'Railway workers and relational history', pp. 607–10. The Jewish workers in mixed areas remained part of the Histadrut but the Arabs were not fully incorporated into the Zionist labour federation.

44. Zachary Lockman and Lev Grinberg have written important articles on this subject of Arab-Jewish cooperation in the Palestine workers' movement in the 1930s and 1940s. Lockman in particular argues that the dual society model of Palestinian mandate historiography does not fully account for instances of social cooperation and interaction. See Lockman, 'Railway workers and relational history', and Lev Grinberg, 'A historical slip of the tongue, or what can the Arab–Jewish transportation strike teach us about the Israeli–Palestinian conflict?', *International Journal of Middle East Studies* 35 (August 2003): 371–91. However, neither historian addresses citizenship or notions of civil society.

45. The Palestinian Arab Workers Society, Tiberias branch memo, undated, ISA/M/5224/19.

46. For example, see Ellen Fleischmann, *The Nation and Its "New" Women: The Palestinian Women's Movement, 1920–1948* (Berkeley: University of California Press, 2003); Islah Jad, 'From salons to popular committees: Palestinian women, 1919–1989', in *Intifada: Palestine at the Crossroads*, eds Jamal R. Nassar and Roger Heacock (Birzeit: Birzeit University Press, 1991); Sayigh, *Palestinians: From Peasants to Revolutionaries* (London: Zed Books, 1979); Matiel Mogannam, *The Arab Woman and the Palestine Problem* (London: Herbert Joseph, 1937).

47. Fleischmann, *The Nation and Its 'New' Women*, pp. 44–8, 81.

48. Ibid., pp. 86–7.

49. Al-Kayyali, *Wathi'aq*, p. 157.

50. Petitions sent to the League of Nations from the Executive Committee of the First Arab Women's Congress, 26 January and 7 July 1932, CO 733/221/9.

51. Laleh Khalili, *Heroes and Martyrs of Palestine: The Politics of National Commemoration* (Cambridge: Cambridge University Press, 2007), p. 22.

52. Matthews, p. 45.

53. The riots have been studied in many other works. In the aftermath of the violence between Jews and Arabs, primarily in Jerusalem and Safed, a total of 133 Jews were killed and 339 wounded and more than 120

Arabs died and 232 were wounded. All offenders were tried in British courts: fifty-five Arabs and two Jews were found guilty of murder. See Kolinsky, *Law, Order and Riots*, pp. 42–4, Y. Porath's two volumes on the Palestinian Arab national movement, and also Norman Bentwich, *England in Palestine* (London: Kegan Paul, Trench, Trubner and Co., 1932), p. 209.

54. Al-Kayyali, *Wathā'iq*, 16 June 1930, p. 174. The three men, 'Atta al-Zeyr, Mohammad Jamjoum and Fouad Hijazi, died by hanging in Acre. In their final statements published for the public, they proclaimed the slogan 'to the Arab nation: complete independence or death'.

55. Al-Kayyali, *Wathā'iq*, p. 180.

56. *Min Awrāq Akram Zu'aytir*, pp. 334–44.

57. Porath, *The Palestinian Arab Nationalist Movement 1929–39: From Riots to Rebellion* (London: Frank Cass, 1977), pp. 35–8.

58. '*Nurīd parliament mumthil*' [We want a representative parliament], 29 August 1931, *Mir'at al-Sharq*.

59. '*Ladīna harakat al-haraja fī itjāha jadīd*' [Our critical movement in its new direction], 17 October 1933, *al-Jamiyya al-'Arabiyya*.

60. The first monograph is in Arabic: Samih Shabib, *Hizb al-Istiqlal al-Arabī fi Filastin, 1932–1933* [The Arab Istiqlal Party in Palestine, 1932–3] (Beirut: PLO Research Center, 1981); and the second, in English, is by Weldon C. Matthews, *Confronting and Empire, Constructing a Nation*.

61. Matthews, p. 2.

62. '*Biyyān hizb al-istiqlal*' [Statement of the Istiqlal Party], 8 March 1930, *Sawt al-Sha'b*.

63. Shabib, *Hizb al-Istiqlal*, p. 50.

64. Ibid., pp. 63–6.

65. Ibid., pp. 73–81, 109–13.

66. *Min Awrāq Akram Zu'aytir*, p. 363.

67. Ibid., p. 113.

68. Al-Kayyali, *Wathā'iq*, pp. 321–30.

69. Weldon C. Matthews, 'Pan-Islam or Arab nationalism? The meaning of the 1931 Jerusalem Islamic Congress reconsidered', *International Journal of Middle East Studies* 35 (February 2003): 2–5. In particular, the Communist Party in the early 1930s included mainly leftist Jewish immigrants.

70. '*Bīyyān al-'amāl*' [Workers' statement], 6 August 1931, *Al-Jamiyya al-'Arabiyya*. For more on the workers' movement, see Lockman, *Comrades and Enemies*.

71. Ann Mosely Lesch, *Arab Politics in Palestine, 1917–1939: The Frustration of a Nationalist Movement* (Ithaca: Cornell University Press, 1979), p. 108.

72. Matthews, *Confronting an Empire*, p. 228.
73. Partha Chatterjee, *The Politics of the Governed: Reflections on Popular Politics in Most of the World* (New York: Columbia University Press, 2004), p. 33.

Notes to Chapter 7

1. Nationality Law and Acquisition of Palestinian Citizenship, Palestine Royal Commission Report documents, May–June 1937, CO 733/347/4.
2. Partha Chatterjee, 'After subaltern studies', *Economic and Political Weekly* 47 (September 2012): 46–7.
3. British censorship of Arabic and Hebrew newspapers increased as tensions rose. The 1933 Press Law gave the High Commissioner the power to close papers that 'endangered' public order but the law 'did not exercise any direct control over the ideas or tone of the paper'. Strict press censorship during the revolt as well as punishments for certain journalists, banning types of information, and closing papers for mentioning certain items of news or opinion all took place during the revolt. The government occasionally suspended all four Arabic dailies at once during the revolt's early phase. As Sandy Sufian shows, both Arab and Jewish dailies attempted to get around censorship through the use of often-satirical cartoons to illustrate opinions on the situation in Palestine. See Sandy Sufian, 'Anatomy of the 1936–39 revolt: Images of the body in political cartoons of Mandatory Palestine', *Journal of Palestine Studies* 37 (winter 2008): 23–42.
4. Noah Haiduc-Dale has written more extensively on the changing relationship between Arab Christians and Arab Muslims during the Palestine Revolt, although he argues against Porath's earlier statements that Christians were apathetic to the revolt. Rather, Haiduc-Dale shows a far more detailed and nuanced account of the types of actions in support of – and against – the revolt in the Christian community. See Noah Haiduc-Dale, *Arab Christians in British Mandate Palestine: Communalism and Nationalism, 1917–1948* (Edinburgh: Edinburgh University Press, 2013), pp. 147–50.
5. The platforms of these parties were largely indistinguishable from one another and their leaders came mostly from the traditional Jerusalem families. The Husaynis (the Palestine Arab Party), the Nashashibis (the National Defense Party) and the Khalidis (the Reform Party) were prominent sponsors of the new parties. This is further explained in the final chapters of Rashid Khalidi, *Palestinian Identity: The Construction of*

Modern National Consciousness (New York: Columbia University Press, 1997), pp. 145–200.

6. Swedenburg, *Memories of Revolt*, p. 2.

7. *Fi Khidām al-Nidāl al-'Arabī al-Filastīnī: Mudhakkarāt al-Munādil Bahjat Abu Gharbiyah, 1916–1949* [In the Midst of the Struggle for the Palestinian Arab Cause: The Memoirs of Freedom Fighter Bahjat Abu Gharbiyah, 1916–1949] (Beirut: Institute for Palestine Studies, 1993), p. 20.

8. These studies include Swedenburg, *Memories of Revolt*; Porath, *From Riots to Rebellion*; Mustafa Kabha, 'The Palestine press and the General Strike, April–October 1936: *Filastin* as a case study', *Middle Eastern Studies* 39 (July 2003): 169–89; Thomas Mayer, 'Egypt and the 1936 Arab Revolt in Palestine', *Journal of Contemporary History* 19 (April 1984): 275–87.

9. Jeffrey Cormier and Phillipe Couton, 'Civil society, mobilization and communal violence: Quebec and Ireland, 1890–1920', *The Sociological Quarterly* 45 (summer 2004): 489.

10. Shepherd, pp. 184–5.

11. *Al-haraka al-wataniyya al-Filastīn: Yawmiyāt Akram Zu'aytir, 1935–1939* [The Palestinian National Movement: Diary of Akram Zu'aytir, 1935–9] (Beirut: Center for Palestine Studies, 1980), pp. 23–6.

12. See Memo, Wauchope to MacDonald, 21 December 1935, CO 733/297/1 and Criminal Investigation Department report, 4 December 1935, FO 371/20018.

13. *Fi Khidām al-Nidāl*, p. 52.

14. Itzchak Weismann, 'The invention of a populist leader: Badr al-din al-Hasani, the religious educational movement and the Great Syrian Revolt', *Arabica* 52 (January 2005): 110–11, 135.

15. Criminal Investigation Dept. report, January–March 1936, FO 371/20018.

16. Subhi Yassin, *Al-Thawra al-'arabiyya al-khubra fi Filastīn, 1936–1939* [The Great Arab Revolt in Palestine, 1936–9] (Cairo: Dar al-Katib, 1967), p. 47.

17. Various petitions on the issue of the April 1936 delegation to London can be found in ISA M/295/17/15.

18. Shepherd, *Ploughing Sand*, p. 187.

19. *Min Awrāq Akram Zu'aytir*, pp. 440–1.

20. The story of the revolt has been written about numerous times and this account is from *Al-haraka al-wataniyya al-Filastīn: Yawmiyāt Akram Zu'aytir*, p. 53.

21. *Yawmiyāt Akram Zu'aytir*, pp. 60–5.

22. Ibid., p. 82. Also: '*Darbāt la darā'ib: wājab al-lajna al-tanfīdhiyya*' [Strike from taxes: Duty of the Executive Committee], 13 October 1926, *Sawt al-Sha'b*.

23. Swedenburg, p. xix.
24. The demands of the HAC differed little from the demands given to Great Britain by the same elites for nearly twenty years: an end to Jewish immigration and land sales, a national elected government and independence for Palestine.
25. Yassin, *Al-Thawra*, pp. 43–5.
26. *Yawmiyāt Akram Zuʻaytir*, p. 400.
27. Mohamed 'Ali El-Tahir, '*An Thawrat Filastīn sanat 1936: wasif wa akbār wa waqaʻa wa wathāʼiq* [About the Palestine Revolt of 1936: Description, News, Facts and Documents] (Cairo: Palestinian Arab Committee, December 1936), p. 67.
28. Al-Kayyali, *Wathāʼiq*, pp. 381, 394–7.
29. Porath, *From Riots to Rebellion*, p. 172; Al-Kayyali, *Wathāʼiq*, p. 384.
30. *Yawmiyāt Akram Zuʻaytir*, p. 87.
31. Swedenburg, p. 123.
32. Al-Kayyali, *Wathāʼiq*, 28 July 1936, pp. 433–5.
33. Swedenburg, pp. 78–80.
34. Michael Provence, 'Ottoman modernity, colonialism, and insurgency in the interwar Arab East', *International Journal of Middle East Studies* 43 (May 2011): 206–7.
35. Monthly intelligence survey, 3 June 1936, FO 371/20030; Weekly summary of intelligence, 30 October 1936, FO 371/20031.
36. Protest by Chamber of Commerce, Nazareth, 24 April 1936, ISA M/274/33.
37. El-Tahir, '*An Thawrat Filastīn* , pp. 22–3.
38. Porath, *From Riots to Rebellion*, pp. 176–7.
39. Matthew Hughes, 'From law and order to pacification: Britain's suppression of the Arab revolt in Palestine, 1936–39', *Journal of Palestine Studies* 39 (winter 2010): 9.
40. Chatterjee, *The Politics of the Governed*, p. 34.
41. Johan Franzén, 'Communism versus Zionism: The Comintern, Yishuvism, and the Palestine Communist Party', *Journal of Palestine Studies* 36 (winter 2007): 12.
42. Michael J. Cohen, 'Sir Wauchope, the army, and the rebellion in Palestine, 1936', *Middle Eastern Studies* 9 (January 1973): 22; Hughes, 'From law and order', p. 9.
43. Shepherd, p. 189.
44. Hughes, p. 7. The first application of collective punishment upon the Arabs under Palestine's civil administration came in 1921 after the Jaffa riots. Similar ordinances for collective punishment were issued through the mid-twenties, always aimed at Arab communities but only applied in specific towns rather than entire municipalities or districts.

45. Collective punishment ordinance, May 1936, CO 733/303/3.
46. Other examples of collective punishment included looting and destruction of household items and crops, incidences of British soldiers forcing male inhabitants of 'bad', or rebellious, villages to stand under the sun for days without access to food or adequate water, house-to-house searches that resulted in deliberate sabotage of property and foodstuffs and mass arrests of all male citizens of various villages. See *Fi Khidām al-Nidāl*, p. 60. Arabs were also made to pay fines for the demolitions and pay the cost of repairs. See Shepherd, pp. 197–9.
47. Petition of the National Committee of Lydda, July 1936, CO 733/287/13.
48. Simoni, p. 100.
49. Sufian, p. 27.
50. Palestine Disturbances 1936 memo, 3 May 1937, WO 32/9618. Military courts did not allow for appeals.
51. Hughes, pp. 9, 17.
52. Petitions on this issue from February 1937 can be found in ISA M/350/24.
53. Nakkara, *Lawyer of the Land*, pp. 94–5.
54. Porath, *From Riots to Rebellion*, p. 268.
55. Nakkara, *Lawyer of the Land*, p. 97.
56. Summary of the Report of the Palestine Royal Commission to the League of Nations, Geneva, 30 November 1937 from *Palestine Royal Commission Report*, CO 733/347/4. The chairman, Peel, was a former Secretary of State in India.
57. Michael J. Cohen, *Palestine: Retreat from the Mandate, The Making of British Policy, 1936–45* (London: Paul Elek, 1978), p. 32.
58. Palestinian Citizenship, 1936, CO 733/296/7.
59. Memo, High Commissioner Wauchope to Secretary of State for the Colonies, November 1936, CO 733/286/1.
60. Palestinian citizenship applications: Hussein Khalil Abu Ziyad, November 1936–February 1937, CO 733/286/1.
61. Nationality Status of Mr. George Rock, October–December 1936, CO 733/306/13.
62. Ibid.
63. A small number of Arab officials supported the scheme. Arab civil servant Ahmed Khalid suggested the formation of an Arab parliament in the Arab zone and a Jewish parliament in the Jewish zone, with an executive council of appointed representatives from both to administer joint and general interests. The two zones were to be named as South Syria and Eretz-Israel. See CO 733/248/20.

64. Roza I. M. El-Eini, *Mandated Landscape: British Imperial Rule in Palestine, 1929–1948* (London: Routledge, 2006), pp. 317–18.
65. Memorandum on the Royal Commission Proposal for the Partition of Palestine, August 1936, ISA/MFA/2278/2.
66. Al-Kayyali, *Wathā'iq*, pp. 500–2.
67. *Yawmiyāt Akram Zu'aytir*, pp. 262–3.
68. Al-Kayyali, *Wathā'iq*, p. 541.
69. *Yawmiyāt Akram Zu'aytir*, p. 271.
70. Palestine Royal Commission: Evidence of Abdul Latif Bey Salah, 1937, CO 733/343/24.
71. Memorandum by the Commissioner for Migration and Statistics, March 1937, CO 733/347/4.
72. Jews could give naturalisation applications to the field officers on the spot and applications could also be made in person in the urban centres of Jerusalem, Jaffa, Haifa and Tiberias.
73. *Palestine Royal Commission Report*, 1937, Cmd. 5479 (London: HM Stationery Office, 1937), CO 733/347/4.
74. *Palestine Royal Commission Report*, 'Nationality Law and Acquisition of Palestinian Citizenship', May–June 1937, CO 733/347/4.
75. Ibid.
76. Ibid.
77. Draft Royal Commission Report Chapter XV' 1937, CO 733/347/4.
78. *Palestine Royal Commission Report*, 1937, Cmd. 5479 (London: HM Stationery Office, 1937), CO 733/347/4.
79. Partition Commission 1936, [undated] ISA/MFA/2278/2.
80. Ibid.
81. Ibid.
82. Ibid.
83. *Arab Higher Committee: Official Documents Relating to the Palestine Question, 1917–1947, Submitted to the General Assembly of the United Nations by the Delegation of the AHC for Palestine, New York*, Oct 1947 (Beirut: Institute for Palestine Studies), p. 5.
84. Cohen, *Palestine: Retreat from the Mandate*, p. 34.

Notes from Chapter 8

1. Petitions of deportees to the Seychelles, September 1938, CO 733/369/3.
2. FO memo, 9 December 1939, CO 733/397/14.
3. Khalidi, *The Iron Cage: The Story of the Palestinian Struggle for Statehood* (Boston: Beacon Press, 2006), p. 107. Many protest letters and

petitions against the atrocities committed by the British in Palestinian villages in 1939 can be found in the file Protests to the Secretary of State for the Colonies and League of Nations, ISA 336/8.

4. The White Paper of May 1939 came after the March conference at St James Palace that resolved to end the conflict in Palestine through discussions between government officials, mandate officials and both Arab and Zionist leaders. See Khalidi, *The Iron Cage*, pp. 114–15.

5. Internal factors of reshuffling in Cabinet and particularly the Foreign Office impacted British policy for Palestine and the perception of Arab nationalism there and regionally after 1936. A discussion of this can be found in G. Sheffer, 'Appeasement and the problem of Palestine,' *International Journal of Middle East Studies* 11 (May 1980): 377–99.

6. Colonial Office memo, 5 January 1937, CO 733/326/8.

7. Palestine Passports, 1938, CO 733/363/1.

8. E. Mills to HC MacMichael, 3 May 1938, CO 733/366/1; High Commissioner memo, March 1938, CO 733/366/1.

9. Annual Report of the Palestine Administration to the League of Nations, 1938, CO 733/399/10.

10. Ibid.

11. Naturalisation certificates, 1938, CO 733/357/2.

12. Palestine Passports: Foreign Office Proposal, January–April 1939, CO 733/393/8.

13. Ibid.

14. Identity cards memo, 16 March 1939, CO 733/413/8.

15. Robinson, pp. 17–21.

16. Citizenship Order-in-Council (Amendment), 1937, CO 733/332/6.

17. Memo to H. F. Downie from C. Parkinson, 13 April 1938, CO 733/366/1.

18. Chief Secretary's Office to Colonial Office, 14 May 1938, CO 733/366/1.

19. Colonial Office to Locker-Lampson, 23 April 1938, CO 733/366/1.

20. Ibid. If the administration put the Locker-Lampson bill's ideas into place, foreign governments would possibly de-naturalise all of their resident Jews whether or not those residents had actual Palestinian citizenship.

21. Home Office to Colonial Office memo, 11 October 1939, CO 733/397/15/5; MacMichael to Malcom MacDonald, 20 September 1939, CO 733/397/15.

22. Citizenship Order-in-Council (Amendment), 1937, CO 733/332/6.

23. Wauchope to Secretary of State for the Colonies, September 1937, CO 733/332/5.

24. Palestine Citizenship Order-in-Council, 1939, CO 733/397/13.

25. Ibid.

26. Home Office to Foreign Office memo, 27 January 1939, CO 733/397/13.
27. Palestine Citizenship (Amendment) Order, 1942.
28. Qafisheh, p. 108.
29. Official report, Palestine Administration, 26 July 1939, ISA 223/21.
30. United Nations General Assembly Resolution 181, 29 November 1947.
31. Anis F. Kassim, ed., *The Palestine Yearbook of International Law*, Vol. I (Cyprus: Al-Shaybani Society of International Law, 1984), p. 25.
32. Robinson, p. 8.
33. Ibid., p. 27.
34. Ibid., p. 69.
35. Leena Dallasheh, 'Troubled waters: Citizenship and colonial Zionism in Nazareth', *International Journal of Middle Eastern Studies* 47 (summer 2015): 467–87.
36. Kassim, pp. 27–9.
37. The Palestinian National Charter: Resolutions of the Palestine National Council, 1–17 July 1968, www.pac-usa.org/the_palestinian_charter. htm (accessed 9 March 2012); my emphasis.
38. Assem Khalil, 'Palestinian nationality and citizenship: Current challenges and future perspectives', in *CARIM (Consortium for Applied Research on International Migration) Research Report*, 2007, pp. 1–48.
39. Ibid., pp. 46–7.
40. Al-Muqtafi Legal Database, 2003 Amended Basic Law, Ramallah, 18 March 2003, www.palestinianbasiclaw.org/basic-law/2003-amended-basic-law (accessed 9 March 2012).
41. Khalil, 'Palestinian nationality and citizenship', p. 17.
42. Nadim N. Rouhana and Nimer Sultany, 'Redrawing the boundaries of citizenship: Israel's new hegemony', *Journal of Palestine Studies* 33 (fall 2003): 10–14.
43. Victor Kattan, 'The nationality of denationalized Palestinians', *Nordic Journal of International Law* 74 (2005): 67–102.

Bibliography

I. Unpublished

Archival sources

1. Israel State Archives (ISA), Jerusalem
   Series: *ISA: Mandatory Material*, M (formerly the Chief Secretary's Office, ISA/RG), 1918–48
   ISA: Ministry of Foreign Affairs, MFA, 1918–48

2. Public Records Office (PRO), London
   Series: *Colonial Office: Palestine Registers of Correspondence* (CO), 1918–47:
   Palestine General Correspondence
   Palestine Original Correspondence
   Foreign Office: Palestine Correspondence (FO), 1918–47
   Foreign and Commonwealth Office, General Correspondence (FO), 1918–47
   Political Correspondence (FO), 1918–46
   Paris Peace Conference (FO), 1918–20
   War Office: Palestine Disturbances (WO), 1936
   Home Office: Naturalisation (HO), 1920–47

3. Middle East Centre (MEC) Archives, St Anthony's College, Oxford
   Series: *Norman Bentwich papers*, GB165-0025, 1913–62

4. The papers of Leopold Amery (AMEL), Churchill Archives Centre, Churchill College, Cambridge

Doctoral dissertations and manuscripts

Barakat, Rena. '*Thawrat al-Buraq* in British Mandate Palestine: Jerusalem, Mass Mobilization and Colonial Politics, 1928–1930.' PhD dissertation, University of Chicago, 2008.

Campos, Michelle U. 'A 'Shared Homeland' and its Boundaries: empire, citizenship, and the origins of sectarianism in late Ottoman Palestine.' PhD diss., Stanford University, 2003.

Nakkarah, Hanna. 'Hanna Nakkarah Book.' Haifa, Israel. Unpublished memoirs.

II. Official Publications

Laws, charters and reports

2003 Amended Basic Law (Palestinian Authority), Ramallah, 18 March 2003.

Crane, Charles R. and Henry King. *King–Crane Report on the Near East, 28 Aug. 1919.* New York: Editor and Publisher, Co., 1922.

Great Britain Colonial Office Reports on the Administration of Palestine and Transjordan

Mandate for Palestine, League of Nations, 12 August 1922.

Minutes of the 24th session of the Council, Geneva, April 1923, *League of Nations Offical Journal*, 4th Yr. No. 6 (June 1923): 567–8.

Palestine Statement of Policy by His Majesty's Government, presented by the Secretary of State for the Colonies to Parliament. Cmd. Paper 3692. London: HM Stationery Office, October 1931[Passfield White Paper].

Palestine Royal Commission Report, presented by the Secretary of State for the Colonies to Parliament. Cmd. Paper 5479. London: HM Stationery Office, 1937.

Arab Higher Committee: Official Documents Relating to the Palestine Question, 1917–1947, Submitted to the General Assembly of the United Nations by the Delegation of the AHC for Palestine, New York, Oct 1947. Beirut: Institute for Palestine Studies.

The Palestinian National Charter: Resolutions of the Palestine National Council, 1–17 July 1968.

III. Books, Articles and Chapters

Abu-Manneh, Butrus. 'The Christians between Ottomanism and Syrian nationalism: The ideas of Butrus Al-Bustani.' *International Journal of Middle East Studies* 11 (May 1980): 287–304.

Al-Tahir, Mohamed 'Ali. '*An Thawrat Filastin sanat 1936: wasif wa akbār wa waqa'a wa wathā'iq* [About the Palestine Revolt of 1936: Description, News, Facts and Documents]. Cairo: Palestinian Arab Committee, 1936.

Arsan, Andrew. *Interlopers of Empire: The Lebanese Diaspora in Colonial French West Africa*. Oxford: University Press, 2014.

—' "This is the age of associations": Committees, petitions, and the roots of interwar Middle Eastern internationalism.' *Journal of Global History* 7 (July 2012): 166–88.

Arsan, Andrew, Lewis, Su Lin and Richard, Anne-Isabelle. 'Editorial—the roots of global civil society and the interwar moment.' *Journal of Global History* 7 (2012): 157–65.

Bailony, Reem. 'Transnationalism and the Syrian migrant community: The case of the 1925 Syrian revolt.' *Mashriq & Mahjar: Journal of Middle East Migration Studies* 1 (2013): 8–29.

Baldwin, M. Page. 'Subject to empire: Married women and the British nationality and status of Aliens Act.' *Journal of British Studies* 40 (October 2001): 522–56.

Banerjee, Sukanya. Becoming Imperial Citizens: Indians in the Late Victorian Empire. Durham, NC: Duke University Press, 2010.

Bayly, C. A. *Empire and Information: Intelligence Gathering and Social Communication in India, 1780–1870*. Cambridge: Cambridge University Press, 1996.

Beinin, Joel. *Workers and Peasants in the Modern Middle East*. Cambridge: Cambridge University Press, 2001.

Ben-Bassat, Yuval. Late Ottoman Palestine: The Period of Young Turk Rule. London: I. B. Tauris, 2011.

Bentwich, Norman and Helen. *Mandate Memories, 1918–1948*. London: Hogarth Press, 1965.

Bentwich, Norman. 'Palestine nationality and the mandate.' *Journal of Comparative Legislation and International Law* 21, Third Series (1939): 230–2.

—*England in Palestine*. London: Kegan Paul, Trench, Trubner and Co., 1932.

Ben-Ur, Aviva. 'Identity imperative: Ottoman Jews in wartime and interwar Britain.' *Immigrants and Minorities* (2014): 165–95.

Beshara, Adel. 'A rebel Syrian: Gibran Khalil Gibran.' In *The Origins of Syrian Nationhood: Histories, Pioneers and Identity*, ed. Adel Beshara. London: Routledge, 2011, pp. 143–62.

Bloemraad, Irene. 'Who claims dual citizenship? The limits of postnationalism, the possibilities of transnationalism, and the persistence of traditional citizenship.' *International Migration Review* 38 (summer 2004): 389–426.

Bradley, Joseph. 'Subjects into citizens: Societies, civil society, and autocracy in Tsarist Russia.' *The American Historical Review* 107 (October 2002): 1,106–19.

Brubaker, Rogers. *Nationalism Reframed: Nationhood and the National Question in the New Europe*. Cambridge: Cambridge University Press, 1996.

—*Citizenship and Nationhood in France and Germany*. Cambridge, MA: Harvard University Press, 1992.

Bunton, Martin. *Colonial Land Policies in Palestine 1917–1936*. Oxford: Oxford University Press, 2007.

—'Inventing the status quo: Ottoman Land-Law during the Palestine Mandate, 1917–1936.' *The International History Review* 21 (March 1999): 28–56.

Callahan, Michael. *Mandates and Empire: The League of Nations and Africa, 1914–1931*. Portland: Sussex Academic Press, 1999.

Çağaptay, Soner. 'Citizenship policies in interwar Turkey.' *Nations and Nationalism* 9 (2003): 601–19.

Campos, Michelle U. *Ottoman Brothers: Muslims, Christians, and Jews in Early Twentieth Century Palestine*. Stanford: Stanford University Press, 2011.

Chakrabarty, Dipesh. *Habitations of Modernity: Essays in the Wake of Subaltern Studies*. Chicago: Chicago University Press, 2002.

Chalcraft, John. The Invisible Cage: Syrian Migrant Workers in Lebanon. Stanford: Stanford University Press, 2009.

—'Engaging the state: Peasants and petitions in Egypt on the eve of colonial rule.'*International Journal of Middle East Studies* 37 (August 2005): 303–25.

Chatterjee, Partha. 'After subaltern studies.' *Economic and Political Weekly* 47 (September 2012): 44–49.

—*The Politics of the Governed: Reflections on Popular Politics in Most of the World*. New York: Columbia University Press, 2004.

Civantos, Christina. *Between Argentines and Arabs: Argentine Orientalism, Arab Immigrants and the Writing of Identity*. Albany: State University of New York Press, 2005.

Cohen, Michael J. *Palestine: Retreat from the Mandate: The Making of British Policy, 1936–45*. London: Paul Elek, 1978.

—'Direction of policy in Palestine, 1936–1945.' *Middle Eastern Studies* 11 (October 1975): 237–61.

—'Sir Wauchope, the army, and the rebellion in Palestine, 1936.' *Middle Eastern Studies* 9 (January 1973): 19–34.

Coller, Ian. *Arab France: Islam and the Making of Modern Europe, 1798–1831*. Berkeley: University of California Press, 2010.

Cooper, Frederick. *Citizenship between Empire and Nation: Remaking France and French Africa, 1945–1960*. Princeton: Princeton University Press, 2014.

—'Citizenship and the politics of difference in French West Africa.' In *Empires and Boundaries: Rethinking Race, Class, and Gender in Colonial Settings*, eds Harald Fischer-Tine and Susanne Gehrmann. London: Routledge, 2008, pp. 107–28.

—*Colonialism in Question: Theory, Knowledge, History*. Berkeley: University of California Press, 2005.

Cormier, Jeffrey and Phillipe Couton. 'Civil society, mobilization and communal violence: Quebec and Ireland, 1890–1920.' *The Sociological Quarterly* 45 (summer 2004): 487–508.

Cronin, Stephanie, ed. Subalterns and Social Protest: A History from below in the Middle East *and North Africa*. London: Routledge, 2008.

Dallasheh, Leena. 'Troubled waters: Citizenship and colonial Zionism in Nazareth.' *International Journal of Middle Eastern Studies* 47 (summer 2015): 467–87.

Daly, Mary E. 'Irish nationality and citizenship since 1922.' *Irish Historical Studies* 32 (May 2001): 377–407.

Darwin, John. *Britain, Egypt and the Middle East: Imperial Policy in the Aftermath of War 1918–1922*. London: Macmillan, 1981.

Davis, Uri. 'Democratization, citizenship, Arab unity, and Palestinian autonomy: A critical reading of the New Middle East.' In *Citizenship and State in the Middle East: Approaches and Applications*, eds Nils A. Butenschon, Uri Davis and Manuel Hassassian. Syracuse: University Press, 2000, pp. 225–45.

—'*Jinsiyya* versus *Muwatana*: The question of citizenship and state in the Middle East.' *Arab Studies Quarterly* 17 (winter/spring 1995): 19–50.

Deringil, Selim. ' "They live in a state of nomadism and savagery": The Late Ottoman Empire and the post-colonial debate.' *Comparative Studies in Society and History* 45 (April 2003): 311–42.

Dodge, Toby. *Inventing Iraq: The Failure of Nation Building and a History Denied*. London: Hurst and Co., 2003.

Doumani, Beshara. *Rediscovering Palestine: Merchants and Peasants in Jabal Nablus, 1700–1900*. Berkeley: University of California Press, 1995.

Dummett, Ann and Andrew Nicol. *Subjects, Citizens, Aliens and Others: Nationality and Immigration Law*. London: Weidenfeld and Nicolson, 1990.

El-Eini, Roza I. M. *Mandated Landscape: British Imperial Rule in Palestine, 1929–1948*. London: Routledge, 2006.

Essaid, Aida Asim. *Zionism and Land Tenure in Mandate Palestine*. London: Routledge, 2014.

Ettinger, Patrick. *Imaginary Lines: Border Enforcement and the Origins of Undocumented Immigration, 1882–1930*. Austin: University of Texas Press, 2009.

Fair, Laura. *Pastimes and Politics: Culture, Community and Identity in Post-Abolition Zanzibar, 1890–1945.* Athens: Ohio University Press, 2001.

Fahrenthold, Stacy. 'Transnational modes and media: The Syrian press in the *Mahjar* and emigrant activism during World War I.' *Mashriq & Mahjar: Journal of Middle East Migration Studies* 1 (spring 2013): 32–57.

Feldman, Ilana. *Governing Gaza: Bureaucracy, Authority, and the Work of Rule, 1917–1967.* Durham, NC: Duke University Press, 2008.

Fischer-Tine, Harald and Susanne Gehrmann, eds. *Empires and Boundaries: Rethinking Race, Class, and Gender in Colonial Settings.* London: Routledge, 2008.

Fleischmann, Ellen. *The Nation and Its 'New' Women: The Palestinian Women's Movement, 1920–1948.* Berkeley: University of California Press, 2003.

Foroohar, Manzar. 'Palestinians in Central America: From temporary emigrants to a permanent diaspora.' *Journal of Palestine Studies* 40 (spring 2011): 6–22.

Foster, Zachary J. 'Arabness, Turkey and the Palestinian national imagination in the eyes of *Mir'at al-Sharq*, 1919–1926.' *Jerusalem Quarterly* 42 (summer 2010): 61–79.

Franzén, Johan. 'Communism versus Zionism: The Comintern, Yishuvism, and the Palestine Communist Party.' *Journal of Palestine Studies* 36 (winter 2007): 6–24.

Gelvin, James. *Divided Loyalties: Nationalism and Mass Politics in Syria at the Close of Empire.* Berkeley: University of California Press, 1998.

—'The social origins of popular nationalism in Syria.' *International Journal of Middle East Studies* 26 (November 1994): 645–61.

—'Demonstrating communities in post-Ottoman Syria.' *Journal of Interdisciplinary History* 25 (summer 1994): 23–44.

Gettys, C. Luella. 'The effect of changes of sovereignty on nationality.' *The American Journal of International Law* 21 (April 1927): 268–78.

Gey van Pittius, E. F. W. ' "Dominion" nationality.' *Journal of Comparative Legislation and International Law* 13 (1931): 199–202.

Gharbiyah, Bahjat Abu. *Fi Khidām al-Nidāl al-'Arabī al-Filastīnī: Mudhakkarāt al-Munādil Bahjat Abu Gharbiyah, 1916–1949* [In the Midst of the Struggle for the Palestinian Arab Cause: The Memoirs of Freedom Fighter Bahjat Abu Gharbiyah, 1916–1949]. Beirut: Institute for Palestine Studies, 1993.

Gonzalez, Nancie L. *Dollar, Dove, and Eagle: One Hundred Years of Palestinian Migration to Honduras.* Ann Arbor: University of Michigan Press, 1992.

Goren, Tamir. ' "Cooperation is the guiding principle": Jews and Arabs in the Haifa Municipality during the British Mandate.' *Israel Studies* 11 (fall 2006): 108–41.

Gorman, David. *Imperial Citizenship: Empire and the Question of Belonging.* Manchester: Manchester University Press, 2006.

—'Liberal internationalism, the League of Nations Union, and the mandates system.' *Canadian Journal of History* 40 (December 2005): 449–77.

Gribetz, Jonathan Marc. *Defining Neighbors: Religion, Race, and the Early Zionist–Arab Encounter.* Princeton: Princeton University Press, 2014.

Grinberg, Lev. 'A historical slip of the tongue, or what can the Arab–Jewish transportation strike teach us about the Israeli–Palestinian conflict?', *International Journal of Middle East Studies* 35 (August 2003): 371–91.

Gualtieri, Sarah. *Between Arab and White: Race and Ethnicity in the Early Syrian American Diaspora.* Berkeley: University of California Press, 2009.

Habermas, Jurgen. 'Citizenship and national identity.' In *Theorizing Citizenship*, ed. Ronald Beiner. Albany: State University of New York Press, 1995, pp. 255–82.

Haiduc-Dale, Noah. *Arab Christians in British Mandate Palestine: Communalism and Nationalism, 1917–1948.* Edinburgh: Edinburgh University Press, 2013.

Halabi, Awad. 'Liminal loyalties: Ottomanism and Palestinian responses to the Turkish War of Independence, 1919–1922.' *Journal of Palestine Studies* 41 (spring 2012): 19–37.

Halamish, Aviva. 'A new look at immigration of Jews from Yemen to Mandatory Palestine.' *Israel Studies* 11 (spring 2006): 59–78.

Hall, Stuart and Bram Gieben, eds. *Formations of Modernity.* Cambridge: Open University, 1992.

Hanley, William. 'Papers for going, papers for staying: Identification and subject formation in the eastern Mediterranean.' In *A Global Middle East: Mobility, Materiality and Culture in the Modern Age, 1880–1940*, eds Liat Kozma, Cyrus Schayegh and Avner Wishnitzer. London: I. B. Tauris, 2015, pp. 177–200.

—'When did Egyptians stop being Ottomans? An imperial citizenship case study.' In *Multilevel Citizenship*, ed. Willem Mass. Philadelphia: University of Pennsylvania Press, 2013, pp. 89–109.

Al-haraka al-wataniyya al-Filasīn: Yawmiyāt Akram Zu'aytir, 1935–1939 [The Palestinian National Movement: Diary of Akram Zu'aytir, 1935–9]. Beirut: Center for Palestine Studies, 1980.

Haste, Helen. 'Constructing the citizen.' *Political Psychology* 25 (June 2004): 413–39.

Henriques, H. S. Q. and Ernest J. Schuster. ' "Jus Soli" or "Jus Sanguinis"?', *Problems of the War* 3 (1917): 119–31.

Herzog, Christoph. 'Migration and the state: On Ottoman regulations concerning migration since the age of Mahmud II.' In *The City in the Ottoman Empire: Migration and the Making of Urban Modernity*, eds Ulrike Freitag, Malte Fuhrmann, Nora Lafi and Florian Riedler. Oxford: Routledge, 2011, pp. 117–34.

Hobsbawm, Eric. 'The nation as invented tradition.' In *The Invention of Tradition*, eds Eric Hobsbawm and Terence Ranger. Cambridge: Cambridge University Press, 1983, pp. 1–14.

Hooglund, Eric J., ed. *Crossing the Waters: Arabic-Speaking Immigrants to the United States before 1940*. Washington, DC: Smithsonian Institute Press, 1987.

Hourani, Albert. *Arabic Thought in the Liberal Age 1798–1939*. Cambridge: Cambridge University Press, 1983.

—'Ottoman reform and the politics of notables.' In *Beginnings of Modernization in the Middle East: The Nineteenth Century*, eds William R. Polk and Richard L. Chambers. Chicago: University of Chicago Press, 1968, pp. 41–68.

Hourani, Albert and Nadim Shehadi, eds. *The Lebanese in the World: A Century of Emigration*. London: I. B. Tauris, 1992.

Hughes, Matthew. 'From law and order to pacification: Britain's suppression of the Arab Revolt in Palestine, 1936–39.' *Journal of Palestine Studies* 39 (winter 2010): 6–22.

Hunter, Emma. *Political Thought and the Public Sphere in Tanzania: Freedom, Democracy and Citizenship in the Era of Decolonization*. New York: Cambridge University Press, 2015.

—'Dutiful subjects, patriotic citizens and the concept of "good citizenship" in twentieth -century Tanzania.' *The Historical Journal* 56 (2013): 257–77.

—' "Our common humanity": Print, power and the colonial press in interwar Tanganyika and French Cameroun.' *Journal of Global History* 7 (July 2012): 279–301.

Isin, Engin F. 'Theorizing acts of citizenship.' In *Acts of Citizenship*, eds Engin F. Isin and Greg M. Nielson. London: Zed Books, 2008, pp. 15–43.

—'Citizenship after Orientalism: Ottoman citizenship.' In *Challenges to Citizenship in a Globalizing World: European Questions and Turkish Experiences*, eds F. Keyman and A. Icduygu. London: Routledge, 2005, pp. 31–51.

Isin, Engin F. and Greg M. Nielson, eds. *Acts of Citizenship*. London: Zed Books, 2008.

Isin, Engin F., Peter Nyers and Bryan S. Turner, eds. *Citizenship between Past and Future*. Abingdon: Routledge, 2008.

Isin, Egin F. and Bryan S. Turner, eds. *Handbook of Citizenship Studies*. London: Sage, 2002.

Isin, Engin F. and Patricia K. Wood. *Citizenship and Identity*. London: Sage, 1999.

Jacobson, Abigail. *From Empire to Empire: Jerusalem between Ottoman and British Rule*. Syracuse: Syracuse University Press, 2011.

Jad, Isla. 'From salons to popular committees: Palestinian women, 1919–1989.' In *Intifada: Palestine at the Crossroads*, eds Jamal R. Nassar and Roger Heacock. Birzeit: Birzeit University Press, 1991, pp. 125–42.

Joon-Hai Lee, Christopher. 'The "native" undefined: Colonial categories, Anglo-African status and the politics of kinship in British Central Africa, 1929–38.' *Journal of African History* 46 (2005): 455–78.

Janoski, Thomas and Brian Gran. 'Political citizenship: Foundations of rights.' In *Handbook of Citizenship Studies*, eds Engin F. Isin and Bryan S. Turner. London: Sage, 2002, pp. 13–52.

Jayal, Niraja Gopal. *Citizenship and its Discontents: An Indian History*. Cambridge, MA: Harvard University Press, 2013.

Kabha, Mustafa. *The Palestinian Press as Shaper of Public Opinion, 1929–1939: Writing up a Storm*. London: Valentine Mitchell, 2007.

—'The Palestine press and the General Strike, April–October 1936: *Filastin* as a case study.' *Middle Eastern Studies* 39 (July 2003): 169–89.

Karatani, Rieko. *Defining British Citizenship: Empire, Commonwealth, and Modern Britain*. London: Frank Cass, 2003.

Karpat, Kemal M. *Studies on Ottoman Social and Political History: Selected Articles and Essays*. Boston: Brill, 2002.

—'The Ottoman emigration to the America, 1860–1914.' *International Journal of Middle East Studies* 17 (May 1985): 175–209.

—*Ottoman Population, 1830–1914: Demographic and Social Characteristics*. Madison: University of Wisconsin Press, 1985.

Kassem, Anis F., ed. *The Palestine Yearbook of International Law*. Vol. 1. Cyprus: Al-Shaybani Society of International Law, 1984.

Kattan, Victor. 'The nationality of denationalized Palestinians.' *Nordic Journal of International Law* 74 (2005): 67–102.

Kayali, Hasan. *Arabs and Young Turks: Ottomanism, Arabism and Islamism in the Ottoman Empire, 1908–1918*. Berkeley: University of California Press, 1997.

Kayyali, A. W. Said. *Palestine: A Modern History*. London: I. B. Tauris, 1978.

Kayyali, 'Abd al-Wahhab. *Wathā'iq al-Muqāwama al-Filastīniyya al-'Arabiyya did al-Ihtilāl al-Britānī wa al-Zioniyya, 1918–1939* [Documents of the

Palestinian Arab Resistance against the British and Zionist Occupation, 1918–1939]. Beirut: Institute for Palestine Studies, 1967.

Keith-Roach, Edward. *Pasha of Jerusalem: Memoirs of a District Commissioner under the British Mandate*. London: Radcliffe Press, 1994.

Kern, Karen M. *Imperial Citizen: Marriage and Citizenship in the Ottoman Frontier Provinces of Iraq*. Syracuse: Syracuse University Press, 2011.

—'Rethinking Ottoman frontier policies.' *The Arab Studies Journal* 15 (spring 2007): 8–29.

Khalidi, Rashid. *The Iron Cage: The Story of the Palestinian Struggle for Statehood*. Boston: Beacon Press, 2006.

—*Palestinian Identity: The Construction of Modern National Consciousness*. New York: Columbia University Press, 1997.

Khalil, Assem. 'Palestinian nationality and citizenship: Current challenges and future perspectives.' In *CARIM (Consortium for Applied Research on International Migration) Research Report*, 2007, pp. 1–48 .

Khalili, Laleh. *Heroes and Martyrs of Palestine: The Politics of National Commemoration*. Cambridge: Cambridge University Press, 2007.

Khater, Akram Fouad. *Inventing Home: Emigration, Gender, and the Middle Class in Lebanon, 1870–1920*. Berkeley: UC Press, 2001.

Khuri-Makdisi, Ilham. *The Eastern Mediterranean and the Making of Global Radicalism, 1860–1914*. Berkeley: University of California Press, 2010.

Klieman, Aaron. 'The divisiveness of Palestine: Foreign Office versus Colonial Office on the issue of partition, 1937.' *The Historical Journal* 22 (June 1979): 423–41.

Kolinsky, Martin. *Law, Order and Riots in Mandatory Palestine, 1928–1935*. Basingstoke: Macmillan, 1993.

Kushner, David, ed. *Palestine in the Late Ottoman Period*. Leiden: Brill, 1986.

Lambert, David and Alan Lester, 'Introduction.' In *Colonial Lives across the British Empire: Imperial Careering in the Long Nineteenth Century*, eds David Lambert and Alan Lester. Cambridge: Cambridge University Press, 2006, pp. 1–31.

Lehmann, Matthias B. 'Rethinking Sephardi identity: Jews and other Jews in Ottoman Palestine.' *Jewish Social Studies* 15 (fall 2008): 81–109.

Lesch, Ann Mosely. *Arab Politics in Palestine, 1917–1939: The Frustration of a Nationalist Movement*. Ithaca: Cornell University Press, 1979.

—*Arab Politics in Palestine, 1917–1939*. Ithaca: Cornell Press, 1974.

Lesser, Jeffery. '(Re)creating ethnicity: Middle Eastern immigration to Brazil.' *The Americas* 53 (July 1996): 45–65.

Lester, Alan. 'Imperial circuits and global networks: Geographies of the British Empire.' *History Compass* 4 (2006): 124–41.

LeVine, Marc. 'The discourses of development in Mandate Palestine.' *Arab Studies Quarterly* 17 (winter and spring 1995): 95–124.

Likhovski, Assaf. *Law and Identity in Mandate Palestine*. Chapel Hill: University of North Carolina Press, 2006.

—'In our image: Colonial discourse and the Anglicization of law in Mandatory Palestine.' *Israel Law Review* 29 (summer 1995): 291–359.

Lockman, Zachary. *Comrades and Enemies: Arab and Jewish Workers in Palestine, 1906–1948*. Berkeley: University of California Press, 1996.

—'Railway workers and relational history: Arabs and Jews in British-ruled Palestine.' *Comparative Studies in Society and History* 35 (July 1993): 601–27.

Louis, Wm. Roger and Robert Wilson Stookey, eds. *The End of the Palestine Mandate*. London: I. B. Tauris, 1986.

Louis, Wm. Roger. 'The United Kingdom and the beginning of the Mandates System, 1919–1922.' *International Organization* 23 (winter 1969): 73–96.

Makdisi, Ussama. 'After 1860: Debating religion, reform, and nationalism in the Ottoman Empire.' *International Journal of Middle East Studies* 34 (November 2002): 601–17.

—'Ottoman Orientalism.' *The American Historical Review* (June 2002): 768–96.

Maktabi, Rania. 'The Lebanese census of 1932 revisited: Who are the Lebanese?', *British Journal of Middle Eastern Studies* 26 (November 1999): 219–41.

Marin-Guzman, Roberto. *A Century of Palestinian Immigration into Central America*. University of Costa Rica, 2000.

Marshall, T. H. *Citizenship and Social Class*. Revised Edition. London: Pluto Press, 1987.

Matthews, Weldon C. *Confronting an Empire, Constructing a Nation: Arab Nationalists and Popular Politics in Palestine*. London: I. B. Tauris, 2006.

—'Pan-Islam or Arab nationalism? The meaning of the 1931 Jerusalem Islamic Congress reconsidered.' *International Journal of Middle East Studies* 35 (February 2003): 1–22.

Mayer, Thomas. 'Egypt and the 1936 Arab Revolt in Palestine.' *Journal of Contemporary History* 19 (April 1984): 275–87.

McCarthy, Justin. *Population History of the Middle East and the Balkans*. Istanbul: Isis Press, 2002.

Migdal, Joel. *Palestinian Society and Politics*. New York: Macmillan, 1980.

Miller, David. *Citizenship and National Identity*. Cambridge: Polity Press, 2000.

Miller, Ylana. *Government and Society in Rural Palestine, 1920–1948*. Austin: University of Texas Press, 1985.

Mogannam, Matiel. *The Arab Woman and the Palestine Problem*. London: Herbert Joseph, 1937.

Dayah, J., ed. *Al-Mu'allam Boutros al-Bustani: Dirāsa wa thā'iq* [The Teacher Boutros al-Bustani: A Study and Documents]. Beirut: Publications de la Revue Fikr, 1981.

Musallam, Adnan A. 'From wars to *Nakbeh*: Developments in Bethlehem, Palestine, 1917–1948.' *Al Liqa'* 30 (July 2008): 7–36.

—*Folded Pages from Local Palestinian History in the 20th Century: Developments in Politics, Society, Press and Thought in Bethlehem in the British Era, 1917–1948*. Bethlehem: WIAM Conflict Resolution Center, 2002.

—'Palestinian Arab press developments under British rule with a case study of Bethlehem's *Sawt al-Sha'b* 1922–1939.' *Bethlehem University Journal* 5 (August 1986), www.bethlehem-holyland.net/Adnan/bethlehem/Sawt_Al-Shab.htm (accessed 15 September 2015).

Muslih, Mohammad. *The Origins of Palestinian Nationalism*. New York: Columbia University Press, 1989.

Myres, S. D., Jr. 'Constitutional aspects of the Mandate for Palestine.' *Annals of the American Academy of Political Science and Social Science* 164 (November 1932): 3–8.

Nadolski, Dora Glidewell. 'Ottoman and secular civil law.' *International Journal of Middle East Studies* 8 (October 1977): 517–43.

Nakkara, Hanna. *Lawyer of the Land and the People*. Haifa: Al-Asawar Publishers, 1980.

Narbona, Maria del Mar Logrono. 'A transnational intellectual sphere: Brazil and its Middle Eastern populations.' In *The Middle East and Brazil: Perspective on the New Global South*, ed. Paul Amar. Bloomington: Indiana University Press, 2014, pp. 199–214.

Ngal, Mae M. *Impossible Subjects: Illegal Aliens and the Making of Modern America*. Princeton: Princeton University Press, 2005.

Norris, Jacob. *Land of Progress: Palestine in the Age of Colonial Development*. Oxford: Oxford University Press, 2013.

—'Exporting the Holy Land: Artisans and merchant migrants in Ottoman era Bethlehem.' *Mashriq & Mahjar: Journal of Middle East Migration Studies* 1 (fall/winter 2013): 14–40.

—'Toxic waters: Ibrahim Hazboun and the struggle for a Dead Sea concession, 1913–1948.' *Jerusalem Quarterly* 45 (spring 2011): 25–42.

Ofer, Pinhas. 'The Commission on the Palestine Disturbances of August 1929: Appointment, terms of reference, procedure and report.' *Middle Eastern Studies* 19 (January 1983): 104–18.

'The Ottoman Constitution, promulgated 23 December 1876.' *The American Journal of International Law* 2, No. 4, Supplement: Official Documents (October 1908): 367–87.

Pandey, Gyanendra. 'The subaltern as subaltern citizen.' *Economic and Political Weekly* 41 (November 2006): 4,735–41.

Parsons, Laila. 'Soldiering for Arab nationalism: Fawzi al-Qawuqji in Palestine.' *Journal for Palestine Studies* 36 (April 2007): 33–48.

Parolin, Gianluca P. *Citizenship in the Arab World: Kin, Religion and Nation-State*. Amsterdam: Amsterdam University Press, 2009.

Pastor, Camila de Maria Campos. '*The Mashriq unbound: Arab modernism, Criollo nationalism, and the discovery of America by the Turks.*' *Mashriq & Mahjar: Journal of Middle East Migration Studies* 2 (fall/winter 2014): 28–54.

Pedersen, Susan. 'The meaning of the mandates system: An argument.' *Geschichte und Gesellschaft* 32 (October to December 2006): 560–82.

—'Introduction: Claims to belong.' *Journal of British Studies* 40 (October 2001): 447–53.

Plummer, Brenda Gayle. 'Race, nationality, and trade in the Caribbean: The Syrians in Haiti, 1903–1934.' *The International History Review* 3 (October 1981): 517–39.

Porath, Yeshoshua, *The Palestinian Arab Nationalist Movement 1929–39: From Riots to Rebellion*. London: Frank Cass, 1977.

—*The Emergence of the Palestinian-Arab National Movement 1918–1929*. London: Frank Cass, 1974.

Pritts, Jennifer. *A Turn to Empire: The Rise of Liberalism in Britain and France*. Princeton: Princeton University Press, 2005.

Provence, Michael. 'Ottoman modernity, colonialism, and insurgency in the interwar Arab East.' *International Journal of Middle East Studies* 43 (May 2011): 205–25.

—'"Liberal colonialism" and martial law in French Mandate Syria.' In *Liberal Thought in the Eastern Mediterranean*, ed. Christoph Schumann. Leiden: Brill, 2008, pp. 51–74.

Qafisheh, Mutaz. 'Genesis of citizenship in Palestine and Israel: Palestinian nationality during the period 1917–1925.' *Journal of the History of International Law* 11 (2009): 1–36.

—*The International Law Foundations of Palestinian Nationality: A Legal Examination of Nationality in Palestine under Britain's Rule*. Leiden: Martinus Nijhoff Publishers, 2008.

Qasmiya, Khariya, ed. *Min mudhakkirat 'Awnī Abd al-Hadi* [From the Memoirs of 'Awni Abd al-Hadi]. Beirut: Institute for Palestine Studies, 2002.

Ramnath, Maia. 'Two revolutions: The Ghadar movement and India's radical diaspora, 1913–1918'. *Radical History Review* 92 (spring 2005): 7–30.

Robinson, Shira. *Citizen Strangers: Palestinians and the Birth of Israel's Liberal Settler State*. Stanford: Stanford University Press, 2013.

Robson, Laura. *Colonialism and Christianity in Mandate Palestine*. Austin: University of Texas Press, 2011.

Rocco, Raymond A. *Transforming Citizenship: Democracy, Membership, and Belonging in Latino Communities*. East Lansing: Michigan State University Press, 2014.

Rouhana, Nadim N. and Nimer Sultany. 'Redrawing the boundaries of citizenship: Israel's new hegemony.' *Journal of Palestine Studies* 33 (fall 2003): 5–22.

Saada, Emmanuelle. *Empire's Children: Race, Filiation, and Citizenship in the French Colonies*. Translated by Arthur Goldhammer. Chicago: University of Chicago Press, 2012.

Saade Kenny and Kathy Saade. 'The power of place: Katrina in five worlds.' *Jerusalem Quarterly* 35 (autumn 2008): 5–30.

Safran, William. 'Citizenship and nationality in democratic systems: Approaches to defining and acquiring membership in the political community.' *International Political Science Review* 18 (July 1997): 313–35.

Saha, Jonathan. *Law, Disorder and the Colonial State: Corruption in Burma c. 1900*. Basingstoke: Palgrave Macmillan, 2013.

Salam, Nawaf A. 'The emergence of citizenship in Islamdom.' *Arab Law Quarterly* 12 (1997): 125–47.

Sayigh, Rosemary. *Palestinians: From Peasants to Revolutionaries*. London: Zed Books, 1979.

Scholch, Alexander. *Palestine in Transformation, 1856–1882*. Washington, DC: Institute for Palestine Studies, 1993.

Schulz, Helena Lindholm and Juliane Hammer. *The Palestinian Diaspora: Formation of Identities and Politics of Homeland*. London: Routledge, 2003.

Scott, James Brown. 'Nationality: Jus Soli or Jus Sanguinis.' *The American Journal of International Law* 24 (January 1930): 58–64.

Shabib, Samih. *Hizb al-Istiqlal al-Arabī fi Filastīn, 1932–1933* [The Arab Istiqlal Party in Palestine, 1932–3]. Beirut: PLO Research Center, 1981.

Shamir, Ronen. *The Colonies of Law: Colonialism, Zionism, and Law in Early Mandate Palestine*. Cambridge: Cambridge University Press, 2000.

Shapiro, Anita. 'The ideology and practice of the joint Jewish–Arab Labour Union in Palestine, 1920–1939.' *Journal of Contemporary History* 12 (October 1977): 669–92.

Sheffer, G. 'Appeasement and the problem of Palestine.' *International Journal of Middle East Studies* 11 (May 1980): 377–99.

Shepherd, Naomi. *Ploughing Sand: British Rule in Palestine, 1917–1948*. New Brunswick, NJ: Rutgers University Press, 2000.

Sherman, A. J. *Mandate Days: British Lives in Palestine, 1918–1948*. London: Thames and Hudson, 1997.

Shuk-mei Ku, Agnes. 'Contradictions in the development of citizenship in Hong Kong: Governance without democracy.' *Asian Survey* 49 (May/June 2009): 505–27.

Sieder, Rachel. ' "Paz, progreso, justicia y honradez": law and citizenship in Alta Verapaz during the regime of Jorge Ubico.' *Bulletin of Latin American Research* 19 (July 2000): 283–302.

Simoni, Marcella. 'A dangerous legacy: Welfare in British Palestine, 1930–1939.' *Jewish History* 13 (fall 1999): 81–109.

Smith, Barbara J. *The Roots of Separation in Palestine: British Economic Policy, 1920–1929*. Syracuse: Syracuse University Press, 1993.

Somers, Margaret R. 'Rights, relationality, and membership: Rethinking the making and meaning of citizenship.' *Law and Social Inquiry* 19 (winter 1994): 63–112.

Speek, Peter A. 'The meaning of nationality and Americanization.' *American Journal of Sociology* 32 (September 1926): 237–49.

Stein, Sarah Abrevaya. *Extraterritorial Dreams: European Citizenship, Sephardi Jews and the Ottoman Twentieth Century*. Chicago: University of Chicago Press, 2016.

—'Citizens of a fictional nation: Ottoman-born Jews in France during the First World War.' *Past and Present* (February 2015): 227–54.

—'Protected persons? The Baghdadi Jewish diaspora, the British state, and the persistence of Empire.' *The American Historical Review* 116 (February 2011): 80–108.

Stewart, Angus. 'Two conceptions of citizenship.' *The British Journal of Sociology* 6 (March 1995): 63–78.

Stoler, Ann Laura. *Carnal Knowledge and Imperial Power: Race and the Intimate in Colonial Rule*. Berkeley: University of California Press, 2002.

Storrs, Ronald. *Orientations*. London: Nicholson and Watson, 1943.

Sufian, Sandy. 'Anatomy of the 1936–39 revolt: Images of the body in political cartoons of Mandatory Palestine.' *Journal of Palestine Studies* 37 (winter 2008): 23–42.

Swedenburg, Ted. *Memories of Revolt: The 1936–1939 Rebellion and the Palestinian National Past*. Fayetteville: University of Arkansas Press, 2003.

Thomas, Martin. *Empires of Intelligence: Security Services and Colonial Disorder after 1914*. Berkeley: University of California Press, 2008.

Thompson, Elizabeth. *Colonial Citizens: Republican Rights, Paternal Privilege and Gender in French Mandate Syria and Lebanon*. New York: Columbia Press, 2000.

Tibawi, A. L. 'Educational policy in Mandatory Palestine.' *Die Welt des Islams* 4 (1955): 15–29.

Torpey, John. *The Invention of the Passport: Surveillance, Citizenship and the State*. Cambridge: University Press, 2000.

Turner, Bryan S. *Citizenship and Social Theory*. London: Sage, 1993.

—'Contemporary problems in the theory of citizenship.' In *Citizenship and Social Theory*, ed. Bryan S. Turner. London: Sage, 1993, pp. 1–18.

Tusan, Michelle. *Smyrna's Ashes: Humanitarianism, Genocide, and the Birth of the Middle East*. Berkeley: University of California Press, 2012.

Ülker, Erol. 'Contextualising 'Turkification': Nation-building in the late Ottoman Empire, 1908–18.' *Nations and Nationalism* 11 (2005): 613–36.

Wasserstein. Bernard. *The British in Palestine: The Mandatory Government and the Arab–Jewish Conflict, 1917–1929*. Second edition. Oxford: Basil Blackwell, 1991.

Watenpaugh, Keith David. *Being Modern in the Middle East: Revolution, Nationalism, Colonialism, and the Arab Middle Class*. Princeton: University Press, 2006.

Wathā'iq al-Haraka al-Wataniyya al-Filastīniyya min Awrāq Akram Zu'aytir, 1918–1939 [Documents of the Palestinian National Movement from the Papers of Akram Zu'aytir]. Beirut: Institute of Palestine Studies, 1979.

Weber, Eugene. *Peasants into Frenchmen: The Modernization of Rural France 1870–1914*. London: Chatto and Windus, 1977.

Weismann, Itzchak. 'The invention of a populist leader: Badr al-din al-Hasani, the religious educational movement and the great Syrian revolt.' *Arabica* 52 (January 2005): 109–39.

White, Benjamin Thomas. *The Emergence of Minorities in the Middle East: The Politics of Community in French Mandate Syria*. Edinburgh: Edinburgh University Press, 2011.

Wilson, Kathleen. *The Island Race*. London: Routledge, 2013.

Wuthnow, Robert. *Communities of Discourse: Ideology and Social Structure in the Reformation, the Enlightenment, and European Socialism*. Cambridge, MA: Harvard University Press, 1989.

Yassin, Subhi. *Al-Thawra al-'arabiyya al-khubra fi Filastin, 1936–1939* [The Great Arab Revolt in Palestine, 1936–1939]. Cairo: Dar al-Katib, 1967.

Yosmaoglu, Ipek K. 'Counting bodies, shaping souls: The 1903 Census and national identity in Ottoman Macedonia.' *International Journal of Middle Eastern Studies* 38 (February 2006): 55–77.

Zachs, Fruma and Basilius Bawardi. 'Ottomanism and Syrian Patriotism in Salim al-Bustani's Thought.' In *Ottoman Reform and Muslim Regeneration: Studies in Honour of Butrus Abu-Manneh*, eds Itzchak Weismann and Fruma Zachs. London: I. B. Tauris, 2005, pp. 111–26.

IV. Newspapers

Al-Difa'
Filastīn
Al-Huquq
Al-Ittihad al-'Arabī
Al-Jamiyya al-'Arabiyya
Al-Jamiyya al-Islamiyya
Mir'at al-Sharq
Sawt al-Haqq
Sawt al-Sha'b

Index

EU representative:
Easy Access System Europe
Mustamäe tee 50, 10621 Tallinn, Estonia
Gpsr.requests@easproject.com

www.ingramcontent.com/pod-product-compliance
Lightning Source LLC
Chambersburg PA
CBHW050632280326
41932CB00015B/2620